The World Needs Dialogue!
Four: Putting Dialogue to Work

This edition first published in 2022

Dialogue Publications
The Firs, High Street
Chipping Campden
Glos GL55 6AL UK

All rights reserved

Book Copyright © Dialogue Publications, 2022
All individual authors featured in this publication retain copyright for their work

Without limiting individual author's rights reserved, no part of this publication may be reproduced, distributed or transmitted in any form or by any means, including photocopying, recording, or other electronic or mechanical methods, without the prior written permission of the publisher, except in the case of brief quotations embedded in critical reviews and certain other non-commercial uses permitted by copyright law. For permission requests, write to the publisher at the address above.

Typeset by Ellipsis, Glasgow, Scotland

Ordering Information:
Quantity sales – Special discounts are available on quantity purchases by libraries, associations and others. For details, contact the Special Sales Department at the address above.

The World Needs Dialogue! / Four – 1st ed.

Classifications:
UK: BIC – Society (JFC): Cultural Studies and JFF: Social Issues)
US: BISAC – SOC000000 Social Science

ISBN Hardback: 978-1-7399911-5-9
ISBN Ebook: 978-1-7399911-6-6

Printed in Great Britain and the USA

On the Cover

The cover photo shows 200 Dialogue Practitioners from the Virginia Department of Corrections gathered at the Convention Center in Richmond in 2019. The standing speaker is Jane Ball. Although the TWND! 4 was held online, this earlier photo was chosen because it includes over half the authors of the case studies in this book.

Contents

Chair's Foreword — vii
Editors' Introduction — ix

PART ONE
CASE STUDIES BY MEMBERS OF THE ACADEMY

Section One
Putting Dialogue to Work in Organisations

Mutual Mentoring – Reducing the Divide — 5
Jane Ball

Promoting a Dialogical Culture in a Gated Community — 11
Thomas Köttner

From Compliance to Choice: Using Dialogue to Improve Safety in Manufacturing — 19
Glenna Gerard

Increased Trust through Dialogue within the Swedish Municipal Workers' Union — 27
Lars-Åke Almqvist

Section Two
Putting Dialogue to Work in Education

Classroom Dialogue and Healthy, Sustainable Communities — 37
Garin Samuelsen

Dialogical Development in Schools — 45
Kati Tikkamäki

Dialogue at Proakatemia — 53
Timo Nevalainen and Alina Suni

Relay Race: Our Next Generation of Practitioners — 61
Heidemarie Wünsche-Piétzka

On Dialogic Relations Transforming from Monologic to Dialogic 67
Tzofnat Peleg-Baker

Section Three
Putting Dialogue to Work for Healing

Dialogic Enquiry Within a Recovery Environment 77
Helena Wagener

Autism Dialogue in Derby City and Derbyshire 83
Jonathan Drury, Kate Salinsky and Jackie Elliott

A Family Dialogue 89
Linda Ellinor

Section Four
Putting Dialogue to Work in Communities

Dialogue Between Police Officers and Multi-Ethnic Street Youth 97
Bernhard Holtrop

Women Weaving Peace 103
Mino Akhtar

Brussels in Dialogue: Connecting Strangers Around a Table 111
Elisabeth Razesberger

Section Five
Putting Dialogue to Work for the Benefit of Society

HOT Challenge – An Outdoor Development Programme for Dutch Homeless People 121
Rijk Smitskamp and Bernhard Holtrop

Community Engagement and Effective Socio-Economic Engagement 129
Loshnee Naidoo

Institutionalizing Public-Private Dialogue in Sierra Leone 137
Chukwu-Emeka Chikezie

The World Needs Dialogue! Dialogue for the Benefit of Society 145
Peter Garrett

Contents | v

PART TWO
CASE STUDIES BY MEMBERS AND ORGANISATIONAL MEMBERS ABOUT ENGAGING AND MANAGING THE IMPACT OF THE COVID-19 PANDEMIC

Section Six
Putting Dialogue to Work in the Covid-19 Pandemic

Seven-Series Dialogues   157
William Isaacs

Intergroup Zoom Dialogues   165
Abigayel Bryce and Rebecca Cannara

Covid Check-Up: Coming Back Together   173
Jennifer Kittrell and Virginia Pauls

Covid-19 vs Religious Services at the Virginia Department of Corrections   179
Jermiah "Jerry" Fitz and Whitney Barton

What's Your Color? Restarting a Random Drug Screening Program   185
Tecora Davis and John Fedor Jr

Operations Dialogue in Pandemic Conditions   191
Matthew Whibley and Eric Fling

PART THREE
CASE STUDIES BY ORGANISATIONAL MEMBERS OF THE ACADEMY

Section Seven
Putting Dialogue to Work for Inmates and Probationers

Vaccinated: To Be or Not to Be . . .   203
Whitney Barton and Carrie West-Bailey

Connecting Probationers to Substance Abuse Disorder and Recovery Services   209
Tessie N Lam and Brandon B Daisy

Dialogue Training for Inmates—Encouraging Pro-Social Behavior   217
John F Walrath and Wardenia Lassiter

Progressive Reinforcement through the Use of Incentives — 223
Joseph P Owen, Dianne Motley and Eric Holloman

Section Eight
Putting Dialogue to Work for Security

Ending Gang Control of Telephones and Showers — 233
Sharon S Burgess

Enhancing Security Procedures to Prevent Contraband — 239
Crystal Butler

Working Dialogue: Managing Gate Pass Cards — 245
Troy "Eddie" Adams

Cooking Up Ideas to Revamp the Kitchen — 251
Vickie Williams, James Brown and Michelle Galyean

Always Ready, Always There: Special Response Team Recruitment — 257
Mahala Carter-Moore, Dianne Motley and Tammy Williams

Section Nine
Putting Dialogue to Work to Improve Operations

Mind the Gap: Bridging Communication between Medical, Dental and Operations — 267
TyKeshae Fowlkes Tucker, Andrea D Wilson and Karen Fleming

Using SWOT and Working Dialogue to Improve and Strengthen our Work Unit — 275
Alfreda M Shinns, Jillian S Mackling and Caitlin M Sweeney

Research Peer Review as Part of the VADOC Healing Environment — 281
Shakita Bland, Tama Celi and Warren McGehee

Employee Retention: How Do We Recover? — 287
Matt Burgess, Michelle Hicks and Angela Hill

Remaining Focused on What Has Proven to Work Best — 293
Shannon Fuller and Gregory Holloway

Chair's Foreword

The case studies in this book demonstrate the conference theme, *Putting Dialogue to Work*. They provide evidence of substantial and beneficial change through the professional use of Dialogue. Dialogue is already recognised by many as a fine way of generating well-being by deepening the sense of inclusion and community, leading people to draw on dialogic skills to enrich the rapport between staff members and to improve team morale. Some of these case studies describe such work, but many of them go much further than that. They describe material benefits reaped through Professional Dialogue. Dialogue frees up the latent energy that is constrained by people's inability to talk and think together well. This enables people to use Dialogue to do work. More specifically, Professional Dialogue can resolve: *organisational fragmentation*, that impedes quality and productivity; *social fragmentation*, that engenders barriers and violation; and *individual fragmentation* that disables and confuses. That is what these case studies describe. You will be impressed by the variety of dialogic applications and the multitude of situations that have benefitted from Dialogue.

These are all first-hand accounts. Each working example was designed and delivered by the authors and their colleagues. The majority of authors have never been published before. We anticipate they will be encouraged by the acknowledgement implicit in this publication, and that it will give them the confidence to extend this part of their professional careers. The first part of the book (Sections One to Five) has accounts of the work of individual Members of the Academy of Professional Dialogue, covering the professional use of Dialogue in organisations, education, health, the community and society. The third part of the book (Sections Seven to Nine) are provided by the Academy's first formally recognised Organisational Member, the Virginia Department of Corrections. These case studies are about work within that large government agency and refer to the generation of concrete outcomes, including: benefits for incarcerated inmates and probation clients; better security; and improved operations. Sandwiched between the two is Section Six that covers the use of Dialogue to understand and accommodate the extraordinary impacts of the Covid-19 pandemic, and this section has case studies from both individual Members and our Organisational Member.

This volume covers our 2021 online conference with participants from Asia, Africa, Europe, South and North America. Over the past four years the numbers of participants attending our annual conferences have increased tenfold, from 55 meeting physically in the UK to the 550 who met online (due to the constraints of the Covid-19 pandemic) in 2021. The first three conferences each considered 12 to 15 Working Papers by Members of the Academy presenting their own Professional Dialogue work that had often stretched over many years. This year was a little different. We invited Members to present shorter case studies about discrete pieces of Professional Dialogue work, to emphasise our theme of *Putting Dialogue to Work*. The 39 case studies are an impressive record of why the world needs Dialogue.

It is very rewarding to document the progress made by the Academy of Professional Dialogue, as evidenced in its initial four annual conferences and their resulting publications, each titled *The World Needs Dialogue!* Although the title of each book is unchanged, the subtitles indicate a steady and purposeful journey, starting with *One: Gathering the Field* (2018) and followed by *Two: Setting the Bearings* (2019), *Three: Shaping the Profession* (2020) and *Four: Putting Dialogue to Work (2021)*. The purpose of the non-profit educational charity is to make Professional Dialogue available for the benefit of Society, and the vision of the Academy is to do so by establishing recognition of Dialogue as a Profession. We are clearly laying a sound foundation to achieve this.

Finally, a word of thanks to Cliff Penwell, who is a long-standing friend, co-founder and the first editor of Dialogue Publications. He has a remarkable skill and sensitivity in encouraging and guiding both new and experienced authors, whilst explaining why he is doing so. This is true coaching and mentoring. Together we have established Dialogue Publications as the world's leading imprint in the niche market of Professional Dialogue. The pleasure that I shall miss of working on this venture with a true professional is only offset by the seamless way in which, with his careful hand, Helena Wagener has worked alongside Cliff to learn the ropes and to play a role in editing next year's volume. Welcome Helena and go well Cliff!

Peter Garrett
Chair of the Board of Trustees
Academy of Professional Dialogue

Editors' Introduction

Helena

This year, I stepped into an opportunity to be both a conference author and a co-editor with Cliff Penwell, who is an empowering mentor, editor and dialogue practitioner. Writing my own case study helped me appreciate the importance of feedback from more experienced practitioners such as Jane Ball and Peter Garrett as well as clear editorial suggestions from Cliff. Stepping in after the conference as a co-editor, in turn, gave me a greater perspective on the bigger body of dialogic work represented by this book. Coming from a background of academic journal editing I was captivated by Dialogue Publications' respect for the nuances of language and sentence structure used by each writer to reflect the unique essence and cadence of their voices. For example, we retained the authors' voices as they were originally expressed (be they British / European or American), by following the spelling and punctuation standards for each language.

In this way I saw how the respect that is such a central part of the Academy's dialogic approach is also integral when creating a body of work that shows how Dialogue is put to work by diverse practitioners in many different places and ways. I like to believe that, together with Peter, I extended this respect when capturing the essence of the smaller group considerations in extracts and editing the postscript reflections. There was a great freedom in supporting each author as they represented their learning in a way that made sense to them several months after the conference. I hope that reading the case studies, extracts and postscripts will give you a glimpse also of how different voices can live together dialogically and make sense without trying to conform to a single format, style or set of rules.

Cliff

Helena describes perfectly the sense of respect we have for those who step forward each year—many without formal training in writing for publication, and several for whom English is not a first language—because it is important and useful to share what they have learned. It is a labor of love, and an act of service to authentically share what it means to convene, sometimes imperfectly, circles where our thoughts, voices and feelings are welcome, and to bring the fruits of that process to this volume.

Speaking of labors of love, I particularly want to highlight the many hours Helena has put into transforming this collection of studies into a useful vehicle for reflection and practice. Working with the 66 authors whose work comprises this year's volume is a complex task, and she has handled it with artistry and grace. She is a joy to work with. Peter and Jane, as always, have guided many of the authors toward clarity and transparency in their thinking--they have been the kinds of muses many writers dream about. And Debi Letham of Ellipsis is the talented, ever-patient (and largely invisible) hand that has shaped the "house style" of this publication. Dialogue Publications is lucky to have her!

From my current perspective this will be the last year I am directly involved with the production of our annual *The World Needs Dialogue!* volumes. While endings are always poignant, I leave with the sense of relief that comes through knowing this body of work remains in supremely capable hands, eyes and hearts.

Helena Wagener and Cliff Penwell
Co-editors
Dialogue Publications

PART ONE

SECTIONS 1 TO 5

Section One

Putting Dialogue to Work in Organisations

We live in what could appropriately be named the Era of Organisations. All manner of human endeavour is now arranged through organisations. The decisions made within and by organisations impact everything we do from birth to death. Our health, education, employment, money, home, water, power, transport, sport, leisure and entertainment are all provided through organisations. It is a sobering realisation that inherently in their structure, the lines of communication and the thinking in all these organisations is disjointed or fragmented through hierarchy, specialisation and physical location. They all need Dialogue! Dialogue is a means of creating inclusive and participatory patterns of communication and thinking that incorporate and run across traditional organisational lines. We open this book with four case studies about putting Dialogue to work in organisations.

Jane Ball *describes her novel design to resolve hierarchical fragmentation in a trading environment through a mutual mentoring programme. Many conversations in pairings, of executives with staff two levels below them and from a different reporting line, generated an organisation-wide Dialogue.*

The exective committee of a gated community of 300 homes in Buenos Aires, Argentina, traditionally communicates little and debates members' demands. **Thomas Köttner** *has been introducing Dialogue to help generate a common understanding of everyone's interests and needs.*

Glenna Gerard *introduced Dialogue at a large microprocessor manufacturing plant in the USA to improve safety. She moved the mindset, from compliance to choice, by creating a safety culture, bringing people closer to their vision of having an incident-free and injury-free manufacturing plant.*

4 | Putting Dialogue to Work in Organisations

The Swedish Municipal Workers Union employed **Lars-Åke Almqvist** *to resolve the conflict between two of its teams – the six administrative staff and the six ombudsmen. Their inability to co-operate has been damaging the effectiveness of the union, and his dialogic approach shifted that.*

Mutual Mentoring – Reducing the Divide

Jane Ball

Context

Integrated Supply and Trading (IST) was a highly successful business within the BP corporation. Their culture was entrepreneurial. Staff were driven, smart and young (compared to other businesses), often working under pressure with high risk and high reward. The London office housed traders alongside mid- and back-office functions.

Social, cultural, and organisational differences between individuals and groups were fragmenting the culture. Though people were highly interdependent, under high stakes this became demanding rather than collaborative, thoughtless and at times disrespectful. Relationships were eroding, and these divisions and their impact were becoming increasingly obvious.

Various local and corporate initiatives were under way to develop a more inclusive culture, and the leadership team took this seriously. They wanted to invest in creating a culture that was based on mutual respect and which allowed everyone to thrive without losing the edge that led to commercially astute business behaviours. The corporate Diversity and Inclusion team had recommended a programme called Mutual Mentoring, but after six months the leadership felt that the potential of what seemed like a good idea had not been met. I was working in the organisation on other initiatives and was commissioned to further develop the Mutual Mentoring programme and help to fulfil its potential.

Aim

The programme aim was *to create a more inclusive workplace by raising awareness of the perspective of others in a non-threatening and confidential way*. Through participant interviews, a review of what had already been done revealed some elements that were needed to enhance the value and address the obstacles.

Method

To create a sustainable Mutual Mentoring Programme, I first established the leadership team commitment. If they knew why the programme was a good idea, advocated for it, and participated it would have more credibility. We still asked them to apply (participation was not an entitlement) and complete a questionnaire. This included questions such as: *How do you think are you labelled by others in the organisation? Choose a colleague you trust and ask them what your blind spots are.* And the easier question, *What are the areas of IST that you would like to get connected to?* The aim was to get them thinking about what they might need to learn. We also asked them to nominate junior mentors. This meant we avoided volunteers who had an 'axe to grind', and nominees inherently had leadership permission to take part. The information also helped us to create effective pairings. *Effective* meant they crossed subgroups in at least two ways – organisationally and socially/culturally – male-female and accounts-trading, for example. It also meant they were outside of structural reporting lines, which could have led to conflicts of confidentiality or accusations of favouritism.

A launch event brought all the participants together. First, they were put into pairs. One by one, senior mentors invited a junior mentor to partner with them. Everyone knew who was paired with whom.

I facilitated a process to help pairs agree on their mutual mentoring contract. The contract included arrangements for meetings – including a protocol for timekeeping, cancelling, re-arranging etc. Confidentiality was considered through a series of prompts or questions, such as *Discuss what confidentiality means to you*; *Name any past experiences that affect how you view confidentiality*. Finally, they talked about their own learning agenda with the stimulus of questions, such as *What do you want to gain from this relationship and what will you invest? How will you continually review whether your expectations are being met?* They located the focus of their learning in seven areas – you, your part of the organisation, your work, your partner, their area of the organisation, their work, or organisational values.

I included guidance on how to give and receive feedback, which people tried out in an exercise – they asked their partner, *Please give me feedback about your first impressions of me today*.

After the launch, each month I sent everyone a stimulus for their Mutual Mentoring session based on one of the organisational values. For example:

> *When is the last time you felt really listened to at work and the person really took on board what you were saying? Think of a situation where you were really listened to by someone who was not a direct report.*

> *Whose growth and success are you contributing to at work and how?*
> *What does this tell you about how you realise the value of Integration – displaying true partnership and teamwork?*

After six months everyone met again to end the process, noticing what was learnt individually and collectively and setting up how the experience might be taken forward and extended through the organisation.

Outcomes

The programme helped individuals from different organisational and social/subcultural groups to develop common understanding. This placed the programme in the context of cultural change. Single meetings were part of a defined, time-limited process to give focus and realise potential.

The senior mentors valued the direct first-hand feedback about what was happening on the floor of the organisation. They had greater appreciation for the real change that was needed to create a more inclusive environment. For example, one junior mentor was female, in her early thirties. She told her partner what happened when she met senior leaders to talk about her career progression – she could see their level of interest disappear when she told them she was recently married. Maternity leave was bound to follow.

The programme certainly met its aim to raise awareness of the perspective of others in a non-threatening and confidential way. Leadership were able to use their greater awareness to keep up other efforts to change the culture.

Learnings

I learnt in practice the limitations of a well-intentioned corporate initiative – the Diversity & Inclusion team mutual mentoring programme – but how powerful and effective it can be to translate this to a local process. Diversity and Inclusion programmes can be of immediate operational value if they reduce fragmentation. A well thought-through pattern, based on clear aims and understanding of the needs of the participants, can provide an effective programmatic intervention. Finally, it was clear that contracting is crucial to create a safe but energetic relationship for mutual learning.

Conference Session Extracts
From the consideration of the case study with conference participants

Speaker: Reading your paper, I found it fascinating that the subordinates were willing to engage in this process and that you were able to create a sphere of trust so that they could do that without fear of retaliation.

Speaker: I would assume that in the oil industry large amounts of profit are involved, so I wondered how receptive upper-level management was to this dialogue process. If subordinates were not performing, there would be profit loss. How did you present it to each of the groups?

Jane Ball: What was it like for the subordinates, then? Why would upper management be receptive? How do you get the different sides talking? What else were people thinking?

Speaker: Well, I think she hit the nail on the head. Whenever I talk to my people about dialogue, I always tell them it's a safe container but this just doesn't resonate with them. They hear the words, but I don't think they really understand or trust that it is a safe container. A lot of that has to do with us as leaders, and how we convey that safety to them.

Speaker: What type of research, if any, had to take place to bring these two groups together in a non-threatening dialogue?

Speaker: There are times the leader needs to call on people to participate in a dialogue because we do have that formal hierarchy still in place. We're working in a closed paradigm environment where people feel like they're respecting the hierarchy. The staff need to feel comfortable to say what's on their mind and not feel that there's going to be retaliation or be told it's a dumb idea. So, it's back to respecting and suspending judgment, et cetera. But the leaders have to model those principles and, in the appropriate manner, we need to call leaders out that are not modeling effective dialogue principles.

Speaker: I read your article and I have a question. Before you worked with the company they had run a program with the same name for six months. What prevented the success of their earlier program, before you did it in a different way?

Jane: The earlier program wasn't successful because people just didn't find it useful. I describe in the case study how I created more of a structure to enable everybody to talk to each other. You have asked how to get subordinates to be willing to raise their voice and how you help senior managers to be receptive. How do you create the atmosphere? The previous structure didn't support an effective engagement so what I did was to create more structure. I made rules that people were willing to follow. As they followed the rules, they found that they could talk together in a different way.

I am wondering if you think it would be useful to bring different subgroups together in your organization, like different levels of seniority, or different genders. If you did, what kind of structure would help that to be useful? Mutual mentoring was my answer to a problem they had. What's the problem that you see in your work? Would a structure like this help? Would you do it differently?

Speaker: Our approach to a mentorship initiative focuses on staff retention – really coming alongside individuals when they come in the door. It is a process whereby we're there, we're coaching, we're encouraging and we're a part of that foundational route to help them through the transition into being a member of the agency. A mentorship initiative within our organization would help, from the beginning and all the way through one's career. I really appreciate the input and hopefully we can have a mentorship developed from this!

Speaker: We discussed the relationship between management and line staff, and the importance of being able to sit down with your constituents as a supervisor and say, "What do you think works well with our relationship and what do you think doesn't work well and how do we improve that?"

Speaker: We were thinking about the first page with your question, where you choose a colleague and ask them to tell you what your blind spots are. It's easy and expected to get feedback from supervisors, but your peer may see things that we need to work on, things that a supervisor may not necessarily see.

Speaker: We talked about confidentiality and trust. For this to work, those are the two things that you have to have. It's really hard for line staff to trust the process. They will say what they think you want to hear, especially if leadership is in the room. They concentrate more on positions than on the issue at hand. But when the dialogue breaks up, then you hear little pockets of people having conversations about the dialogue and saying, "I wish I said this", or "I wish I said that". But they don't say it while they are in the main group. They tend to be reserved because there are leadership present.

Jane: A one-to-one learning environment can be really productive when you add it to everything else. And the contracting where I, as a senior person, say to somebody more junior than me, "I'm trying to learn this. Can you help me?"

Postscript

The author's reflections written some months after the conference

I chose to bring the Mutual Mentoring programme to the conference because I believed it was simple enough to inspire others to try something similar in their organisations. At the time the work was done I wrote an internal report that recorded the process and feedback from participants. This provided a great source document for writing the case study. As I wrote I was struck by the level of structure in the programme and realised, more than I had at the time, how important that structure had been for its success. Despite the energetic entrepreneurialism of the business, like any large organisation people were used to following rules, policies and procedures. The Mutual Mentoring rules provided a pattern for engagement to enable conversations that the organisational norms restricted. I recognised the impact a well-designed and structured process could have, enabling people to create common ground across organisational boundaries without the constant presence of a facilitator.

In the session people were most interested in how to create safety for junior staff to speak openly with senior staff. Their questions reinforced the importance of the whole process, from application to completion, rather than a single feedback conversation. Safety is not a prerequisite for the process – rather the process creates safety as people engage. However, safety remains a big issue for people in hierarchical organisations, and despite my confidence that this was a straightforward process I think most people had real reservations about the possibility of people talking openly across hierarchical boundaries.

Since the conference I have continued reflecting on and working with how to create a powerful environment for learning, and the relevance of mutual learning in doing so. I have never felt comfortable with an expert trainer dynamic. In my early work in the charity Prison Dialogue, we used the strap line *where everyone learns, and nobody teaches* – I was more comfortable with that. In the conference session I tried to create this dynamic. On the one hand I was the expert who wrote the case study and people wanted me to answer their questions. On the other hand, I also had something to learn from others. With a collective enquiry we could all benefit from hearing how people reacted to the story and exploring how it might be applied in their setting. It takes discipline to maintain the dynamic of collective enquiry (as you can see in the transcript extract), rather than reverting to question and answer, and explanations!

Promoting a Dialogical Culture in a Gated Community

Thomas Köttner

Context

The following is a work in progress, fostering Dialogue initiatives within a gated neighborhood slightly north of Buenos Aires, Argentina, where I live with my family. Ours is a 200-year-young country with a peaceful society, fragmented by the still-strong cultures of its immigrant descendants.

Today the strongest, most predominant presence is of Spanish and Italian descent, carrying the imprints of the Spanish cultural social hierarchy and the Italian body-expressive, outspoken communication style, both of which have created an interesting mix of social interactions. In the absence of a clear national identity, the tendency has been toward building individual images, or identities, the defense of which, over time, have mainly turned into ego-based social interactions. This generates a certain difficulty for respectful and balanced dialogical attitudes and relations.

This same dynamic is playing out at a traditional and quite renowned middle-class golf club, which, over time, has evolved into a so-called country club, given the availability of land that initially allowed members to build weekend houses and, in the last few decades, permanent residence homes. The property is home to 300 permanent resident families.

I have often considered that, if institutional and political Dialogue is to have a chance in our larger society, a good way to test it would be within the local politics and non-dialogical attitudes of this small community where I live.

As a member of the club's executive committee, which is in charge of the organization's relations with its members, I became aware of the members' demands to receive more communication than the currently sparse amounts emerging from the different authorities that guide and rule over the place. Truth be told, there has not been a policy of open communication, and I have tried to contribute toward changing this.

Method

Under these general conditions and circumstances, a couple of years ago the club's executive committee agreed to start an initiative that it code-named *The Club Listens*.

Members would enroll three at a time, every second Friday evening, and meet with the committee for whatever conversations that might emerge. It was partially positive; however, the weak point in my perspective was the implicit assumption of asymmetry between the "authorities" offering to the "regular" members the right to be listened to.

The name *The Club Listens*, combined with the scarce opportunity to interact with the authorities, could only result in what actually happened. Members presented themselves in the meeting with a list of claims, which would then be counter-argued, turning many of the meetings into arguments and unfortunate discussions.

Starting 2021, I insisted on the intrinsic fallacy of this approach, which I knew would just further stimulate the enrollment of members wishing to present their complaints about club matters. I suggested we re-conceptualize and rename the initiative the *Club Dialogues*. We started by enrolling, one-by-one, the most conservative members of the committee, who slowly began to understand the possible benefits of the Dialogues.

A bit further on I submitted some papers about Dialogue basics to illustrate what a Dialogical approach could look like. We also created a process to help people understand that their personal values would not be challenged. Finally, I was able to get to get all members to commit to experiencing a conversation among us that would reflect Dialogical attitudes, and we used the spaces to conduct some basic Dialogue education.

We progressed, and began to perceive some benefit from our engagement. The use of Zoom added some order to the conversations which, if done in person, would have had people overtaking each other in simultaneous conversations in the typical Latin way.

On realizing that we had reached—and even enjoyed—a Dialogical exchange, the next step was to invite a few members to a *Club Dialogues* space with the purpose of thinking together about the kind of Club we would all wish for.

By way of explaining and launching this "new" initiative, we had the publisher of the monthly newsletter conduct an interview with me about the differences between the old and new approach, and how we wanted to emphasize that the committee is just a team of regular members; we want to take our conversations to a space of mutual and joint exploration of our common interests. I also noted the conditions and nuances required for a Dialogue, and how it relates to other kinds of verbal interaction.

Outcomes

When we held our meeting the invitees, while thankful for the invitation, arrived with the usual list of complaints and proposals to demonstrate how they would do things better than the committee. We took the time to explain how we expected to carry forward; hopefully, soon, the meetings would become Dialogues.

The *Club Dialogues* space was increasingly successful. We recently started promoting the meetings with the board members; some of them, after some insistence, agreed to join us in a Dialogue meeting.

We also intend to create Dialogue between the different committees, management and employees, both in administration and field operations. As the initiative progresses and word keeps getting around, we hope to bring Dialogical interactions into the community of residents at large.

So far, it is slow but quite good going in this journey.

Learnings

While it is a work in progress, I have taken lessons from this process:

- Cultural worldview impacts almost everything in the ways we interact.
- Our cultural beliefs and practices sometimes complement—but more often tend to collide with—other people who have been educated in different cultural perspectives, even within the same nation.
- Power is a determinant of people's attitudes. This may be out of respect for or even in dogmatic submission to what authorities determine. In others power fosters rebelliousness towards what is perceived as power-exhibiting behaviors.
- Time management for fruitful Dialogues is a cultural matter. For some time is abundant, for others it is scarce.
- Self-pride is relevant in ego-based, individualistic societies, and this needs to be taken into consideration.
- In societies that tend toward the anarchic, it may be helpful to take the first steps with Dialogues online, only later stepping into in-person circles.

Conference Session Extracts
From the consideration of the case study with conference participants

Speaker: How do you address the issue of power in an HOA [Homeowner Association], because when people pay money they surely expect an element of power, and they expect things to be done? How did you get people on equal ground?

Thomas Köttner: I go into the conversation with the awareness that we are all paying to keep this place running, but in reality we are paying for our lifestyle. We are not paying for others to serve us. My personal approach is to turn my power down. If people are listening to me they are giving me power. I check my own power attitude in a way that gives it the potential to become contagious. If people raise their voices, I lower my voice.

Speaker: I think the key thing is relationships. Maybe you're not talking about systems or dialogue per se, but rather about relating to the people you encounter in their own language.

Thomas: Yes. We open a conversation by inquiring, by asking something. We ask, "Where is the other one coming from about what he is saying?" or, "Does any one of us ever say something when we believe that we are wrong?" I speak about the power each of us holds in that we are able to do something. Living here as neighbors, we can see everything, the beauties and the miseries. We can see everything because we live here every day.

Speaker: Our managers strategically identified people that are a little bit more open to listening to different points of view and who may have some influence over other people. It can be an easier way of doing things.

Speaker: How did your community made a decision to meet each other, and has leadership been open to participating in the space? I chose to come here today because I am in an HOA and I feel like you were doing a case study on my community! I live in Puerto Rico, so many of us speak English and many speak Spanish, and there's a lot of unnamed cultural issues. Also, Puerto Rico is a colony of the United States, so it comes with those political issues too. Some of the issues that we have related to colonizers living on the island are not being named. How did you manage to have these club dialogues?

Thomas: If you want to generate change in an organization, bring together four or five persons who are able to agree at least to start working in a different way, which will hopefully get better results. Then other people might ask themselves, "What are these people doing that helps them to get better results?" It starts people acting through contagion. As far as I know this is the only way of creating real cultural change. I first engaged the leader of the executive committee, and we visited each other for a few conversations—we had a glass of wine. I told him about my activities in dialogue. He got engaged with what I was saying. Others from the committee followed him because of his hierarchical authority, and they started listening too. We have a WhatsApp group started by the executive committee about our dialogue initiative. I sent some interesting videos, and we are slowly creating an awareness of how the dialogic attitude is different from other approaches. Sometimes we have dialogues for just the executive committee to practice and observe all the deviations. We started off by making it clear that there is a regular executive committee meeting to decide actions in a dialogic way, to just explore what kind of club we would like to have five years from now. Only once that happened did the leader of the executive committee invite people from the board. Three out of 16 came, and we told them what it was all about. This was the first meeting to happen in 20 years! It was a new experience. They came into the room and they said, "Where's the table?" We answered, "Oh, there's no table! It's just our chair circle." In this way we flattened the power dynamic as much as possible from the first meeting and onwards.

Speaker: You talked about the contagious nature of dialogue . . .

Thomas: What is contagious is that the people respond to a nice feeling, it creates expectation. People heard that some of their friends had a good time in the dialogue circle. We had to make clear the difference between a dialogic meeting and an action executive committee meeting, as for now these have different dynamics. Hopefully the executive committee in its action-oriented meetings will become more dialogical as well. I don't know how far this would have progressed if we didn't have our first meetings about dialogue on Zoom, because it brought order. You cannot all talk at the same time!

Speaker: I'm taking several themes away from this session. The importance of going slow to start with. The cultural uniqueness—each organization or group of people has a cultural uniqueness to consider. You showed people what dialogue was, and they came to value it from being exposed to it and from understanding its benefit. You had the vision to see what was needed, and you put in the work to make it happen. That's the lesson I want to take as I am finishing my career with Corrections soon and I want to look at how I can best impact my own communities through dialogue. I thank you for that.

Postscript

The author's reflections written some months after the conference

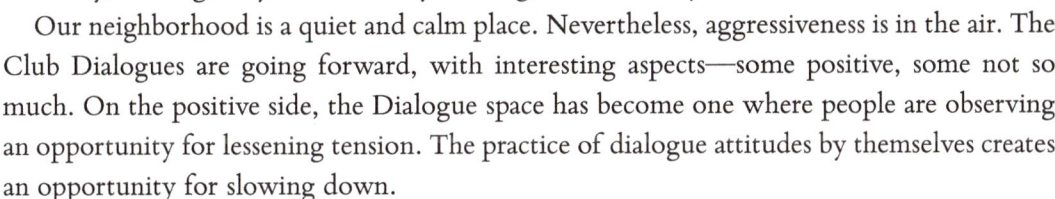

I am reflecting on the process of this case study since its writing in 2021 and several perspectives have unfolded . . .

The social mood in Argentina is harsh these days. There is high political instability, 100% inflation and obstructive state intervention in the economy, making daily life in society and organizations very emotional and unstable.

Our neighborhood is a quiet and calm place. Nevertheless, aggressiveness is in the air. The Club Dialogues are going forward, with interesting aspects—some positive, some not so much. On the positive side, the Dialogue space has become one where people are observing an opportunity for lessening tension. The practice of dialogue attitudes by themselves creates an opportunity for slowing down.

On the negative side, what had progressed in using Dialogue in the Board meetings has receded into often confrontational discussions, in the pursuit of quick decisions, given the permanently changing contexts in which those decisions need to be reached.

As for the experience of writing the case, it is always a challenge to explain a situation of high implicate complexity in a short script. Yet rereading it, I am quite satisfied with it, and its structure allows me to identify what has evolved, changed, what is new, and what has gone since then. The complexity of introducing a dialogical practice in a neighborhood with quite individualistic ways of living is not easy to describe.

The session presentation allowed nice learnings. I felt challenged by presenting an experience which I thought culturally and geographically remote in relation to most convention participants home places.

But the Dialogue that unfolded was very interesting and allowed us all to become aware that we are all neighbors, wherever we live, we can almost not avoid being the neighbor of someone if we live in society.

And the challenges to at least get along in the best possible ways with each other, and the opportunities to generate a community spirit where some agreements can be reached for social well-being, are the same in every geography, culture and society.

Observing social interaction in a tiny community, and the small but steady improvements in the dosages of trust and respect between members, makes us aware of the immensity of what is ahead in order to bring Dialogue into society at large. At the same time, it renews the meaning of the saying that is often attributed to Margaret Mead: "Never doubt that a small group of thoughtful, committed citizens can change the world; indeed, it is the only thing that ever has."

From Compliance to Choice: Using Dialogue to Improve Safety in Manufacturing

Glenna Gerard

Context and Objectives

The story begins at a large microprocessor manufacturing plant. In 1996 the number of recorded injury cases was in the high 50s per year. This was dangerous—it was bad for morale and productivity, and it was embarrassing. Manufacturing leadership created a strategic initiative and gave it the highest priority. The goal: to dramatically reduce the number of incidents and injuries. In 1999 the recordable cases dropped to below 10. Though this is significant, the measure was still not acceptable to leadership. Their vision was for an Incident and Injury-Free (IIF) plant. That meant zero recordable events per year.

The primary processes employed between 1996 and 1999 were based on compliance and punitive consequences. Though they reduced numbers, they also engendered a culture of workarounds and nonreporting. It became clear a new way of thinking about and engaging with the problem was needed.

One of the senior consultants in the Organizational Development team took up the challenge. She had read the then-recently published *Dialogue: Rediscover the Transforming Power of Conversation,* by Linda Ellinor and me, and was convinced that dialogue could be instrumental in anchoring the values and skills for changing the safety culture and outcomes within the manufacturing plant. She saw that it would also help them realize their vision of an incident- and injury-free workplace at the plant and meet their goals of moving from compliance to choice.

Method

Through conversations with managers and teams in the plant, we began to clarify and adopt design assumptions. The process would be choice-based and voluntary instead of mandatory. Individual teams would own the process they would use to achieve the IIF Next Steps outcome. To move from compliance to choice would require shifting focus to strengthening relationships and creating opportunities for people to change the way they thought about safety. Only then would team members be able to coach each other on safety behavior and have this received as an expression of caring rather than criticism.

First, we would engage people in an individual introspection activity where they would reflect on what personal commitment around safety meant to them. Then team members would share personal commitments that made sense to them and how they could support each other.

The two activities were followed by two team conversations. The first was a form of divergent/opening conversation, or dialogue, for an hour. The dialogue closed with a reflection harvesting insights and learnings the team wanted to take forward into the second conversation. This conversation was also an hour and was convergent in nature; that is, moving towards decision and action. It culminated with an agreement on next steps the team would implement towards accomplishing their goal of an IIF manufacturing floor.

Participation was by choice, and individuals would share responsibility for the quality of the conversation and the results. Further, the process of dialogue highlights and strengthens the relational component of the issue at hand (safety) while simultaneously opening the door for people to change the way they think about safety.

To support managers and team members in leading the Team Conversations, we designed and facilitated a two-part, three- to four-day (depending on shift requirements) program. In Part I we focused on learning about the value dialogue could add to the IIF Next Steps process and strengthening the skills needed to facilitate the Team Conversations. In Part II we focused on preparing volunteer managers and team members to facilitate the process for the Dialogue and the Action Planning conversations.

Manufacturing managers and team members then facilitated a series of IIF Next Step conversations within the manufacturing plant over the next year. In all areas where this process was engaged, reportable incidents and injuries further decreased.

Outcomes

Here are two direct quotes from people who participated in the process:

> *"I've never seen a company where safety is so highly valued. After seeing the safety practices at other semiconductor facilities, it's one of the big reasons I've stayed [here] over the years."*

> *"IIF Next Steps is a terrific initiative. I've seen team members gain a full new respect for each other's safety and build deeper relationships through the process. People love it. We should more actively promote it!"*

Learnings

I will limit myself to those that focus on successfully applying dialogue within organizations.

It is crucial to check carefully for alignment between:

- the business problem/issue
- the working context
- the vision of success
- the process that dialogue brings to the table and what is needed to support people in participating

A corollary to this first point is to remember to *embed dialogue*, and any skill building required, *within a business initiative/application* rather than doing *training and/or development* and then looking for an application. It is important that dialogue be able to deliver value immediately and in ways that are fully integrated into the work of the people.

Personal choice can be a powerful vehicle for change. I was surprised at the levels of commitment and skillfulness of the managers and team members who stepped up to lead/facilitate the conversations. I also hold a hypothesis that the degree of caring that they embodied for their fellow workers was a key ingredient to their success.

Creating a container where judgment is suspended, even temporarily, can support people in catalyzing deeper levels of listening, speaking and new ways of thinking.

Using managers and team members as facilitators for the conversations vs. bringing in consultants (even internal ones) can foster ownership of the process and the outcomes.

Developing the capacity to respond to and support the "pull" that a voluntary process creates is crucial. Leadership had not fully anticipated the desire to expand such an effort and/or was unwilling to provide sufficient follow-on resources. As a result, once the initial goal was reached, the process lost its priority position within strategic initiatives the executives were supporting. The will that is required from leadership to sustain and regenerate culture change is perhaps the most important ingredient to the adaptation of dialogue within an organization setting.

Conference Session Extracts
From the consideration of the case study with conference participants

Glenna Gerard: The question is: "What distinguishes compliance and choice, in your experience? I am interested to talk about why dialogue makes a difference in helping people to move from compliance to choice. How does dialogue help that to happen?"

Speaker: First, I have a question. In your paper you mentioned that participation was by choice. I'm interested to know what the overall numbers for participation in the initial dialogue session were.

Glenna: You're asking about participation among members on the manufacturing floor, correct? It started out with 30%, and then it grew because people became ambassadors. People were joining because they were hearing from their peers, rather than their managers saying, "You need to do this!" It was never a hundred percent, but it did get up into the seventies, which was remarkable.

Speaker: I have a follow-up question. Once you got through and every change was made, leadership said they couldn't afford to keep doing this. What happened after that?

Glenna: The folks who had been involved in the program continued to do what they were doing, and their safety record remained high. Then, because they began to have some turnover and because leadership changed, the program didn't have the same kind of priority and resources behind it so it began to slip. There was some lasting effect but it was not what it could have been if they devoted resources towards continuing the program.

Speaker: I'm still struggling with the idea of moving from compliance to change. I often work in the ethics compliance space in organizations, and I am trying to understand what you mean by change. I imagine it starts with the leadership. Are they in the position to open a dialogue on the compliance issues that are on the table? If we're going to move anything, that is where it should start. Otherwise, you just have to comply. There's does not seem to be a lot of choice in it, it's just how you do it. Is there something else to unpack?

Glenna: I think part of your struggle relates to the difference in how we use the word *compliance*. When *compliance* is used within the ethics world, it means there are certain things that you can do and things you cannot do, and there is a very strict boundary within organizations around compliance. There is a right way and that's all there is to it. When you use *compliance* in that sense, you don't have choice. You do have a choice to not comply but then you can get fired or whatever else the consequences are. But in terms of this program, they had what they called a "compliance system." It wasn't an ethics compliance issue, rather it was a case of, "If you don't do this, there will be negative consequences to your salary." It was therefore more of an enforcement model that they used to get people to pay more attention to safety. People were talking to each other about what they noticed about how their behaviors could be safer. An ethics compliance is where you have a legal issue.

Speaker: I still think the same applies in both cases because I don't think there's one right answer. Often what happens with compliance is that things haven't been worked out between parties, and without people trusting each other there is more and more compliance. The measures are merely put into place to course correct the group. There wasn't always so many compliance rules and regulations. It is because people can't be trusted for whatever reason. It's my interest then to bring us back to ethics, which to me is a form of inquiry.

Glenna: I think you bring up a really interesting point, which is valid from my perspective too, about how compliance systems get put in place because people aren't trusted or because people have different ethical value systems.

Speaker: I don't even know if it is based on values, on a lack of trust or on a habit and a lack of imagination. I work in international development and in a government-owned organization where it is often just the way that things are done. If you want something done, you create a rule. You speak to leaders, and they actually think that people know all those rules. But they don't because it's bigger than the Bible. Everything is regulated, even down to whether you can accept a packet of crisps on a plane, because it's the taxpayers' money paying for it!

Glenna: I think it's fascinating how we structure things. They get structured in a certain way for a reason and that reason always makes sense within a particular context or in somebody's mind. But then at some point the reason becomes a habit, and then the system continues to create all kinds of things around it, including the high degrees of fragmentation that Peter talks about. Unless we pause and become willing to look at what it is that we've created and some of the unfolding results, we won't see the consequences. Yet we often can't really open up that conversation. So we have to ask ourselves, "What is it that we really want, what is it that we really value?" and "How do we then look at our rules and our compliance structures?"

Postscript
The author's reflections written some months after the conference

When the first conference of The Academy for Professional Dialogue was held, I was deeply curious to discover what the "new format" for papers would yield. Participants reading the papers before the sessions, followed by a conversation and inquiry about the work, and discovering what unfolded, was intriguing. Now, some four years later, having experienced this process, I continue to find it evocative and inspiring.

I originally did the work described in this paper as part of a Strategic Safety Initiative in the early 2000s. My organizational development partner at the company and I presented it at the Systems Thinking Conference in 2000.

I wrote this brief paper for the 2021 Academy Conference because I believed it demonstrated key learnings relative to applying dialogue within a large action- and results-oriented organization. It seemed it would be useful to others who devote much of their professional lives to bringing dialogue into the world. The responses of session participants affirmed this perception.

The postscript included here, from the latter part of the session, expanded on my original intention for the paper. As I read the excerpt, I remember thinking, "What an interesting and powerful dialogue could be seeded by the questions that surfaced in a very few moments that day at the 2021 Conference."

The conference experience and preparation of this addendum did not evoke a desire to "have done the work differently" in the early 2000s. I *did* find the inquiry evocative of a larger conversation about working with dialogue in organizations and the many choices we make as leaders and consulting dialogue professionals. I do remember wishing there were another hour to continue the inquiry that day.

The Inquiry: Do we as dialogue professionals choose to surface the larger conversation about underlying thought systems that source a system's culture? With whom? The executive leadership? The workers on the manufacturing floor? Or? Is this conversation available? Regardless, can we bring dialogue into the system in ways that bring value? Whose well-being are we serving? What will be our contribution to healing incoherent thinking and fragmentation that often lie at the foundation of organizational structures and decisions? What is work worth doing?

I think the above questions are evocative dilemmas that all dialogue professionals have met, and are "worked by" regularly. There are no "right" answers. Rainer Maria Rilke wrote: *"Live the questions now. Perhaps then, someday far in the future, you will gradually, without even noticing it, live your way into the answer."* (Rainer Maria Rilke, *Letters to A Young Poet*).

With continued dialogue we will unfold our answers, pulling them from the implicate into the explicate of our personal practices. As we do, we learn more about ourselves and the choices we make as we bring dialogue to the world.

Increased Trust through Dialogue within the Swedish Municipal Workers' Union

Lars-Åke Almqvist

Context

Kommunal is Sweden's largest trade union, organizing staff in municipal operations as well as in private companies that have been hired to perform municipal services. The district office employs an administrative manager and a team of six administrative staff and six ombudsmen who negotiate with employers and support elected representatives in local unions.

Because the local office manager felt that the business did not work well enough – there were too many interpersonal conflicts within and between the two staff teams – I was hired in February of 2021 to work with the entire staff group.

Aims

My aims were to improve cooperation within each team and between the teams in order to a) provide better service to elected representatives and members; b) change the workplace atmosphere, or climate; and c) achieve better working results from the teams.

Method

All the activities had to be carried out via Zoom due to Coronavirus restrictions. I began with confidential, individual interviews with all employees. After the interviews summarized an overall impression in a way that made it impossible to trace what individuals had said, I reported the results to the local office and administrative managers and listened to their reflections.

The results of the interviews included issues such as:

From administrative staff:
- Cohesion and atmosphere in group
- Distribution of responsibilities
- Personality differences
- Cooperation with ombudsmen
- Relationship with the local office and administrative managers
- Dealing with what goes wrong
- How decisions are made
- Information and participation in decisions
- How to continue the work with new routines and structure
- High workload and many new tasks

From the ombudsmen:

- Different needs for structure, both within the group and in relation to the administrative group
- Uncertainty about trust in the administrative group
- Inability to receive feedback
- Status differences: us and them, regulated vs. unregulated working hours
- The union as top-down, with short notice, poor coordination
- The workload, taking a break and having lunch, 40-hour work week
- Changes in cooperation with elected representatives, new ombudsman role
- Relationship with local office and administrative manager
- Better collaboration with the administrative group
- Recommendation to continue the work of developing new routines and structure

Based on the interviews, I created a separate two-day program for each team, attended by the local office manager and administrative managers. We began with a check-in: What expectations and concerns do you have for the work we are going to do during these two days? I presented a summary of the interviews and an introduction to our process. Then we worked with different theories or exercises, each followed by individual reflection, conversation in breakout rooms and a Dialogue in the whole group.

For the administration team we began with the question, *Why are we at work?* This was followed by an introduction to Simon Sinek´s theory about "The Golden Circle", working with these questions: *What is our mission? What value are we supposed to create for those for whom we are there?* We used a method called 'Visual Dialogue', which ends with the teams each creating a vision summarizing how they view their mission and what benefit they should create.

Administrative staff: *We are a well-oiled machine that contributes with good service, stability and continuity. We do this through good collaboration, in which we support and coach local members and elected representatives.*

I asked the ombudsmen to reflect about the following: How do you use your work hours? What is value-generating time? What is opportunity-generating time and lost time?

> **Ombudsmen team:** *This is what we ourselves can influence: How we use our time; how we plan our calendar; how we plan and prioritize; how we overbook team meetings. We need a handbrake! These are influences from outside: Orders from the central union and emergencies.*

We also introduced Dialogic Actions and David Kantor's Four-Player Model and we had a Dialogue: *How do we function as a group? What is our strength? What is our weakness? What do we as a team need to develop?*

The participants filled in self-assessment forms to evaluate how they each function as a team member, and they gave each other feedback in pairs. Everyone talked to each other and then reflected together on what had been learned from the exercise.

Finally, we introduced Susan Wheelan's theory of effective teams; our whole-group Dialogue and reflection was: In which development phase is our group currently? What will be required for us to improve our cooperation?

Based on the results of these sessions I designed a program for the entire staff group together. This also took place over two days.

The program began with a check-in about participants' expectations and concerns. We repeated some of the earlier sessions and introduced Johan Galtung's ABC (Attitudes, Behaviour and Contradiction) model for conflict resolution. There was an individual reflection on experience of conflicts privately and at work, before small-group breakouts and the whole-group Dialogue. Participants completed a self-assessment form about how they experience their own listening. Then we looked at conflict in the group through an individual reflection: How do I experience the conflicts that arise in the group? What are they about? We held conversations in mixed groups in breakout rooms and a whole-group Dialogue: How shall we deal with conflicts in the future?

At the end of that session, Alamanco's model for an action plan was introduced. Work on the action plan was completed during an employee day led by the local office manager.

Several individual conversations were conducted with some employees and the local office manager, and we ended with an evaluation interview with the local office manager in September.

Outcomes

As a result of the work the office staff agreed to several new working arrangements:

- A review of administrative procedures
- A division of the employees into pairs with an ombudsman and an administrative staff member to improve cooperation in the daily work

- Joint planning and decision-making meetings
- An agreement to work regularly with feedback

Learning

- The interviews created trust and openness
- It is possible to facilitate a process like this via Zoom
- Individual reflection and breakout rooms help people talk
- During the work with feedback and the ABC model people showed courage

References:

Alamanco model for an actionplan, Arbetslust och Utveckling and Alamanco, 2018.

Jordan, Thomas. "Konflikthantering i arbetslivet-förstå, hantera, förebygg", 2014.

Kantor, D. (2012). *Reading the Room: Group Dynamics for Coaches and Leaders*. San Francisco: Jossey-Bass.

Sinek, S. (2009). *Start with Why: How Great Leaders Inspire Everyone to Take Action*. London, England: Penguin Group.

Wheelan, S., Åkerlund, M. and Jacobsson, C. (2020) *Creating Effective Teams: A Guide for Members and Leaders*. London: Sage Publications, Inc.

Conference Session Extracts
From the consideration of the case study with conference participants

Speaker: I am touched by the way you dealt with the situation and brought the two teams together in a mutual agreement. You realized that both teams have their own values and that the conflict was a result of the values they wanted to protect. There was no trust between them because they were protecting their values. They did not feel safe enough to share what they held with the other team, maybe because they felt they might be devalued. One way or the other, they probably felt like they couldn't open up. The main call I see here was that they were all trying to achieve the same goal but the lack of trust between them meant they were denied the opportunity to achieve that goal.

Researching to understand the individual view and bringing everyone together to discuss the findings in a safe container helped them see that they can trust each other, which meant they could collectively work together to achieve the goal. It is remarkable how much I have taken from this presentation. If I look at how everybody is working in my unit, I can see that we create conflict when we don't understand that we all are working towards one goal. Only when we get to understand that we share one goal, and we understand trust can we feel comfortable. We will feel safe and secure and we want to be together collectively, to plan together and work together to achieve our goal. I think the presentation is very powerful.

Speaker: I really like this conflict management model. One thing is universal no matter where you're trying to bring a group together: if there's mistrust you have a challenge. Your model brings in attitude, and to me that is the real key. Attitude is going to be a source of continuing mistrust. If you try to bring people together the biggest challenge to overcome is if they have an attitude of, "I don't trust them". I've had success bringing people together, but I've also had failures. It can be very difficult. I enjoyed seeing how you went about this.

Speaker: I'd like to piggyback on that. It's all about the attitude.

Speaker: Thanks for sharing your case study, Lars. When you started to talk about the mistrust within the groups it reminded me of 'suspension' in Dialogue. It seems that each team had some idea in their mind about how somebody claimed a part of what they've created. The distrust is there because of something they believe, and that signifies that they're not suspending their judgement to allow the process to go forward and for them to create new meaning together.

Lars-Åke Almqvist: One important reason that I wanted to talk about this was that I conducted individual interviews where I was able to create trust towards me as a person. Then I could see that I needed to work with feedback. We don't normally give feedback to each other in Swedish workplaces. In the United States you are much better at giving positive feedback, but we are too shy to do that. This changed when I created these mixed teams, and we now always give people time for few minutes of individual reflection:

"What are your experiences of conflicts at your workplace and how can we use dialogue to solve conflicts and create trust at workplaces? Let's reflect on those two questions".

Speaker: You were saying in our country, we were better at giving feedback, but we feel it's still a work in progress for us too.

Speaker: I hear in a lot of places that Americans are outspoken and that Americans freely share their opinions and offer feedback, negative or positive. What built that belief for you about Americans? What experiences have you had?

Lars-Åke: I'm thinking more about your capacity of giving positive feedback. I've been to America several times and I have also been working through Zoom and you are also so polite, open and confirming. I was reflecting on that aspect more than about your ability to give critical feedback. I have, on the other hand, heard that at some organizations people tend to be very afraid of saying what they think because they are afraid of losing their job. What about conflicts at your workplaces? What are they all about and how do you deal with them?

Speaker: Within our group, the focus was on feedback. I've seen that getting people to engage with one another in order to give feedback can help them move forward. Progress is slower in those districts where feedback is missing. To start establishing that trust it can sometimes be really important to have one-to-one meetings.

Lars-Åke: I think confidential, individual interviews beforehand are very important because then the whole group knows that I know their big problems and they can't fool me. I can ask the right questions. They feel confident after our interviews to talk about things. I think that feedback is the only way that a group can develop in their collaboration over time.

Postscript
The author's reflections, written some months after the conference

The work I was asked to do was to support people working in a regional office to create trust between individuals and two teams. My first reflection was that confidential interviews with each person were very important to understand the culture of the organization. I think I was able to create trust through how I listened and asked open questions. Besides trying to reach each individual it was also important to understand the culture in each team, ombudsmen and administrative staff. That part of the work made it possible to create a process that could start building trust between the two teams. Working with Johan Galtung´s ABC model for conflict resolution and feedback created an openness that brought people together.

It is always difficult to describe a process through writing about it. Writing about it in another language does not make it easier, but it is an important challenge. Writing about work that I have done helps me to reflect about what really happened. Presenting this kind of work to people who live in another country and work in totally different organizations is another challenge. Never the less it is also important to reflect together with people who have a different background.

I think that we had an interesting conversation during the seminar. The participants showed great interest in trying to understand the work I presented. The ABC model created a lot of interest as a useful method that makes it easier for people to understand the different reasons behind the conflicts they are involved in. To be able to use those insights as feedback is important to make constructive communication possible.

Section Two

Putting Dialogue to Work in Education

Education is way of preparing people for the future, and without Dialogue in education we cannot expect to see Dialogue emerge in the world. It is helpful that people are taught the principles of Dialogue, but it is more important that they have the experience of Dialogue. They should get a taste of how subtle and powerful collective thinking can be. It affects people's perception, understanding, disposition, intention and even their sense of identity. This requires learning rather than teaching, and at times teachers will need to step back from their position of authority to become more facilitative in how people form their own views and stories of life. Since our first conference in 2018 we have been considering examples of Dialogue in education. This year is no exception, and our five case studies cover a children's classroom in Vermont, educational administration in a municipality in Finland, dialogic entrepreneurship in a university also in Finland, European-wide Youth Dialogues, and a way to address social fragmentation that originated in Israel.

Garin Samuelsen taught 9- to 12-year-olds at a small school in Vermont for 18 years. He introduced Dialogue as a way of talking together and realising the value of each person's voice. It brought people closer together, helped to solve problems and was an effective way of addressing conflict.

Within a larger funded project to bring dialogue and well-being into Finnish workplaces **Kati Tikkamäki** co-facilitated a pilot project with a municipality's five schools and the welfare and family counselling services to bring 'special needs' children into 'normal' classrooms for equal access.

Timo Nevalainen and Alina Suni present their whole unit at Tampere University in Finland as a 22-year-long dialogic case study. Their approach to entrepreneurship is based on generating knowledge through doing, with stumbles or conflicts helping students learn to be more personally responsible.

Youth Dialogues began as part of the three-year EU-funded project that led to the European Network for Dialogue Facilitation. **Heidemarie Wünsche-Piétzka's** case study describes the Youth Dialogues for German pupils to learn skills, enter the labour market and participate in democracy.

Tzofnat Peleg-Baker proposes a dialogic approach derived from experiments in Israel of *living by* democratic values in public schools rather than *learning about* democracy. To move beyond an adversarial approach she advocates a reflective practice (insight) that is embedded through action.

Classroom Dialogue and Healthy, Sustainable Communities

Garin Samuelsen

Context

Our society has many issues, all of which come from a dysfunctional root—one that is built from the narrative that we are separate from the world.

The education system is the foundation from which our culture is constructed and maintained. Over time the system, through fear and coercion, perpetuates the belief that we are separate from one another and nature. Because of this, most of us live in conflict and dysfunction within ourselves, in our relationships, and collectively with the world at large.

Generally speaking, children don't have a say in their learning and are taught that their voices don't really matter. Instead, we have been taught to follow what we are told and to push down our voices and sense of wonder. We are essentially coerced by fear through rewards and punishments to follow the prescribed curriculum in school. John Holt, a long-time educator, shared, "For many years I have been asking myself why intelligent children act unintelligently at school. The simple answer is, 'Because they're scared.'"

Aim

I used to suspect that children's defeatism had something to do with their bad work in school, but I thought I could clear it away with my hearty cries of "Onward! You can do it!" What I now see is the mechanism by which fear destroys intelligence and the way it affects a child's whole way of looking at, thinking about, and dealing with life. Instead of fear and a forced curriculum, what would happen if we were to give space and opportunities for our children to keep their voice and wonder and, at the same time, we were to model and build dialogic skills to help facilitate open, direct, safe, honest conversations?

I had the opportunity to teach nine- to- 12-year-olds at a small, holistic school in Vermont for over 18 years. All student voices were important at this school. From almost the beginning, I created space each day for dialogue practice. Over the years, I began to recognize the deep importance of dialogue in not only creating a healthy classroom environment, but also for the world at large.

These were the expectations for our dialogues:

1. Be open to each other
2. Listen to understand
3. Have patience—there is no goal or outcome that we are trying to arrive at
4. Notice what you are feeling. Don't react, but find a way to present your thoughts without blame or judgment.
5. Try not to agree or disagree
6. Be aware of your own beliefs and assumptions

Method

One person would share at a time, explaining their perspective without trying to blame or judge. While the person shared, their classmate or classmates would listen. Because the sharer was expressing themselves in a thoughtful way, the other students were able to hear and seek understanding. As each person shared in a circle, the group began to understand the problem. By the end of the process, either we discovered that there was a misunderstanding or the person who made a mistake took responsibility. This led to compassion and forgiveness as people were able to understand not only what the problem was, but also what led up to the problem.

We also spent every Thursday outside in the wetland at the school. We would often circle up and dialogue about our experience with nature. One day, one of the students who was sharing said, "Wait. Hold on. Just listen." As we all were quiet we heard a beautiful flute-like sound emanating from a red maple a few yards away from us. The sound was mesmerizing. I am not sure how long we listened, but it was for a while. Finally, the wood thrush flew away. The student continued, "That seemed to be part of this dialogue. That bird was a part of our circle. Maybe the trees, the soil, and insects are also a part of our circle . . ." The student finished by saying, "I think if people could come out here and just be quiet for a second, they may hear something really beautiful and learn something that makes them feel joy."

Outcomes

Through this practice, students began to change the way they spoke to each other. Because they learned to appreciate differences in perspectives and didn't need to become defensive, students grew closer and more thoughtful in their relationships with each other. They became more patient in their interactions. They learned to trust their voice and see that each voice in the classroom was important. Dialogue illustrates a true democratic approach to life itself. We learned that for us to move together as a community, we needed to make sure that we were all participating in learning and that nobody had more power than anyone else.

They also began to use the dialogue process to solve their issues. Instead of the conflict becoming an argument and creating more issues, dialogue would not only help them find a solution to the problem, it actually brought the class or the pair closer together. When a conflict arose, we learned to confront it thoughtfully.

Learnings

As I reflected on what dialogue teaches us, I thought about what dialogue can do not only in the classroom, but also in building an ecological community of engaged community members.

Dialogue illustrates that there is no hierarchy. Dialogue illustrates that we are all in this together and that there is no "other." Dialogue pushes us to be patient and not react. Dialogue builds trust and connection and helps the teacher let go of control. It mirrors back that learning happens in an open safe space. Dialogue teaches us how to listen into thoughts and emotions and how to let go. Dialogue points to presence and listening with a quiet openness. This made me ponder. Isn't this what is essential to education?

I came to see that if we can bring dialogue into the classrooms, it can transform the students' experience from one of fear into one of joy and wonder, and can help build a foundation that, when these children become adults, could potentially transform society.

Conference Session Extracts
From the consideration of the case study with conference participants

Speaker: I love that you're bringing Dialogue to youth, giving it to the youth. It's similar to what we're doing in the Department of Corrections where all the staff know how to dialogue, yet it was a closed network. So now we're bringing it to the inmates and the probationers, and folks like that. It spreads out to the streets. That's really our goal with dialogue—to not just have a dialogic organization but to have a dialogic state, the State of Virginia, a dialogic country, the United States, and a dialogic world! And you're bringing Dialogue to the youth to spread it throughout all organizations. So great work!

Speaker: I was wondering how you were able to get the children to suspend what they had been taught by their parents as well as the individual environments that shaped them because children's personalities are developed by their environments. So how are you able to basically start off with a clean slate?

Garin Samuelsen: That's a great question. What I've come to understand is that children's unique experiences—from their home lives or the experiences they had outside of the school—were actually wonderful. They could teach their friends, and me as well, because they were able to listen to their peers and thereby illustrate that many different experiences and different values are possible. That's part of the dialogue. It's what can come out of that kind of listening. I wasn't trying to change them. It was more trying to listen in and help to understand where those stories came from.

Speaker: What was the demographic makeup of your students? Was it more of a homogeneous group or were they very diverse?

Garin: That's another great question. I worked at a private school. We had students from all socioeconomic situations, but Vermont is 98% white, I believe, so that's an unfortunate aspect resulting in a lack of diversity.

Speaker: How do you teach the kids to listen without judgment?

Garin: It is one of those things that takes time. Especially in the beginning of the year judgments definitely came out as we dialogued. Instead of running away from those things, we talk about them and looked at them. We talked about how judgments can make another other person feel as well as where a judgment is coming from. And we ask, "What does that mean?" The beautiful thing about dialogue, for all of us, is that it teaches us about ourselves. The dialogue can become a mirror of who we are. For these children it is an opportunity to start to get to know who they are at a very young age. One of the greatest journeys that we can ever take is to learn who we really are. And I love seeing these kids in this process so early, not only learning who they are, but also seeing different perspectives or different ways by learning from their peers.

Speaker: I learned that you can probably start this at a pretty young age. I figured about 10 or 12 was probably the right age, but some people believe it could happen a lot sooner.

Speaker: Our group decided to start at birth, engaging with your kids biologically, because they're going to emulate what they see their parents doing, and that becomes their pattern and their lifestyle as well.

Speaker: We decided that preschool (kindergarten) or first grade is the opportune time for children to learn different languages. If this is a language we are trying to teach them, it would be the opportune time to introduce these skills.

Garin: I'll share one cool thing that started as a dialogue. One of my students said, "I'm really interested in history." She felt history can tell us a lot about why we are where we are today. The next student is itching to go and says, "What about if we started learning about Columbus?" Then the other students said "Yes." We started learning about Columbus and the impact he had on people when he traversed across the Atlantic. After this discussion the student said, "What if we put him on trial for human rights violations?" All the kids got really excited about this idea, so we created a courtroom. Some of the students got to be lawyers, some were Christopher Columbus and some were Latino people. Then the parents decided to participate, and they came in as a jury. A couple of the teachers came in to play the judge.

It was an amazing process because they had to learn about all the different perspectives and then put it together to create this trial. The parents had no idea about the direction the dialogue would go, except that they were going to vote for whether Columbus was guilty or not. They created this performance, and it was amazing how well they brought information representing all the different perspectives. And, in the end, he was found guilty for human rights violations, unanimously. Unanimously! The kids probably couldn't tell you the date of 1492, but they could tell you all the information about what happened, the impact it had on them and how what they saw happening in our world is connected to that piece of history. The learning that took place was amazing. It was something that was integral to their own passion.

Postscript

The author's reflections, written some months after the conference

I was excited to have the opportunity to share my case study and was curious about the case studies that I would be attending during the conference. There seemed to be a great potential for learning.

With regards to my case study, I was concerned that I would struggle to articulate myself well in my writing and in presenting orally in my session. Yet I felt at ease as everyone made me feel welcome and embraced. I found the whole experience invigorating and surprisingly relaxed.

I was blessed to have a wonderful partner, Elizabeth Razesburger, who was assigned to help me navigate my Zoom room. She was wonderful to work with. She helped me process and practice beforehand, which helped calm my nerves. Elizabeth also provided support during the session by putting people in breakout rooms when needed and made the session flow with ease. I really enjoyed the people who joined my case study. They all seemed engaged, and presented wonderful questions. It appeared that not many people had thought about using dialogue in a classroom setting. Many of the participants of my case study seemed intrigued on how dialogue can be used in a child's educational experience. I am deeply motivated to find ways in which to educate the public about dialogue's multiplicity of benefits for students.

The Virginia Department of Corrections brought a large congregation to the conference. I was surprised and thrilled that dialogue was something that they practiced and used throughout their organization.

The sessions I attended illustrated the different ways in which dialogue is being used and has sparked healthy change in the world. I felt energized to participate more with people in the Academy of Professional Dialogue in the coming years.

By the end of the session, I experientially learned that people are open to questioning their own educational background and seeing how dialogue can transform education. I am not sure I would have recognized this without having participated in presenting this case study. As a result, I am now more deeply motivated than before to find ways in which to educate the public about dialogue's multiplicity of benefits for students.

The conference also inspired me to continue my ongoing practice of dialogue in all areas of my life. One last thing to note: I did not see much with regards to nature and dialogue. With our earth system becoming more and more out of balance because of the consequences of our culture's actions, we are now getting to a critical point where we either change our ways with her or it will most likely be the end of humankind. I feel like dialogue could have a huge potential for our re-enchantment with the wild. I am curious to see if the Academy would ever be interested in a conference around this.

Dialogical Development in Schools

Kati Tikkamäki

Context

This paper deals with dialogical development in basic education within one Finnish municipality. More specifically, it is development work done together with professionals working with students with special needs.

The development has been carried out through the project *Renewing Dialogues in Social and Health Care – Leadership, Well-Being and Productivity* (European Social Fund Development, 2019–2021). The project aims to promote dialogue and well-being in Finnish workplaces. The project is national and will be implemented in nine Finnish provinces, coordinated by Tampere University and funded by the European Social Fund (ESF, Ministry of Social Affairs and Health) and consortium organisations. The project's pilot organisations are providing services for the elderly and child welfare services (child protection and special education). The main goals are to learn dialogue and embed the management of well-being at work as well as renew work processes through continuous development into the everyday processes and structures of work communities.

In the case of basic municipality education, the participant group was comprised of personnel from the municipality's five schools and welfare and family counselling services that students use. The head of the local education department also has been an active participant in this development collaboration, which started in autumn 2020 and will end at the end of 2021. Two of us have been facilitating the development process.

A key principle of Finnish education is that all people should have equal access to education and training; that is, the same educational opportunities should be available to all citizens regardless of ethnic origin, age, wealth, or where they live, as described in the Finnish National Agency's paper, "Finnish education in a nutshell".

As a result of the new education curriculum for basic education, created in 2006, and changes in the law that took place in 2010, aims have included integration and inclusion. In practice, pupils with special needs are integrated into 'normal' classrooms, and support for special needs students is tailored, based on the 'three steps' support model: general support, intensified support, and special support. These changes also have affected the work of teaching staff through encouraging concurrent teaching and closer interprofessional collaboration.

Objectives

The project and development goals were negotiated together with representatives from the target organisations. The main goals were to promote:

- dialogue and multiprofessional collaboration between professionals working with special-needs students'
- professionals' well-being at work
- sharing best practices

Multiprofessional collaboration is a crucial factor in education that is based on integration and inclusion. Students with special needs are a matter for the whole school staff and different professionals, not just special teachers or student welfare services. This calls for sharing tasks and responsibilities, as well as organising collaborative efforts between professionals so that all students have equal opportunities for learning and growth. It also concerns professionals' attitudes, habits, and professional competence. This calls for collective learning and multiprofessional collaboration. Dialogue plays an important role. As William Isaacs points out, it's about listening, voicing, suspending, and respecting (Isaacs 1999.)

Method

The target organisations' needs provided the basis for research-assisted, collaborative, and dialogical development. Core development principles based on dialogue comprise inclusion, participation, polyphony, systematicity, reflectivity and renewal. Based on ideas from Generative Dialogue, the aim is to facilitate dialogue and other interaction that breaks ground for new action and knowledge to make real change happen (Isaacs 1999). We created a flexible development structure and carried out development activities based on the principles of dialogical development:

- At the beginning of the project, we established a representative, multiprofessional *development team* comprising 10 volunteer representatives from each school, different professional groups, and the head of the local education department.
- We conducted a wide *work well-being survey* of the schools' personnel at the beginning of the project. We then provided feedback, along with a written report on the results, to the participants. We also provided individual results and development proposals to each school.
- We carried out *participatory observations* and spent one day in each pilot school to learn more about the teaching and guidance of students with special needs.
- We *interviewed professionals*. We have heard from school social workers, a school psychologist, the head of the local education department, and other professionals from a family child health centre and the adolescent psychiatry field.

- Professionals were invited to *'dialogue spaces'*, which are meetings that focused on encounters, in-depth discussions, and learning from each other. These spaces were organised for the development team, different professional groups (e.g., special needs teachers), primary and upper comprehensive school personnel, and the five pilot schools' principals. The head of the local education department has been an active participant in all these dialogue spaces.
- After each dialogue space we wrote *a development memo* in which we summarised dialogue content and gave schools development tasks.

At the final facilitated dialogue event for the project, we will meet staff from the primary and secondary schools with the aim of promoting pupils' transition from primary to upper secondary school by enhancing collaboration between personnel from different school levels. Due to Covid-19, we've been forced to conduct these 'spaces for dialogue' mainly virtually. Hopefully, these final development actions can be carried out face-to-face.

Outcomes

The development remains ongoing but, based on feedback, the project has been successful so far. Participants have been experiencing the dialogue spaces as an opportunity to get to know each other, reflect on themes relevant to their work, learn from each other, and develop new ideas. The project has promoted several new practices and development in schools. As the local education department head stated, "A genuine dialogue has permeated the whole development project and all its development activities. The project has increased the appreciation and coping skills of children and young people, and strengthened positive pedagogy and inclusion". Thus, the dialogue holds enormous potential.

Learnings

Promoting dialogue requires that the facilitator her/himself believes in the dialogue and strives for it in his or her own actions. Dialogue calls for authenticity, vulnerability, incompleteness, and learning together. A dialogue is possible, both technology-mediated and face-to-face. It requires that we find the courage to use our hearts.

References
"Finnish education in a nutshell". Retrieved from https://www.oph.fi/sites/default/files/documents/finnish_education_in_a_nutshell.pdf.

Isaacs, W. (1999). *Dialogue and the Art of Thinking Together*. New York: Currency.

Conference Session Extracts
From the consideration of the case study with conference participants

Kati Tikkämaki: Our project is ending this year. We still have couple of dialog spaces left and a couple of meetings with the participants, but we are going to end the development actions quite soon. We asked participants' feedback on what we have so far. They told us that they experienced the dialog spaces as an opportunity to get to know each other better, reflect on themes that are relevant to their work and to them as professionals, learned from each other, and had the to develop new ideas. In a way I could call it collective sense making, the ability to really think together and create renewable possibilities.

They have also developed new ideas and new practices, asking, "How we can do things in a different way than we have done previously? What could be a smoother way to do this or that?". We have reached concrete new practices. We have changed reality in a way. The feedback that delighted me the most came from the local education department head. She shared that authentic dialogue has permitted the whole development project and all its development activities, and, in turn, the project increased the appreciation and coping skills of children and young people and strengthened positive pedagogy and inclusion. It was very nice to hear that we have reached the goals that we saw as important at the beginning of the pro project. We too developed through the dialogue and learned new skills.

Speaker: The children you worked with looked fairly young. Were they, mostly six- and seven-year-olds, or did you expand into 12, 13, 15 and 16 years as well?

Kati: Yes, and yes. Here in Finland basic education starts when you are seven years old and goes up to students of around 15 years.

Speaker: How long did this study take? I know that it is ending soon but when did you begin it?

Kati: Even though we do the research-assisted development work it was not really a research project. Rather it was a developmental-project, and the main point was do practical changes and to help people find new practices and develop their work practices. It took approximately one and a half year because they entered into our project a little bit later than other organizations, and due to Covid we had only Zoom and team meetings and we were not able to see face to face. It was very challenging to start the development project through virtual and technological means.

Speaker: How long did it take you to convince the schools to participate in this project? Was anybody resistant?

Kati: There were many feelings when they were told, "OK, now you have a possibility to join this type of development project". I'm sure there were teachers who though, "Oh my gosh, I can't take on anything more. What I'm doing already is enough" or "Not a new project once again". That is the reality. It is very important that you get cooperation and that you convince people that it is worth it, that they really will get something out of it is they use their energy for this. Still, I have to say that people were very motivated. I believe it's due to dialogue. We really tried to listen to them and to their needs and to give them space and not to talk with our voice, rather in each meeting to let them voice their possibilities. As a result, they understood that this is important and meaningful for them and, in return, we were heard also.

Speaker: Was the fundamental objective to bring dialogue into the classroom or was the fundamental objective to help teachers support each other?

Kati: The main, the objectives were to promote multiprofessional cooperation. In that case, I see it more as bringing dialogue to get cooperation and to serve the professionals to do things together. But it will, of course, transfer to the classroom level through the professionals.

Speaker: The way our public schools are structured is kind of political. You got a school board of supervisors for the county. So as implementation dialogic practices in the school system would probably be difficult depending on who sits on those boards. I'm not really sure how you guys are structured. I would like to know the difference between your structures and ours and what the contrasts are between how you implemented your program and how we would implement it.

Kati: It really depends on the context and the size of municipality or city and the educational culture in each country, and so on. We carried this out in quite a small municipality, which was an advantage as people knew each other and even the parents of pupils knew each other. It might not always be good thing but in this case, it was because the number of participants was small, and the head of the local education department was intensively involved in the process.

Regardless of structure, what is important is how enthusiastic the key persons are because as a facilitator, you cannot do everything. One of the most important things is to get people motivated and enthusiastic because they are the ones that will continue the development when we leave. But, of course, there are many things affecting the results and the aims that are possible.

Postscript
The author's reflections, written some months after the conference

The research-assisted development project presented in this paper and conference session was a huge learning process. School as a work context not only has similar possibilities and challenges to any other workplace, but also contains unique characteristics. As a developer, it is important to get to know your environment, and you must also know the people with whom you are doing the development. Dialogue must be learned and supported in everyday work so that it can flourish and promote cooperation. The prerequisite to this is that participants experience dialogue and are motivated to further develop it.

Working as a developer in different work contexts provides great learning opportunities. Facilitating dialogue requires a desire to learn new things and renew and develop oneself as a dialogue partner. Dialogue is a learning process and a possibility with which to grow as a human being and professional.

Writing a paper is a great opportunity to reflect on your thinking and actions and become aware of your learning. When writing a short paper, one must crystallize essential themes. Written text helps you become conscious of your thoughts and reflect on your learning experiences.

Discussing the paper with a multicultural audience created a space for learning. As a presenter, one must explain and question the cultural assumptions one has. For example, in this case these assumptions related to school systems, which differ between countries. It was challenging to explain the essence of a large development project in a short time. I remember thinking after the session about whether I understood the participants' questions correctly and whether I was understood in the way I hoped. Understanding another is not self-evident; it often requires much effort and many open questions.

It was interesting and useful to read the discussion of the conference session as a written text. This helped me recall the questions and answers encountered during the session. Once again, I realised that constructing a common understanding requires sincere curiosity, sufficient time and a desire to understand and be understood.

Dialogue at Proakatemia

Timo Nevalainen and Alina Suni

Context

Proakatemia is a unit in the School of Business & Media in Tampere University of Applied Sciences (TAMK) in Tampere, Finland, that specializes in entrepreneurship and team leadership. Currently there are about 160 team entrepreneur students (TEs) in Bachelor of Business Administration (BBA) and MBA degree programs and 12 team coaches. Last year, Proakatemia started the first bilingual (English and Finnish) international BBA degree program in Entrepreneurship and Team Leadership. This year marks the 22nd anniversary of Proakatemia.

Aims/Objectives

The aim of Proakatemia is to teach through experiential action learning, educating highly skilled entrepreneurs and leaders who have the capability to change business life in Tampere region and in Finland.

Method

Proakatemia is structured around the model of a knowledge-creating company developed by Nonaka & Takeuchi in in Japan in the early 1990s. Their model, often called "SECI", is based on creating and maintaining four different kinds of spaces (*ba* in Japanese) for different knowledge processes: socialization, externalization, combination and internalization. In Proakatemia's model, many of these spaces rely heavily on building and maintaining dialogic relationship between participants.

As its pedagogic framework, Proakatemia relies on team entrepreneurship, team learning and team coaching, all of which depend on dialogical and relational practice and culture and democratic leadership structures within the Proakatemia learning community, comprised of current team entrepreneurship students and their team coaches, as well as hundreds of active alumni members.

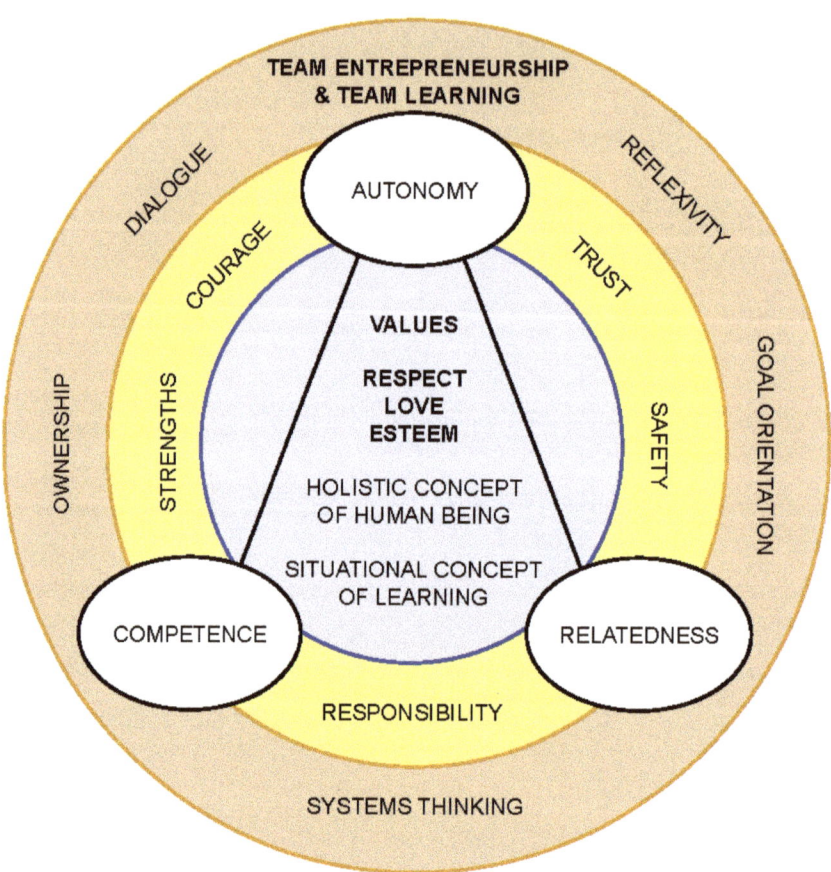

Figure 1. The dynamic model of Proakatemia operating principles (Nevalainen, Lindell & Parkkila, 2021)

Outcomes

Personal outcomes: These are stated best in the words of a TE:
I have learned not to focus my energy on comparing my background and style of doing things to others in a negative light. Though it is important to have a well-functioning team, it is more important to focus on what it is I do rather than focus on what others are not doing. After all, I'm here to study for myself to become the best possible version of myself.

Team outcomes: Team entrepreneur students learn by doing, and they teach one another through dialogue. Topics are chosen together as a team to first build our common knowledge and then to sharpen our expertise.

Usually these dialogues are carried out in a circle, where everyone sits in an equal place. This enables everyone to see each other throughout the session, which helps in the interaction.

Any distractions such as phones are prohibited as a dialogue requires the full presence of its participants for fluent flow.

In addition to learning new information, TEs practice some very basic yet crucial skills such as listening, voicing outcome in the form of different opinions, respecting and understanding the opposite side. Many teams often bring up the dichotomy of the extroverts and introverts. It does take time and nerve to find the balance between speaking up (introverts) and toning down (extroverts).

Contextual outcomes: For several years now, Proakatemia has been at the top of student satisfaction measurements in TAMK, and it is the only unit in Finland to consistently achieve some of the highest marks in almost all of the measurements. Proakatemia graduates currently lead a number of high-profile businesses in the Tampere region and work as managers or specialists in businesses, the public sector and NGOs. Also notable is the number of Proakatemia graduates working as teaching staff or specialists in secondary or higher education.

Learnings

This study model does not just teach team leading; rather it all starts from learning to lead oneself first. Since Proakatemia students are of different ages and come with a variety of backgrounds and work experience, teams can stumble and end up in conflicts if the individuals cannot lead themselves properly. Students with more working experience and – often – age, have already had the time and pressure to learn taking responsibility for their own actions and act more independently. From a coaching and learning point of view, this stumbling often creates spaces for dialogic learning. Different backgrounds, a potential source of conflict, can also be very useful in fuelling the conversation. TE students described their experience as follows:

> *In my opinion one of the most complex things is to build actual, strong trust between the team. Since we get all the tools and time to build team trust, you'd think it comes easily. We have spent a lot of time as a team and a lot of dialogue about our past lives, values, hopes, and fears and traumas. Even with this, the trust might not be built. For our team this has built an atmosphere, where we discuss more of the social aspects rather than work based. If I could lead differently looking back to the beginning with my team, I would focus more on building the trust by doing things in the present than discussing of the past or future.*

> *Our old head coach once told us that many graduates from Proakatemia have wide networks and are equipped with both theory and concrete skills, but there are also those who just sailed along through the program at the expense of others. I have seen this distribution also in my team. Even as I should focus more on what I'm doing rather than what the few others are not, I wonder if my motivation*

and future would look different if our team had everybody fully motivated and focused in this method of studying?

The experiences of TEs vary according to their own interests and those of their teams. As in any organisation or study program, this is perhaps unavoidable also in Proakatemia. What we can do is to turn, through dialogue, these different and sometimes frustrating experiences into material for learning and growth.

Besides the countless different learning outcomes for almost a thousand entrepreneurs in Finland, we have learned that this kind of a program can not only function within a Finnish university of applied sciences, but it also can flourish and achieve impressive results in both learning and student satisfaction. Sometimes it seems that the challenges and frustrations, when overcome together, can even feed into a deeper sense of personal growth and satisfaction.

Conference Session Extracts
From the consideration of the case study with conference participants

Timo Nevalainen: In Proakatemia there are multiple levels of learning. There is the individual level, the team level and the whole community, and they are there to support each other. The traditional view is that university studies is an individual enterprise. In other words, you are there as an individual, your work is judged on an individual level and you get graded as an individual. Our system, however, is based on team learning as we believe it's the team that counts. Each of our teams is fairly large with about 20 people in each team. We do this because when you start a company it would mostly likely be with 20 other people and you would probably not know most of them beforehand. So as coaches we always try to move the attention from an individual towards asking how individual actions affect the team.

Speaker: I find this very interesting because when you do something as a team you create a group identity. What tension do you see between the individual identity, which I think is still very important in some aspects of learning, and the bigger group identity? Group identity can create a lot of conflict because it creates a close-knit system around the team. Do you feel sometimes you sacrifice the individual for the team?

Alina Suni: Is it part of the ethos that the team, the group comes first?

Speaker: I think that relationships build stronger individual identities, and so we never sacrifice individuals for the team and we also never overlook the individual experience.

Speaker: The students actually accomplish very significant practical things, perhaps even solving real-world problems. Is that true Timo?

Timo: Yes. As an individual you have to learn to understand the hopes and needs of others and how you can fit into that. If we do these studies as individuals it would come as quite a shock to enter the workplace where all of a sudden you have to be a part of a team and learn to do things, not just from your own perspective and your own hopes and wishes, but also for the common good of the company you are working for.

Speaker: In my corporate training around team development the individual contribution was emphasized as a unique and special part of a mosaic. Everyone contributes in a unique way. It's not about just team identity or individual identity, rather the whole is greater than the sum of its parts.

Timo: I follow what you say. If you try to get rid of the differences between people and you try to get rid of the tensions that it causes you lose key insights to team learning.

Speaker: Have you found that this approach attracts a different type of student or learner? Or do you see hesitation or resistance at the beginning? I'm curious how students are introduced to the concept.

Timo: In our area of Finland we are well known and we attract entrepreneurial young people. Any student who has been to high school is welcome to do our entrance exam and enter our selection process.

Speaker 2: A question about how dialogue comes into things. Is it involved in everything you do or is it regarded as something that you do in certain areas?

Alina: I'd say dialogue is present every day and in every moment, even when our communication happens in WhatsApp. It is something we try to always remember, and we will surely be reminded of it by our teammates when we are not bringing our part in making it work. We have weekly training sessions together, eight hours with the team, where we sit in a circle with no lap laptops and no phones. We just sit with our pencils and a notebook. We make notes and we try to learn together. We rarely have situations where somebody comes to just teaches us something and where we are left with just information. We are very good at giving feedback.

Timo: It's the only program that I have seen with a dedicated space, of two times four hours, reserved for dialogue each week.

Speaker: Can you speak a little about the dialogical training you do to become good communicators? I'm interested in that.

Timo: The people who have been at Proakatemia for a year or longer take care of the initial training sessions. They bring in the practices of listening, suspending, respecting and voicing one's experience.

Speaker: It is a soft approach of teaching by role modeling and coaching rather than a formal training . . .

Timo: It could be described as soft but I sometimes feel we challenge the students much harder than in normal programs. You are basically running your own company, a real company registered in Finland. You have to run it like a real company, which puts you under pressure. There is high tension within the team at times about the goals of the team the company. A big part of working as a coach in Proakatemia is about creating and maintaining a safe space with a sense that we are in this together. It takes time before most people realize that we are in this together and that it is everybody's responsibility to take care of the quality of interactions in a team and to use and provoke the tensions needed to encourage learning.

Postscript

The authors' reflections written some months after the conference

We presented a case study in The World Needs Dialogue! conference 2021 on TAMK Proakatemia, an innovative degree program in Entrepreneurship and Team Learning in Tampere, Finland, which has a history of more than 20 years. Writing about Proakatemia came quite naturally and we reflected on two perspectives, that of a Team Coach and that of a graduate (a former Team Entrepreneur) in the program.

In our session we reflected together on the inherent tensions involved in teamwork and starting, building and running an enterprise with others, whom you may not have even met before and whose goals in life and business can differ greatly from yours. We also discussed the role of continuous and disciplined practice of dialogue in making sense of a team, its goals and the whole community and, perhaps more importantly, one's own unique role in relation to them.

Reading the excerpt reminded me of a phrase from Patrick Lencioni, an expert on building teams, "*Teamwork ultimately comes down to practicing a small set of principles over a long period of time. Success is not a matter of mastering subtle, sophisticated theory, but rather of embracing common sense with uncommon levels of discipline and persistence*". (Lencioni, 2002). In Proakatemia, it is dialogue that is at the core of this common sense.

Relay Race: Our Next Generation of Practitioners

Heidemarie Wünsche-Piétzka

Context

My opportunity to work with Dialogue began in the 1990s. The German Unification process was a real challenge, especially for citizens of the former German Democratic Republic (GDR), also known as East Germany. Various East-West projects were developed and implemented to support this process, including dialogic approaches in which I was able to participate.

In more recent years I have had many opportunities to work with dialogue in the European Union. These included projects helping new member countries to meet EU gender equality legislation, collaborating in Learning Partnerships, working in Small- and Medium-Sized Enterprises (SME), and in administration to enhance the understanding of dialogue.

In a three-year, EU-financed project we engaged two interested people from each of eight different countries (including Iceland and Turkey) for dialogue facilitation and, finally, founded our European Network for Dialogue Facilitation.

We had many impressive experiences in Youth Dialogues in these EU projects. For example, we worked with students from the University of Oviedo (Spain) and post-graduate students on the Erasmus Mundus programme at the Centre for Women's Studies, with young prisoners from the Buzias Re-Education Centre (Romania) for juvenile offenders and with 10-year-old pupils of a school in Ankara, Turkey. As a result, we also focused our attention in Germany on the young generation – pupils and students. The public school system in Germany does not provide opportunities to train in dialogic skills, yet co-creative dialogic communication can and should be a valued part of schooling to establish respect and deep listening, and to provide skills for common thinking. Introducing dialogue skills in education would also provide what is needed for young people to actively participate in dealing with current problems and in designing a future for the individual and society. Based on our firm conviction that young people are entitled to and able to play a big part in designing their future, we saw, and still see, a specific need to equip them with dialogic skills, which are widely unpractised in youth culture.

Aims

We wanted to spark interest among young people in the quality and possibilities of dialogue based on our understanding of the approach of David Bohm. We wanted to enable interested young people to learn dialogic skills to use in their peer groups and families, and in cultural and political engagement. The themes and problems of young people are important and cannot be ignored when decisions are being made for the development of a sustainable future of society. We aimed to provide individual skill development to help young people enter the labour market and to participate in democracy on various levels. Also we intended to offer a course to become a certified Dialogue facilitator for interested and engaged students. We were interested in finding suitable regional partners (NGOs, youth organisations and enterprises), and engaging our certified Dialogue facilitators in German Federal States to continue Youth Dialogues (including all organisational requirements) in a cooperative and co-creative way.

Method

Our preparation team decided to organise Youth Dialogues (YD) as pilot events in each of the 16 German States. These would serve as the basis for the regional follow-up that would be led by Dialogue facilitators in cooperation with participants of YD. The preparation and follow-up work were undertaken by volunteers from the institut dialog transnational.

We cooperated with the Schwarz Medien-Center in Meerane, which is also a printing firm. The director is an engaged Dialogue facilitator and practitioner and was part of our preparation team. A corporate design was prepared for all the YDs nationwide. This was used for participants folders, which contained an invitation, information about our intention to offer and experience a new kind of creative communication, and a short description of the cooperating organisations. Afterwards all participants and cooperating organisations received documentation (photos and short texts) about the event.

We decided to start in Meerane (Saxony, Germany) and in 2015 we began our preparations.

We visited secondary schools in the region and explained our intention. Most of the school directors were interested in opening up this chance for their pupils. Selected pupils were invited individually with a personal letter, asking for the written consent of their parents. Participation was free of charge.

When we met, our agenda for the day/half day was nearly the same as in our well-evaluated previous Youth Dialogues. The YD was led by a duo of Dialogue facilitators.

The process is still ongoing. We have arranged Pilot Youth Dialogues in six German Federal lands, and three are now in preparation. Follow-up YDs are taking place in the regions. In total, 150 young people participated in Pilot Youth Dialogues.

Outcomes

Our approach to working in a dialogic setting with youngsters proved to be successful. The quality of dialogic communication – that is, slow down, show respectful behaviour, listen deeply, use the talking symbol, don't interrupt – was a new experience for them. It met their needs to come to a deeper understanding and for common and mutual learning.

All reflections after the event placed emphasis on the cultivated and beneficial atmosphere. Participants wished to learn and to experience more of it. Some expressed their interest to work as a Dialogue facilitator. Meanwhile, five students passed a one-year course and now work as certified members of the institute with their different peer groups. They just took the initiative and founded a Youth Dialogue Academy.

Learnings

We were surprised at the speed at which an atmosphere of trust developed between the participants. Furthermore, the seriousness with which they dealt with the subjects was impressive. In the same way, we were astonished at the capability of self-reflection expressed by some of the participants. We also did not expect such a long-lasting interest in implementing dialogic skills and in spreading dialogue messages.

This future-oriented YD project is a great learning opportunity for all the people involved. After the Pilot Youth Dialogues we got much feedback from our colleagues regarding the joyful intergenerational dimension and effects.

Author's Addendum:
Heidemarie Wünsche-Piétzka's comments during the small-group consideration of her paper

I was born in the western part of Germany and grew up in the eastern part. In the unification of Germany in 1990 it was a real challenge to have fruitful conversations between East and West. We all had the same language, but we didn't understand each other. It was very hard for those who came from the eastern part of Germany – in the first days of the breakdown of the wall the interest from the western side of Germany was very large, but it tended to be a one-way learning process. The western Germans were already familiar with their democratic system, but we were not. It was a situation in which we were not on the same level. The NGOs especially tried to bring together people in a unifying process. From the Eastern side, it was difficult to integrate because our whole economic system was broken down and the political system was completely new to us.

Over a lot of transnational projects in Europe I had the possibility to work in dialogic settings. I also got the opportunity to work with children. You can see from the paper that we worked with children in a school of Ankara. We worked in a prison with young offenders, and with students in Spain, as well as in Iceland, Turkey, and in other countries. In working with people in eastern European countries we had to take into account that they were not able to learn in a free setting; for example, they were not able to sit in a circle without any tables. They needed something to hold in their hands, or to have books on the table in order to learn. That was one of the great challenges.

Since 2016, based on our European projects, we've been developing dialogue in order to engage young people in their peer groups, for example, and in their classrooms or in their families. We have developed a model for youth dialogues which we intend to implement in all 16 German states. We now have six youth dialogue pilot projects and are preparing for three more.

I would like to describe a little bit how we did these projects. We prepared and certified a group of facilitators in our Institute to prepare for one pilot dialogue in each German state. These facilitators took over the responsibility for conducting the youth dialogues. The youth dialogues are implemented in different timeframes – sometimes for half a day, sometimes a full day.

In some cases, when the students were not 18 years old, we needed the permission of the parents so they could travel to the place of the dialogue session. A large number of pupils tried to apply to participate, but we couldn't take everyone because we decided to have a maximum of 25 people in each session. We felt they should always be male-female mixed groups, except for in the prison.

We started with a small introductory session, where they told us why they were participating. Then we explained a little bit about the history of dialogue, connected with some information about David Bohm. After some key impressions about dialogue from the dialogue facilitator, the participants had time to think about what type of problems or themes they wanted to deal with in a dialogue. We collected these all on the floor in the middle of the circle, where we had flowers, a singing bowl and a candle. We called this place the didactic center, to help focus people on the words, ideas and thinking of the others as participants collected and placed the subjects the center of the room.

And then the dialogue faculty left the room while the pupils agreed upon which subject, theme or problem they wanted to deal with in their dialogue. After a short break we introduced the rules we wanted to implement for dialogue. This was important, as our idea was to build relatively strong rules in order to meet their interest in a certain kind of disciplined communication. We introduced not only the core skills and competencies of dialogue, but we also gave them the opportunity to participate actively in the dialogue by integrating their own activities.

On Dialogic Relations Transforming from Monologic to Dialogic

Tzofnat Peleg-Baker

Context

Though we live in a reality filled with opportunities to connect across continents and time zones, we are not guaranteed connectedness—authentic and meaningful experience wherein new possibilities are co-generated for ourselves and others. However, our experience in a culture dominated by Western, individualist ethos is typically monologic, a Buberian *I-It* instrumental relational structure—unidirectional, subject-object relationship. A *self* relates to the *other* as secondary, less valuable. Relationships are fragmented, and always subject to suspicion. When cast as separate, bounded beings, people don't carry much responsibility toward one another, perpetuating transactional relationships with less caring, empathy or concern.

This formula between *constructers*, historically, white educated men, and those *being constructed*—people who are not included in the dominant group, as women, non-Western, people of color, people with different sexual orientation, or of a different perspective, preserves an adversarial, blaming discourse. In this context, the idea of dialogue has attracted many scholars and practitioners.

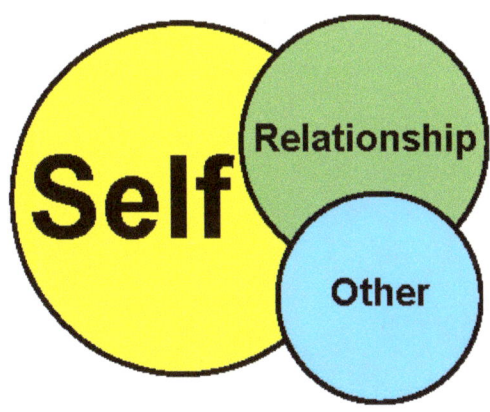

Figure 1: Positioning of *Self* & *Other* in Western Tradition

Aims

While presenting the theoretical and practical foundation of my dialogic perspective may be beyond the scope of this paper, I hope to trigger some thought. I set a goal to help people and organizations build alternative ways of being together to address social fragmentation.

Method

I began my dialogic journey in Israel two decades ago when I joined the Institute of Democratic Education. Our goal was to expand democratic education in two ways: building democratic schools and integrating democratic practices in public schools. We supported 20 new projects in the first five years. Children in democratic education are accorded the same human rights and freedom as adults. They *live by* democratic values rather than learning *about* them. All stakeholders—staff, students, and parents, make decisions jointly within participative practices, such as a parliament, various committees, project teams and learning gatherings. These schools—more than 30 today—report significantly less violence than conventional schools. However, because we felt the culture was still adversarial, we increased our emphasis on relationships in the *Dialogic Experience* program, where we combined what I later termed *insight* and *action*.

Insight refers to reflective practice: deliberate consciousness-raising efforts about assumptions and perceptions of self, other, and relation. Using reflective models, participants reexamined their views and manifestation of relational notions, such as respect, power, inclusivity, freedom or conflict. *Action* denotes participative practices to cement stakeholders' new relational understandings in daily life. For the new understandings to take seed, I have engaged organizational stakeholders, workshops participants and students in questioning assumptions and practicing new insights in whatever they do with family, community or at work while learning from each other's experiences.

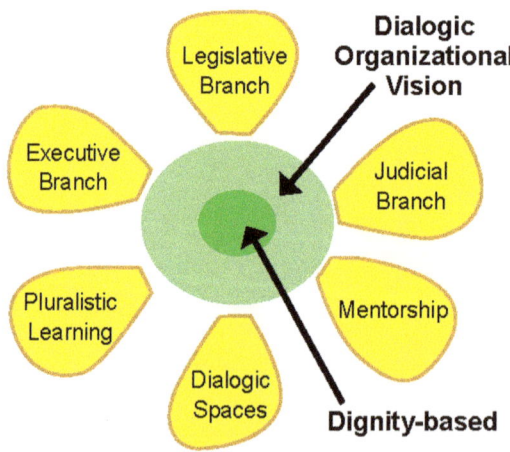

Figure 2: Democratic Platforms in Dialogic Education

Outcomes

Here are a couple of examples of the impact of the dialogic approach that I continue developing and applying in all projects, workshops and classes. When Idit, a student of the *Dialogic Experience,* became the principal of a struggling school in a rough neighborhood in Israel, she applied her new skills to transforming a school where students dropped out and teachers, demotivated, were leaving. She led a dialogic organization for 16 years, engaging staff, students and parents in both reflection and collaborative practices. Forming a dialogic vision, she emphasizes, helped rebuild trust and a sense of belonging and set a safe container for legitimizing and addressing differences and conflicts. Vision was followed by strategy and a detailed plan for specific dialogic practices and programs to support stakeholders' daily dialogic actions. Idit: "Dialogic platforms turned the new understandings into a way of life. All actions were evaluated in light of the vision to ensure it is reflected in all school activities." Parents were encouraged to give feedback and were even involved in curriculum planning. Stakeholders regularly convened in the parliament to make decisions on various issues from uniforms to trips to curriculum issues. Routine gatherings like *Hot Chocolate* morning dialogues introduced students to different perspectives and helped in embracing differences.

An MBA student in my conflict course offers another example: "Initially, I thought that the skills learned in this course will be necessary only for rare situations when there is contention, or for times when I'm negotiating a high-profile business deal . . . I began to see the value of what we learn for all daily interactions, from making a decision on which movie to go with my wife to managing a project with my co-worker or talking with my supervisor about a project. Every day, there are all these opportunities waiting for me to improve my relations with others and learn from them . . . if only I can see the value in others and our relations."

Learnings

My understanding of relational accountability has evolved over the years through my practice, combined with pursuing advanced degrees and studying social constructionists' ideas. Improving our capabilities to form a more dialogic human experience is an uphill battle in an individualist culture. We must move beyond the default individual unit to a relational one—to the space we co-create. This challenge requires surfacing what is taken for granted and transforming stubborn confrontational patterns deeply ingrained in our culture. It takes a more complex, multidirectional outlook of social interactions. Combining *insight* and *action* seems necessary to ensure lasting relational forms of being.

Dialogic relation is rooted in recognizing that we construct one another; therefore, we share responsibility for the quality of our interactions and their individual and collective outcomes. Being dialogic is neither a single event nor a particular intervention. It is an alternative to the dominant monologic relational mode, recognizing our mutual embeddedness in each other's lives. While the Western, monologic formulation separates us, encouraging us to avoid one another, the dialogic alternative defines our freedom not as being disconnected *from* others but being actively interconnected *with* one another. If we can deepen our understanding of the nature of our relations as we have been studying the individual mind to explain the human experience, we might be able to open new horizons for reducing hostility and paving innovative ways to connect.

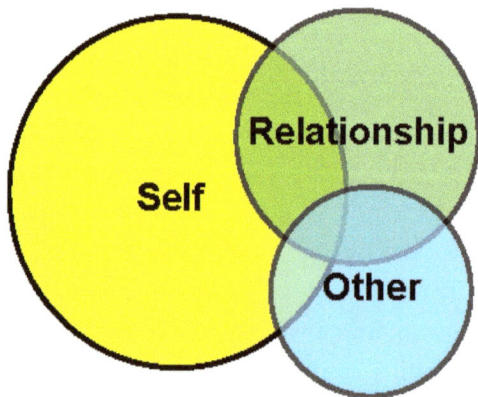

Figure 3: Positioning of *Self* & *Other* in Dialogic Relation —egalitarian, inclusive formula

Conference Session Extracts
From the consideration of the case study with conference participants

Speaker: I'm a superintendent in the Virginia Department of Corrections. I think our actions and how we treat others come from our environment, from the thinking and experiences that we've gleaned through the years. However, I also think it's our personal responsibility to treat others as we would have them treat us. I'm very open minded and will listen to anybody and what they have to say, because I'm not always right. I like to believe I am, but that's not the case. Sometimes when you deal with another person with understanding of where they're coming from, despite their values being different to yours, it can affect your life in a positive manner. So I'm very open to what other people have to say.

Tzofnat Peleg Baker: Please share your thoughts with everyone, whatever you have on your mind.

Speaker: I experienced two conflicting experiences. Mr. Clarke got here 10 or 15 years ago, and we transitioned out of a more monologic organization. At the same time, I was still affiliated with groups in the education field where I met with a leader who conducted business as a monologue on a regular basis. So I had to attend meetings and conferences engaging with both modes. For me, the dialogic practices we utilize today are much more inclusive of people and their viewpoints, and that produces good results and buy-in. Staff members have a voice, they get to help make decisions and they buy into the direction we head in. It is not to say we won't have to come back to meet, and maybe tweak, whatever we came up with before, but there is a certain amount of buy-in. In the other organization I saw how the monologue led to the downfall of that leader. He was dismissed and is no longer in the organization. I think we're heading in the right direction, and I do think we need to continue this journey.

Speaker: In my job as a warden what I find challenging on a daily basis is the relationship with inmates. You mentioned a protective mode. Okay. Establishing rapport with inmates every day is a protective mode. You have to learn dialogic skills to be able to have a conversation that establishes some sort of rapport. I have been in the Department of Corrections for 26 years, and when we started it was, "Do what you were told to do and don't ask any questions." With Mr. Clarke's arrival we have been committing to dialogue, and it's been very helpful to our organization.

Speaker: I agree with you. I think modern culture is marinated in a view that each individual is a self-contained unit and that, somehow, each individual has their own behaviors and their own knowledge and so on. Even when we do dialogic training we very often still think it natural to train only the individual. You have an instructor who gives instructions to individuals, who then has to learn it. It's a mode of transferring knowledge from a trainer to a student. It misses that the human mind is fundamentally dialogical. Our thinking is, to a great extent, an inner dialogue which we have with ourselves. We are also constantly in relation with other people who influence our thinking so we never have our own thoughts. They're always shared with others, and at the same time there's always an inner dialogue. Unfortunately, for a lot of people today, it's more of an inner discussion or an inner debate than an inner dialogue. I think that understanding the view you are advocating is an important aspect of learning dialogue. There has to be firsthand learning in the way that Peter Garrett talked about it earlier today. Obviously there is an introduction, which is going to be secondhand learning, but real learning happens firsthand where it is fundamentally relational, and this happens through reflecting together with other people about our experiences.

Speaker: I find that there is a place for both monologic and dialogic modes. In my work the planning phase is dialogic; we ask to hear all the ideas and we figure out how to solve a particular problem together. Then, when we are in the middle of the operation, the mode becomes monologic. There is no time to talk about it; no, we have to go and take care of this, and when we come back for an after-action report it becomes dialogic again. I always said to my guys, "Once we've made the plan, we all have to go in with the same frame of mind. When we come back, then we can discuss all the good things that happened, all the bad things that happened and ways of changing it for the next time."

Speaker: A while ago I was in a dialogue training with native Americans, and somebody said it was enlightening because it was a completely different perspective than a Western approach to things. Somebody else said that emotion always happens first and then reasoning occurs based on that emotion. So reasoning is always conditioned by emotions. First we feel, and then we reason. I see a feeling going around that is mostly fear. And people act from that sense of fear and, so, they act protectively all the time.

Postscript

The author's reflections, written some months after the conference

The work of helping people re-examine their connections and acquire new skills to restructure these through *Reflective Practice* (as opposed to reflection) has been illuminating and transformative for participants and me.

Writing this paper was an opportunity to present the idea of transforming how we relate to each other from a monologic to a dialogic mode by focusing on the environment—the system, context and relationships—instead of on the individual. It was challenging, mainly because of the strict number of words that did not enable capturing the depth of the theoretical and practical foundation of a dialogic perspective.

I found openness and curiosity toward systemic relational ideas among the conference participants, who expressed their desire to learn more and use this lens to re-reexamine their interactions.

The case study captured very generally two decades of dialogic work. Reviewing the excerpts from the conference session reminded me of what people expressed about moving from monologic to more dialogic modes of relationship, and the examples they shared from daily work in the Department of Corrections. I found the use of the relational lens I offered for reflecting on the relationship between a guardian and inmates useful for re-examining participants' personal and professional experiences. A participant said, "Even when we do dialogic training, we very often still think it natural to train only the individual . . . an instructor who gives instructions to individuals . . . It's a mode of transferring knowledge from a trainer to a student," which reinforces our default monologic state of being.

I feel enriched by having a conversation with people about my work. Different perspectives nurture my thinking. One speaker talked about phases. Some call for a monologic mode and some for a dialogic mode, like the planning phase the speaker thought should be dialogic versus the operational phase that, according to this speaker, should be monologic. I hope to continue exploring this question.

Section Three

Putting Dialogue to Work for Healing

It is healthy for people to talk and think together about things that matter to them. When people cannot do so for whatever reason, it results in challenges about how to participate with others and contributes to social fragmentation. Thinking on one's own is different from talking and thinking with others. It is what cannot be talked about that drives stress, disengagement and violation. When things can be talked about, then respect and appreciation emerge naturally. Clearly Dialogue has a fundamental contribution to make in any socio-therapeutic process. The participation with others changes awareness, understanding, assumptions and implications. It even changes what people realise they can do. We have three papers on this theme related to recovery from substance abuse; the inclusion of experts, families and autistic people in a common enquiry; and a novel example of placing Dialogue into a contentious family disagreement to enable healing.

Helena Wagener has considerable experience coaching people with substance abuse disorders. She incorporates a deeply dialogic approach to building awareness of triggered reactions within safe co-learning spaces. Her online weekly Pocket Rehab sessions are a testament to her effectiveness.

Including autistic people with family members, support workers and academics is very dialogic and very effective. **Jonathan Drury, Kate Salinsky and Jackie Elliott** consider the commissioned Autism Dialogues they held in the UK, and report highly nurturing experiences within a safe environment.

Linda Ellinor is candid about her family challenges when a sister was ostracised by other family members at Thanksgiving. She addresses the matter successfully by convening a Family Dialogue that uses fun exercises, enquires into assumptions, and enables painful issues to be talked about.

Dialogic Enquiry within a Recovery Coaching Environment

Helena Wagener

Context

The Ubuntu Addiction Community Trust (UACT) is a non-profit and public benefit organisation that supports individuals, families, organisations and communities in addressing substance use disorders. David Collins, the founder of UACT, recognized that recovery coaching could add a forward-thinking, solutions-driven approach to the therapeutic and group support work already supporting the addiction space in South Africa. In 2016, UACT established a Workplace platform to support and empower professional recovery coaches as they complete practice hours for certification, build and maintain recovery coaching businesses and create supportive communities of practice.

In the early days of establishing the workplace platform, I witnessed an enlightening dynamic at a training event. A conversation on absent fathers triggered strong reactions among a group with diverse histories and experiences of inequality and racial injustice. As conflict fragmented the group, I was unable to speak. Others were also stuck. Some chose to attack or support viewpoints while others offered solutions. And some, like me, pulled back and silently observed. We were fragmented not only because of our differences but also in how we talked together. In that moment my theoretical understanding on worldviews, triggers and of dialogue became a lived reality. I, therefore, decided to introduce dialogic concepts to a recovery coaching class I facilitated on Workplace each week. The purpose of the class was to review and practically apply coaching models and skills from our five-day recovery coaching training.

Aim

My aim was to address group dynamics among coaches and trainee coaches through building an awareness of links between triggers and habitual communication styles, as well as how we could talk together to create safer co-learning spaces. I would introduce dialogic theory and relate it to recovery coaching concepts and models to build on existing knowledge. I wanted to create an open, generative, voluntary group, free from financial exclusivity or rigid structures so that we could model a psychosocial support system that is flexible and resource light, run by and for participants, where learning occurs in our own contexts and is driven by our own questions.

Method

We meet weekly in a dedicated Zoom room, which forms part of the 'Pocket Rehab' community Workplace platform. The group runs for an hour and starts with a check-in. The check-in is followed by a short learning piece, which is then unpacked with people sharing their thinking around a topic and how it applies to their lives and coaching practice. At times I also invite guests or collaborate with core group members to bring more specialized information or processes.

The group is open to anyone on the UACT Workplace platform. Between four and 10 people attend at a time, and about 180 people have attended over the last two-and-a-half years. Currently 95 people are registered to receive regular updates on Workplace, and they often invite others. Most people attend one to 12 sessions, but some have attended up to 50 sessions and some only one.

Outcomes

Based on participant feedback, the groups demonstrate a socio-therapeutic impact with increased awareness of their inner processes and how they affect the outer lives of participants. Both regular and new members often comment on the safety and authenticity of the peer-led space and how it supports their recovery. The space is generative, with people reporting new understanding of the training concepts both personally and professionally. Because the space is voluntary, open and free it remains accessible and current. Here are a few participant comments:

> *"A great class with fantastic people. Tools which one can apply in everyday living and to use for clients."*

> *"So grateful for the safe container to experiment in."*

> *"Beautiful. Today and, actually, this whole lockdown brought to mind how very dependent all of us are on mostly everything and that's okay, actually, more than okay because we are not only receiving*

but also giving. I always felt I had to give more than I received. Now I realise, there is no competition, no way to measure, we just all do the best we know how."

"Realising how resilient I am with my own situations and circumstance but get bumped out of the resilient zone when it comes to my son and his."

"Thank you for showing up each and every week, our time is always so thought provoking and moves me to go just that little bit deeper, I much appreciate your commitment."

Learnings

My initial attempt to present dialogue concepts and skills theoretically was not successful. Now most learning takes place through knowledge exchange, communication and collaboration. Because we relate openly about our own experiences and understanding, respectful suspension of thought is modelled and assimilated rather than 'taught'. This approach, however, might work well because many participants are familiar with the fellowship and 'spiritual principles' of AA (Alcoholics Anonymous) and NA (Narcotics Anonymous), and these concepts relate well to the dialogic principles of non-judgement, authentic sharing and listening with respect. At the same time, the safety of the container is sometimes seen as more important than authentically confronting any views or comments that might be experienced as intrusive or disrespectful.

With regards to inner processes and how these affect the outer lives of participants, a dynamic tension seems to exist between the psychosocial insights needed for resilience and the need to create and implement goals leading to more sustainable lives. For example, as I take on more of a leadership role in UACT, I am frequently challenged. Unless I consciously address these challenges, I disproportionately focus on spiritual and psychological processes and, therefore, fall behind with work and household commitments. At the same time, when I apply process-related insights to leadership and relational challenges, I become more competent, and my ability to generate income and support increases. This learning encourages me to collaborate with others who engage with recovery, dialogue, trauma resilience, coaching and sustainable livelihoods. Talking together could increase our understanding of how socio-psychological groups can more directly address the dynamic between healing the past and creating the future.

Conference Session Extracts
From the consideration of the case study with conference participants

Speaker: Could you elaborate about the two portions of suspension? I realize that it is a must when trying to build a safe container, where people feel the freedom to express things.

Helena Wagener: Thank you for the question. It made me realize that I left out an important part. I think for suspension to happen, there are two parts that I talked about (the way Peter and Jane taught me). One is that we want to be able to suspend our thinking and just really listen to someone as if we don't have any assumptions or judgements - we just want to hear them. The other suspension (Peter always says) is like suspending something up in the air - we take something that's happening in our own minds, that nobody will be aware of unless we speak it, and we suspend it outside for all to see. To make that kind of suspension safe we need to contract with one another, and that's the part that I left out. In all our groups we are very clear about what we can and cannot say.

Speaker: I am from mental health and wellness services in the Virginia Department of Corrections and this concept of healing through dialogue came up in my author session a little bit earlier. I would like to hear more about healing through dialogue.

Helena: Healing through dialogue happens in many ways, but in my community it mostly happens through being able to say things that we are not normally able to say. Like saying, "I know I should use this model to plan my time, but every time I pick up that piece of paper and I start planning, I actually just feel like crying. I don't want to do it!" Then someone else will say, "Oh my gosh, I feel the same way", and somebody else will say, "Well I think that you should just put it behind you". Another might say, "Ooh, I feel very uncomfortable when I hear you saying that . . ." And there's this ongoing conversation where there's respect for what people are saying. There's also a tracking where we often just stop and ask, "What have we achieved?", or when the trauma feels overwhelming we might ask, "What do we need in this group? How can we support one another? How are we unable to support one another, what other help is needed?" It's been a very informal process, and my suspicion is that there's more that can be done.

Speaker: Helena, I love that you created a safe space. This space for people who are recovering, would really remove a lot of barriers and stigma here in

America. We have a lot of stigma still – in even our language. In the safe space that you're creating through dialogue, I feel some of that could even be confronted if, for example, someone used language that was offensive. Have you found that there are some specific steps that can create that safe space and make it even more effective? Are your groups gender specific, or are there other ways that you have designed the groups besides using dialogue practices?

Helena: I've got a trauma aware approach, so I always give people choice. I find that people in recovery have had many places in their lives where they haven't had choice - either as children or with whatever else caused the trauma. They might have been self-medicating. Or even when you're addicted or you've got a substance use disorder (and here I'm speaking only for myself) there was a sense of not having a choice. In some ways the substance started driving my choices, right? So, I find it's very important to always give people choice. If I have a check-in question, only answer if you want to. Giving people choice empowers them and this creates safety.

Speaker: I heard you talk about triggers and people getting stuck when they're triggered. That resonated with me. When I am trying to steer away from conflict, I will stay in a follow mode or try to connect with someone else in a dialogue to avoid that conflict. When you sense that going on, how do you bring that out into the open? I think that's a really powerful skill to be able to do that in a group.

Helena: As a group, we regularly talk about what kind of things trigger us, and why. It's building a resilience and some language about it. I'll also often call myself out - because when I feel triggered I tend to bystand, but I don't voice what I see. I'm scared that if I say something, I'll get into trouble or I'll say something wrong. So I really step into my courage and I'll say this is what's happening for me. I will ask permission. I'll say, "I'm noticing something, and can we look at it?" Then I will name it and ask other people in the group if they are prepared to share how it affects them.

Speaker: I think first and foremost is to establish that degree of feeling comfortable in a group. Then, aside from being brave enough, I guess it is important to be vulnerable and to share things that challenge the way people had originally been thinking. I appreciate your guidance and suggestions on ways I can bystand a lot more and on how to ensure more inclusion by the group collectively to help one another.

Postscript

The author's reflections, written some months after the conference

When I first introduced dialogic theory to the UACT space we all got a bit lost in the theory. However, when I changed my approach and related the dialogic actions of move, follow, oppose and bystand in small increments during a weekly peer-learning space it offered us a new way to relate to familiar concepts of triggers, habitual ways of reacting and being bumped out of the resilience zone. Next I introduced the principles of listen, voice, respect and suspend. All I needed to do was introduce a relevant check-in question, briefly relate a principle to information the group was already familiar with, set clear time and communication boundaries and occasionally share my inner process when challenged by an outer process – and the group did the rest. What struck me was how trusting each voice, including my own, enabled us to create safer co-learning spaces.

Rereading my case study reminded me how the process of writing what was – up to that point – quite an organic process, allowed me to see emerging patterns that I was not consciously aware of, such as the struggle between processing things internally and acting on them externally. I also got a better idea of the scope and impact of the project, which made me more confident to step into new projects and collaborations.

Reading through the extract, I was struck by a question asked about how the composition of a group contributes to its safety. At the time my answer was that giving the group ongoing choice was what created much of the safety we experienced. However, now that I am more consciously engaging with groups outside the recovery space, I realize that the process of going through recovery, as well as completing the recovery coaching training, preselected certain individuals who felt safe with one another and the topics. Working in less contained spaces I now recognise a need to put more thought into who is in the room, speaking about what and why, and how this combination affects the safety and authenticity of every person involved.

Autism Dialogue in Derby City and Derbyshire

Jonathan Drury, Kate Salinsky and Jackie Elliott

Context

In 2021 the Derby Clinical Commissioning Group (CCG) hired our firm, Dialogic Action CIC* to work with them to improve and develop their services for autism and neurodiverse communities. This case study describes and evaluates this piece of work; the study was co-produced by the stakeholders and participants in the project itself.

CCG faced several problems: specifically, they noted that their different services were fragmented, leading to a lack of coherence. Waiting lists were growing and people were 'falling through the net'. Parents, caregivers and children were suffering from a lack of support with knock-on effects to mental and physical illness, despondency and anger. The Clinical Group recognised that, over the long term, lack of appropriate provision was creating an unknown future, since today's neurodivergent young people are tomorrow's adults.

They also acknowledged that there are many existing (isolated) examples of good, enthusiastic initiatives but that staff, stakeholders and users who care were feeling disempowered and powerless because not all autism voices were being heard sufficiently. Derby CCG also appreciated that community is very important. The picture of service provision in January 2021 was a complex range of public-, private- and third-sector services that needed to demonstrate cost-effectiveness and success.

Dialogic Action CIC created the Autism Dialogue Approach® with the aim of improving the lives of autistic people by tackling isolation, reducing social anxiety, raising acceptance, increasing community cohesion and addressing fragmentation in organisations. Our experience in this work has shown that including autistic people directly benefits them socio-therapeutically. Sharing stories, thoughts, and experiences of autism in a safe and confidential micro-community nurtures familiarity, reducing the negative effects of social anxiety that are increased by isolation. This approach raises morale, empowers people and leads to an improved sense of well-being and quality of life in a holistic, systemic fashion that benefits families and communities too.

---

* A CIC (Community Interest Company) is a UK limited social enterprise company which exists to benefit the community, using their profits and assets for the public good.

Aims

Derby CCG's aim for their work is compatible with our own:

To empower autism and neurodiverse communities and organisations, to facilitate and nurture a sense of belonging and empowerment. For example, help individuals and groups to become more reflective, offer peer group support and encourage self-help."

Their stated objectives made us a good fit to work together: to support communication universally, to renew empowerment of core staff and teams, to release systemic blocks and latent energy, to clarify common understanding and purpose, to revitalise both staff and clients, to improve health and well-being for staff and service users, to overhaul economics and save costs and, finally, to create a more dynamic, inclusive and accessible hub. We used dialogue to build toward these goals.

Method

Initial interviews. Before the dialogues we conducted nine individual interviews with the participants who were both stakeholders and leaders. We asked the following questions:

- If you look at the Derbyshire autism system today, what is your experience of it?
- If you could wave a magic wand, what would you change and how?

These interviews informed the two dialogue facilitators about how the prevailing system presented itself to the people using the services, and they provided improved understanding and relations with individuals in the cohort prior to the group work. Subtle characteristics of both individual and systemic influences were acknowledged by the interviewers, who were then better equipped as facilitators. The interviews were held in confidence; no feedback was provided to any other parties.

The Autism Dialogue format. A typical 'Autism Dialogue' on Zoom is usually up to 30 people and lasts from 90 minutes to three hours, including breaks. The number of sessions in a series varies from six to 10. Participants are consenting autistic adults (invited rather than referred), parents, workers and academics connected to autism. There should be a minimum of two experienced facilitators and one of them should identify as autistic (Asperger's included). Sessions open with a short, guided mindfulness session and, after a check-in, the group generates its own topics of enquiry and aims for slow-paced, free-flowing conversation using the four dialogic practices. It is a safe, confidential, and generative atmosphere, but not without discomfort. Silence is equally welcomed.

The Sessions. We facilitated six, two-hour generative 'Autism Dialogue' sessions (with up to 26 people) and a final thematic (non-Generative) session focusing on pulling together themes, which provided the opportunity for co-production of a report and recommendations, which was sent to the client.

Outcomes

This Dialogue series met the need for nurturing a sense of belonging and empowerment. Participants reported that we need more conversations where we really listen: *proper conversations*. They also reported that Dialogue *has heart*, contrary to tokenistic meetings where decisions have already been made for autistic people. The group raised the importance of this kind of peer support and friendship, and how vital it is in the wake of diagnosis for autistic people to understand and accept themselves. Autistic people find solutions to problems through accessing the wisdom in the community rather than having to justify why something is a problem to begin with. There is an autistic need for freedom from the neurotypical (non-autistic) *gaze*, "doing things our own way in our own time, without being excessively managed".

Learnings

Many people carry good intentions, but there is a lack of understanding, seen to be rooted in the pathological origins of autism. There is widespread confusion around terminology, with inappropriate and even harmful language and assumed power or expertise within the predominant neurotype. Services offer little or no support beyond diagnosis. Yet there is a desire for more autistic people to be meaningfully employed within the system, in such roles as mentors and counsellors, and a desire for specialist services.

Dialogue is seen as a supportive environment where neurodiversity can be celebrated and where people feel nourished. There is value of a dialogic approach in creating a sense of community between autistic and non-autistic people in Derbyshire, empowering seldom-heard voices to affect systemic change. There is positive impact on the well-being and personal growth of those attending the dialogues.

Conference Session Extracts
From the consideration of the case study with conference participants

Kate Salinsky: We were quickly asked to join in various meetings and to become part of the special educational needs strategy and discussion on what was needed for the system. We felt increasingly uncomfortable. Is this what we set out to do? One of our learnings was staying true to who we are and what we are doing and trusting the dialogue itself to do what dialogue does best. Bringing people together and allowing them to hear each other and to build together was the way that we were able to move forward. And it was very powerful for some of the commissioners of services to really hear what some of the autistic people were saying. This listening was made possible by the safe container we all created. It was extremely powerful, and also challenging at times. I think it left a big imprint in terms of the realization amongst those people about what they can do to make change.

Speaker: I do have a question. How did the participants partake? You had individuals that had autistic family members, and individuals that were actually autistic. So that's great but what's the dynamics of that? Having a different scope of levels when it comes to the autistic individuals and not all individuals communicate effectively like we do. How was the scope? I'm trying to visualize it.

Jonnathan Drury: There's an assumption that the less abled autistic people will not be in dialogue. We had dialogues where people have used AAC (augmentative and alternative communication machines) or had someone with them that can speak on their behalf - because they don't use the English language and use a different way of communication. But, generally, in the dialogues we run, people want to attend and use English as their spoken language. We make sure that we are clear with people that being part of the dialogue is simply being there, attending and listening with respect and suspension. If they are just listening, then that's fine. You are still as much of a part of the dialogue as when you are speaking. We ask people to have their video on as long as they're comfortable with it. If they're not, and quite often we see people turn their video on and off, it is generally because of sensory overload and they need to quiet down. The breadth of what's acceptable is much wider and because of that people are comfortable to express themselves.

Speaker: The comfort of being yourself. I love that. I have worked with autistic students for years and have been trying to find a way to let them know that it's okay to be yourself - especially when you have sensory sensitivities. So I just want to say thank you for that. I've never put it that way even though I have years of working with different individuals. The comfort of being yourself - that's what it's all about. Bringing in dialogue just to make them comfortable in groups and able to talk and communicate. I loved reading the paper as it helped me find really useful ways to change the dynamic of a situation.

Speaker: I have a lot of neurodiverse people in my life for various reasons. Yesterday I was giving a Covid vaccine, and I realized pretty quickly that the person I was administering the vaccine to was not neurotypical. I don't know her diagnosis, we didn't talk about it, but she was really very nervous about needles, which is a separate issue from her being neurodiverse. But her expression of not wanting to have a shot was different than what my expression might have been. I found myself wondering what to do in this situation. I was doing my best to keep her calm and say, "You don't have to do this". I was trying to do grounding things with her to see if that helped and asking her what she needed, but she was in a place where she couldn't even respond to me. We ended up getting through it by her putting on headphones and listening to music. It would've been pretty interesting if we had a framework of dialogue that helped us to talk to one another. We didn't, and there's no societal structure set-up where she and I can move into a mode of dialogue allowing us to talk to one another. So we did the best we could. We got through it, and she was okay and I was okay, and everything was fine. But in that meeting with the commissioner, it would be really interesting for them to hear about a shared framework of dialogue. I just applaud you all for using dialogue in such a useful way. Altering life for people, which this should be about, rather than checking a box.

Speaker 2: That's a brilliant way to finish the session.

Postscript

The authors' reflections, written some months after the conference

One participant from Derby attended Autism Dialogues in Sheffield for two years, which then resulted in an introduction being made to the right person within their local authority, who had the open-mindedness to listen and understand, and the power to make something happen. This organic human process is as much a part of dialogue and its proliferation as the initial felt-sense, years previously, that there are people out there who desperately need dialogue. Personal contacts and professionalism are required to create the trust that's needed in this field at a systemic level, in order to give way to the impersonal and generative. A good chemistry between both leadership teams carried through and the required final report was edited for this paper, as a matter of course.

One thing our small team didn't anticipate was the confusion that came at us from several elements of the system – including parents who seemed angry and almost hostile and consultants with complex agendas – and each took equal amounts of effort to unravel ourselves from. As the extract shows, we the facilitators quickly grew a heightened awareness, and once attuned to these fault lines it's almost like a managed trauma. When similar language was used in the conference presentation, such as one person saying, "not all individuals communicate effectively like we do", our language-awareness spotlights the privilege of the predominant neurotype. Facilitators are like the canaries in the coal mine – a phrase also commonly used in relation to the very high sensitivity of autistic people.

It was a powerful learning experience for me, the team and reportedly most of the participants. It has made my vision sharper and, without lasting damage, increased my resilience and professionalism. As I write this, I have the image of walking into the middle of a raging battlefield and laying down a red rose, which I hope has taken root, and whose scent is picked up by the right people.

A Family Dialogue

Linda Ellinor

Context

Six or seven years ago, when I was living in Arizona and coming back to California for family gatherings at Thanksgivings, my niece, Tina, told me that Ann, her sister, was being ostracized that year. What? (!) How could this happen? My brother's family consists of six kids. I couldn't believe that my brother wouldn't allow one of his kids to come to Thanksgiving. Tina tried to explain, but I needed much more explanation.

I started calling family members for their versions of the story. I talked to some of the other nieces and nephews and found that it was all true. No one wanted Ann to attend. She was too disruptive, too critical of everyone. Everyone was sick of the darkness she brought to such gatherings. She was no longer wanted there. I was shocked.

When I checked in with Ann, she was still planning on traveling to California for Thanksgiving, even though she knew she wasn't welcome. As I explored her feelings about this, she thought being ostracized was outrageous. But she was unwilling to own her part of the feelings that had been generated within the family interactions.

Aim

It occurred to me that, perhaps the day before Thanksgiving, we might plan a "family Dialogue." I had a clear vision of what it might look like and how I might facilitate it. My goal was to build some Dialogue skills: listening, suspending judgment and attuning to underlying assumptions that were getting in the way of the brothers and sisters actually having a good family time together.

Method

I had private chats with each family member to see how each felt about Ann and what they perceived to be the real problem. I spoke at length with Ann and asked her if she were willing to come to a two-hour family Dialogue. At first she was against it. She was angry that they weren't even letting her stay at the family home.

Tina's mother wasn't keen on a family Dialogue either, though her father—my brother—thought it might be helpful. The other nieces and nephews were willing to attend. They all thought it might lead to a breakthrough if they could just talk about their feelings in a real way without Ann throwing darts at them. I promised to keep everyone safe.

They all knew that I did this thing called "Dialogue." They didn't know much about it, but they trusted that I could hold the family together for the two hours. They all felt the pain of having to ostracize a family member, so they were willing to try. Even her mother eventually agreed to attend.

I kept working on Ann. I told her that this was a chance for her to be heard in a non-judgmental way. I said she might hear from her family members about why it was so difficult for them to interact with her. She had nothing to lose and everything to gain.

Finally, at the last minute, when I had almost given up on Ann's coming and was just going to do a family Dialogue with the rest of the family, she agreed to come. I feel it was my ability to release my need for Ann to be there that allowed the Dialogue to happen.

We started with check-ins. Everyone was quite depressed about the whole affair, and yet there was a certain anticipation of wanting to bring Ann back into the family. Ann had little to say in the beginning. She had been scapegoated and was acting defensively and was emotionally unavailable as one might expect.

We started with a few "listening exercises" to get things started in a fun and light way such as what it is to be "good and bad listeners." We then did a quick round exploring what it means to suspend one's judgement so that listening could be deep and not clouded with criticism.

We then did an exercise in pairs that helped everyone assess what it was like to deal with conversations that don't go well. This helped us all connect more deeply with each other. We each shared our own painful experiences with others in conversation. We practiced ways of inquiring into underlying assumptions so we weren't just making up stories of why the "other" was acting and saying what they were. We processed our learnings in the whole family and realized how we all have issues and painful experiences when conversations don't go as we would like them to.

Outcomes

The last thing we did was an inquiry circle. This was where the real magic happened. I don't remember the initial question, though it was probably related to how it might feel to be ostracized. As we went around the room the questions deepened. When it was Ann's time to respond to a question she finally sank into her feelings. Tears streamed from her eyes. She melted in front of her siblings and parents. She softened, which was the first step of re-entering the wonderful tribe that her large family is. Everyone else melted as well. After one round we kept the Dialogue going. Everyone was present and attentive. There was no judgment, and the listening was keen. When the two hours were up we were one family again. Hugs all around.

I can't say that we have kept this family Dialogue alive over the years. But I can say that, every now and again, one of my nieces, nephews or my brother will mention that family Dialogue and say what a breakthrough it was.

Learnings

My main takeaways from this experience were 1) even in a closely knit family, Bohm-inspired Dialogue can work well; 2) one does not have to teach the skills of Dialogue directly, but through structured exercises it is possible to provide enough safety for shared meanings to develop over two hours that can be quite healing; and 3) working in a family setting focused on developing communication skills is valuable, even if it isn't followed by ongoing practice. Family members will remember the breakthrough experience for some time.

Conference Session Extracts

From the consideration of the case study with conference participants

Speaker: Your paper really inspired me, because as a psychologist I have always been discouraged from doing any kind of self-treatment. I've also been told we should not treat people that we know, especially our own family. I also believe that using dialogue for a family—not just my family but any family—is very difficult because of the emotions that exist in the people. But the way that you used dialogue with the members of your family was very interesting. What was key to me was how everyone was able to agree on one common issue. When you talk to a family they often remember lots of issues and they don't allow you to concentrate on just one. But in this situation everyone agreed to talk about one situation only.

Linda Ellinor: You're right, this was really not meant to be family therapy. Rather, I stuck to a communications model, and I made it clear to everyone that we were not going to therapize anybody. We're going to learn how to listen together and see if we can hear something that we hadn't heard before. I kept it at that level, and I made sure that there were clear boundaries, which we limited to fairly structured things to do. I knew once people started to accuse each other they would go into defensive behaviors. We thus kept to the one issue, what it would it feel like not to be invited to a family gathering. That issue hit everyone right in the heart. You're ostracized. Everyone could feel that pain and everyone really wanted to move beyond it. So I got everyone to agree, before we even came into the dialogue, on that one simple issue.

Speaker: I'm a victim-offender dialogue facilitator in Virginia within the Department of Corrections. One of the things that we focus on is remaining unbiased as a facilitator. Because you are a part of the family, were there any concerns about potential bias? You said you were closest to Ann and the oldest daughter. Did that create any level of tension in your preparation or facilitation of the dialogue?

Linda: Well, I'm 'Auntie Linda' and I'm a pretty safe auntie. People see me as a nurturing aunt, someone they can bring issues to and who they can talk to offline. I think people felt safe with me. I had already done significant trust-building over the years.

Speaker: You made clear for everyone the point you were going after, but in the midst of the session, how did you ensure that somebody didn't go off the rails or

	start going off topic? How did you make sure that the situation didn't run out of your hands?
Linda:	Well, in this particular case, it didn't; I was lucky. It could easily have gone off the rails at the end when I allowed the free-form dialogue to happen. But by then, which you might recognize if you've ever done an inquiry and reflection circle, the process had slowed down and by that time it had such an intimate pace, and that's when you want to let go. Still, someone could have brought up a very critical, defensive and reactive comment. If that happened, I would have needed to make an intervention. Typically, I would just stop, and ask for clarification, and maybe say that that's not really what we are here to do or I would mention that it is off topic.
Speaker:	Were you astonished that your family was able to participate along with you in this dialogue? Or were you very sure that they could do it?
Linda:	Because I had spoken to every member before we gathered (other than the mother who just flatly said she wouldn't participate and she didn't believe in this) I kind of knew they were all on board for helping to heal this dynamic.
Speaker:	It makes me think of Bill Isaacs' article about the Southeast Asia work he did. He said that the most important thing was the conversations he had with each person ahead of time.
Linda:	It is not unlike what we would do as consultants when we do action research. You really have to develop a relationship with each member before they come into the dialogue.
Speaker:	What is the current family dynamic? Was the dialogue sustainable, what was learned and has the learning carried forward?
Linda:	Well, there's still difficulties in the family's communications and Ann continues to be a problem, especially for her parents. But the dynamics between the kids are better. They are all talking amongst themselves more freely than they ever were before.
Speaker:	When doing a dialogue with your family do you recommend a certain environment or a place to do it in or perhaps also a place to not dialogue in?
Linda:	Well, you want to make sure it accommodates everyone and that it is quiet. I wouldn't do a dialogue in a restaurant setting or in a public setting. We were outside in the fresh air, and it was quiet and contained.

Postscript

The author's reflections, written some months after the conference

I found the whole process quite satisfying. I shared an experience that showed the power of "Bohm-inspired dialogue" in one's personal and family life. The process provided me with a platform to share an intimate story with colleagues in dialogue. I was pleased to have the opportunity.

As the process unfolded within my family, my main anxiety was that my niece wouldn't come. Everything depended on her being willing to step into a family that was trying to say she was no longer welcome at family gatherings. That was a tough sell. I didn't, however, worry about the basic process I was using. I knew it would keep people safe and it would help them connect in new ways.

Writing the paper helped me reflect on the whole process and prepared me to clearly present it at the conference. What it has stimulated in me is that it is our *stories* of dialogue, integrated into our lives, that bring it alive for others. It is a way of modeling and being Bohm's vision of radical interconnection.

Section Four

Putting Dialogue to Work for the Benefit of the Community

The health of any community depends on how the people in that community talk together. In a flourishing community there is lively engagement between a broad cross-section of people as they go about their daily affairs. In recent times the opportunities for interaction are being reduced. In the past you may have been served by an assistant in a shop, but now the staff serve the shelves and you serve yourself before paying a machine. That may be fast and efficient, but it is socially lacking. Similarly, waiting on an automated telephone system when you call for help can be surprisingly frustrating. Without social engagement people become lonely, communities fragment and less trust is extended to those you do not know. This occurs at a broad level between people of different age groupings, ethnic backgrounds, levels of wealth and so on. It is ever more apparent that our communities need Dialogue! The three case studies describe powerful examples of Dialogue being put to work to improve the relations between youth and police, to understand the commonality of faith, and to connect strangers.

A Dialogue between street youngsters and police was co-facilitated by **Bernhard Holtrop** in a notoriously tense neighbourhood in Rotterdam. The cynicism and resistance displayed by both the youths and the police gave way to understanding and changed practices as the Dialogue developed.

Mino Akhtar describes her work in New Jersey, USA, engaging Muslim, Jewish, Christian and non-religious women in open and ongoing dialogic engagement in each other's homes and after dinner. Many small shifts in understanding each other's faiths reinforced the basic human values of peace.

Brussels in Dialogue created conversations across stereotypical social boundaries in cosmopolitan Brussels. Groups of 10 strangers met to listen to each other's experiences. **Elisabeth Razesberger** facilitated many such two-hour sessions, leaving participants feeling enriched and more connected.

Dialogue Between Police Officers and Multi-Ethnic Street Youth

Bernhard Holtrop

Context

Between 2003 and 2016, a group of co-facilitators and I facilitated dialogue programs in neighbourhoods and vocational schools in Rotterdam. These dialogic interventions aimed to de-escalate tensions and create mutual understanding, thus restoring or building relationships. After several neighbourhood interventions the City of Rotterdam asked us to facilitate a dialogue between a group of street youngsters and police officers of Delftshaven, an old, notorious neighbourhood in the city.

Method

Step 1: In the preparation phase, I met with the local police superintendent and her second-in-command, and with the social work organization's boss. They explained the situation, and we planned the steps to be taken.

I met 25 officers, almost all in uniform, some still wearing their bullet vests in their home base, in a circle. I felt cynicism and resistance at the start. I could feel empathy for them, men and women hardened by their job in the streets, showing their instinctive guardedness for an unknown situation. I confessed that I felt nervous and told them that I thought I felt resistance –thus showing myself as vulnerable.

I explained the basics of working with a talking stick and we started. After some first defensive, cynical remarks, balancing remarks began to be shared. Officers reflected on their work: about the pressure and situation on the street, where it was necessary to judge instantly. Impressive openness in which some tears were flowing.

Step 2: The contact with the youngsters was via the youth workers and social workers. After the youth workers gained trust in me, they invited me to walk the streets and contact some youngsters. I had our first dialogue with some informal leaders at the street corner and took it from there. We gained initial trust from them.

A co-facilitator and I met with 25 young people. Not surprisingly, we went through a similar pattern. After starting with cynicism and 'showing your tough self', sincere questions and dialogue gradually brought them into reflection.

Step 3: We met in a community centre in the neighbourhood. We were 55 persons in the room: 50 participants and 5 facilitators. The police officers tried to shake hands with everyone, as the youngsters replied hesitantly or refused to speak.

In the large opening circle, it was mostly officers and youngsters sitting on separate sides. I welcomed everyone. The police superintendent explained the reason for this meeting: Seek mutual understanding, an improved relationship, and, if possible, come to some agreements for better interaction.

We started with a one-word check-in. With what feeling are you sitting here, and why? We always work with a so-called 'talking object' like a stick, a stone, or sometimes a tennis ball with a smiley on it. In smaller circles we started with a lot of silent passing of the stick. It brought a gradually growing uneasiness in the group, until someone took the courage to speak first. Then people began to share about their life and their struggles with each other.

Understanding gradually grew. Although the police officers stayed more 'professional' on the surface. After some initial sharing the same theme arose in almost every small circle: ethnic profiling by the police. The officers collectively refused to admit they were practicing ethnic profiling. This caused the dialogue to stall. Several youngsters were enraged. Some were ready to leave. I asked one young man how many times per month he was halted and asked to show his ID. "Per month? Better ask per *week* or per *day*", was his reaction. I compared this to my white 16 years old daughter who went to school in the same neighborhood and was never asked for her ID. A long silence followed, then one police officer admitted that he did practice ethnic profiling and hated it. He sketched the cases in which he had to judge in an instant with on an average night: burglary, fights, home violence, drug dealing. Dilemmas in which he felt forced to apply ethnic profiling. He shared about his fears when leaving his wife and his young child home when doing night patrols.

Gradually all the officers admitted their ethnic profiling dilemmas. A great sigh of relief went through the group of young men and women. This confession gave space for compassion towards the officers. One concluded, "You police officers are just like us. A gang that has to stick together to survive, no matter what".

Outcomes

Both sides realized how much they were responsible for keeping this game going – how much ethnic profiling raised anger, which, in turn, raised the young persons' rejection of authority. The only way to get beyond it was together.

That was the opening to start envisioning a brighter future. We inventoried what all wanted with this neighbourhood and what agreements were needed. The circle came to basic but essential agreements: meeting more frequently, getting to know each other. Contacting the neighbourhood police officer with questions first – and vice versa. Preventing, as much as possible, armed police vans entering the neighbourhood. Plans were made to build a relationship with the parents of these youngsters.

The check-out was promising. Police officers and youngsters sat mixed in the large circle. Many encouraging words were spoken. I asked them to keep this understanding of each other; it was vulnerable, and people make mistakes. There would be moments where people slip into old behaviour. It takes perseverance to let this trust grow and for old pain to heal in the community and ourselves.

Step 4: The group, or parts of it, continued to come together. It bettered the relationship considerably. There were problems when some new police officers joined the neighbourhood. Regrettably, this caused some confrontations – all the more cause for investing in a consequent follow-up and a dialogic approach with the community, social workers, police, and city workers. Individual and collective development takes healing, time, and trust.

Learnings

Short-term reflexes are everywhere: It took true perseverance to convince the city officials to invest in a consistent follow-up after the initial success. To my frustration, I only succeeded partially in this. Healing doesn't come overnight.

Trust the circle: this dialogic healing asked a lot of inconvenient suspension from us facilitators – not intervening, allowing the circle take responsibility for their painful silence. It brought both youngsters and police officers more in connection with their inner self and with owning their problems.

NOTE: *This paper has been condensed from a longer version that appeared in the* Täter-Opfer-Ausgleich *publication.*

Conference Session Extracts
From the consideration of the case study with conference participants

Bernhard Holtrop: Now for your questions. Are some questions popping up?

Speaker: I was wondering, "Do you see any potential opportunity to reintroduce the dialogic process to get things back together with the neighborhood you described and the police?" Because I know it's been some time since you did those dialogues.

Speaker: As it is predictable that it will fall back to the previous situation I am also wondering, "What kind of structures can be put in place to allow the interaction to continue?" If you didn't have some deliberate structures you could find the culture reverting back to the common culture and the state it was.

Speaker: What do you think caused the push towards being open? Was it mostly acknowledging the issue or was it based more on accountability on the sides of both the youth and the police?

Speaker: No matter how young or how old you are certain behaviours needs to be reinforced and there needs to be accountability. What incentive does the city have for the police have to continue to have an open conversation? What goal does the city have? Were they really devoted to addressing this issue or was it meant to be a short-term fix to a bigger problem?

Speaker: Getting buy-in from leadership is so important. You mentioned that there was a new kind of sheriff in town, a new organization as far as the police department was concerned. It seems like there might be some strong anecdotal evidence that it made an impact and maybe that's something that could be used to get that buy-in again?

Speaker: Was it just a breakdown with the new police or did the breakdown happen with the city overall, and is that why the dialogue stopped after so long? A lot of the focus was on the police but then we shifted and we focused on the youth, and suggested possibly introducing dialogue into the schools and focusing on the youth from that point onwards.

Speaker: We talked about the data to sustain this. The Department of Corrections is a data-driven agency and we were wondering if there is any data to support the claim that everything was going well for eight or nine years? Because that will be part of sustainability, to show that during a period of time, for example, the crime rate went down, or something like that.

Speaker: Our discussion centered around purpose. What was the purpose of the police department? Did they identify what their purpose was and what their goals were? If their purpose is to control, do you really need dialogue? But if their purpose is to serve, like we believe most police departments and law enforcement agencies should do, wouldn't it be in their interest to identify how you best serve? And having dialogue with those folks you serve would be critical. If dialogue was the vehicle used to identify what the goals are it should also be used to identify how you would go about serving people appropriately, in the way they feel like they need to be served.

Really identifying your purpose can help you transcend through changes in leadership. The flip side of that is what someone mentioned about the accountability of the community. There's a level of accountability for people who live in that community as well. It is not just about the community identifying what the problems with the police are, it is also important that they are helping themselves and serving themselves as well. So when the two groups come out of their corners still holding on to their beliefs and their thoughts the first thing is to identify what their shared purpose is.

Bernhard: Something I also struggled with was the discontinuity of leadership in the political arena. Rotterdam has elections every two years, either in the big city or in the smaller city municipalities. So every two years we had a different leadership. While the left-wing party embraced this program the right-wing party would not embrace it. As a result, I had constant talks with deputy mayors, convincing them that the program was a good thing. What I learned from it is that it would have been a great thing to have more dialogues with those at the top, such as the deputy mayor and with the commander of the police, and to let them experience the dialogues themselves. It was difficult for me, and it difficult that the lesson to bring in some structure happened in hindsight.

It was a bottom-up initiative, and it was a struggle. Even though we did beautiful miraculous things in the neighborhoods it was difficult to constantly convince the deputy mayors and the mayor that we were doing a good thing, especially because there was a discontinuity in their regions. That was a challenge for me. Looking at it in hindsight I could have done it differently. It gives me new thoughts on how to make such an approach integral, to gather data in a more constructive way and also to invite the authorities to put in place a parallel program to gather this data.

It is inspiring to hear you. Thank you very much.

Postscript

The author's reflections, written some months after the conference

While doing the work and reflecting on it I experienced how tough it is to bring a 'new' concept into a strongly control-driven, multistakeholder system such as a municipality. To bundle the many parties involved, both public (like the police) as well as private (like the social-work organizations) is a big challenge. Therefore, to give such an intervention a successful embedding, strong support is needed from higher up.

On top of all of this, a deputy major (or mayor) is, in the end, strongly driven by elections and thus fluctuating public opinions, and a dialogue initiative goes against many control-and-suppress reflexes which understandably pop up under these circumstances.

Later, writing the paper and sharing it during the conference helped me to summarize my insights around this project. It also made me realize how *avant la lettre* the intervention probably was – and how our even more strongly polarized society in the current time can be helped through such formats.

Rereading the case study and going through the excerpts from the conference stipulates for me the importance of sound embedding, a well-anticipated follow-up and record keeping of the outcomes of what many would perceive as an unconventional intervention. This is especially the case in a politically driven, multistakeholder environment.

Women Weaving Peace

Mino Akhtar

Context

Even before 9/11, many Muslim activists and community leaders were involved in dialogue with other ethnic, race or faith-based groups. It stemmed from a desire to be understood as media and Hollywood continued their negative stereotyping of Islam while hiding the political underpinnings to those conflicts. I got involved with many such groups, as I loved the promise of dialogue for our new multicultural world, having grown up on four continents myself. I had been enchanted with Bohm's writings as I was doing my Master's in Human and Organizational Transformation. My corporate expertise in collaborative methods and my growing practice of Sufism added to my own passion for dialogue as a path for peace.

My first such project involved bringing Arabs, Israelis, Jews, Muslims, and Christians together in Manhattan to discuss the Israel/Palestine conflict—it gave me my first taste of the challenges and transformations that dialogue enables. Another was a national Muslim/Jewish national study project with men and women, which several of my friends were involved with. It splintered as soon as the political rights of Palestinians were raised. Fortunately, one Muslim and one Jewish woman decided not to let the idea die and formed the Women's Interfaith Initiative of Bergen County, New Jersey. We invited women of the Muslim, Jewish and Christian faiths and felt we could develop a more heartfelt circle of conversation. I was nominated to be a co-leader, which was a fortunate coincidence as the 9/11 backlash triggered an acceleration of my spiritual journey.

Aims

First, develop deeper understanding and appreciation for each other's faiths, and how faiths could be more effective in bringing about peace.

Second, educate the public through educational events such as seminars and film showings, and to share with them the unity and the diversity of the faiths.

Third, practice our faith together by conducting joint action projects to help underserved groups such as women's shelters, food kitchens, etc.

I personally wanted to continue my own development as a practitioner and to see what processes and methods could be of practical benefit for nonpractitioners.

Method

Over a period of eight years we met monthly in living rooms after dinner, hosted by rotating faith groups. It became a social club with lots of time for personal sharing before and after the formal dialogue. Several mother/daughter pairs were members too, which was quite encouraging. We had several members not affiliated with any religion or faith, and we appreciated them even more, as "humanism" was the root unifying all faiths.

The host faith group would select a topic, such as "welcoming strangers," and speak about it using their scriptures and teachings. The other faith groups would then add their own perspectives and their formal teachings and would share how these were practiced. This would be followed by a dialogue which could go into totally unpredictable terrain. The dialogue would last an hour or so, followed by planning the next meeting, choosing the topic, the host, etc.

I began to document our processes and methods and published a guide that described our aims and our methods. It is a reflection on how we designed the container in an evolutionary manner:

Faith: As seekers, each in our own faiths or humanism, we all believed that there is a purpose to humanity and hope for a better world. This faith encouraged us to seek understanding and knowledge of all paths to love, peace and unity which is what God represents to us.

Relationships: Our deep personal relationships and fellowship became a solid foundation for genuine sharing, vulnerability and exposure of our innermost feelings and thoughts. The bond of friendship was strong enough to allow one to understand even when one does not agree with the other.

Values: We discovered common values that we hold dear, and those became the glue and guide to our conversations and any common actions we undertake.

- Inclusion & Diversity
- Respect & Dignity
- Curiosity & Learning
- Growth & Development
- Community
- Spiritual Union and Connection

Practices: A group of practices evolves, allowing for all types of conversations, especially difficult and challenging ones, to take place without harming the strong bond of the group. These practices included the typical norms for dialogue such as generous listening, gentle speaking and practicing all our espoused values.

Outcomes

We constantly had to remind ourselves that our small shifts in mindset were just as precious as any action project. Over time there were many shifts, such as biases being lessened or dropped altogether, which led to new actions in members' daily lives. For example, if someone saw a member of another faith being bullied or talked down to, they self-reported that they were more inclined to intervene.

Members learned about themselves, about their faiths and about other faiths. The most common reactions we heard were "Oh, we are so alike!" or "I love that you have such a nice tradition!" We learned a lot about each other's practices, but also about how to navigate and honor differences, no matter which type.

Learnings

My own observations and reflections:

a) It takes a lot of time and socialization for a group to get to a point where they can have difficult conversations, especially where large political conflicts or faith misunderstandings are present. However, once the relationships are strong enough, the conversations can be very powerful and transformative.
b) We as human beings operate from so many myths and biases, and media plays a huge and underestimated role in this. We are not aware of these. As we meet with the "other," we can slowly peel away these layers. It is very hard work, and it is so much easier to grab whatever the media, social media or Hollywood film says and make it your truth.
c) Unfortunately, Covid-19 stopped all our meetings, and our Zoom meetings had only a handful of people attending. We eventually stopped scheduling the meetings. I was surprised by this development and realized that perhaps the fun social setting was a key attractor to the meetings; "online dialogue" could not replicate that!

Conference Session Extracts
From the consideration of the case study with conference participants

Speaker: I am wondering if the values that you identified were what drove you to form the group? Did the values happen first, or was it faith-based and about your genuine desire to learn about each other's faith, or was it more based on social interconnections?

Mino Akhtar: There were groups that were predecessors to us, and I think they were all started from a faith orientation. A rabbi met with an Imam and said, "Let's do this, because our people are always criticizing each other." Faith was the wellspring of it. However, the other group from Manhattan was more multicultural. It consisted of people who were saying, "We have to learn to talk with each other about a very difficult subject—the Middle East." It was a huge challenge to do that, but we stuck with it. All those values are important, but inclusion and diversity are especially important to me.

Speaker: It is very interesting that the group started out with both male and female participants, and when things got heated, the male participants stopped coming . . .

Mino: Yes.

Speaker: . . . and that the women decided that they were going to continue with this group. I wonder how that dynamic may have been different had the men stayed in the group. It would be interesting to see if you'll have the male participants back in future. It's also interesting that the greatest amount of productivity happened after the males dropped out.

Mino: Yeah. We felt very proud of it!

Speaker: From my own experiences with dialogue the camaraderie happens more with women, and when they're in that kind of setting what happens is just beautiful to me.

Mino: Well, I noticed we have one male participant right now. I would love a comment from you at this point.

Speaker: You're talking to me, Mino?

Mino: Yes, about the male participation.

Speaker: I agree. I think women should be leading the world! My tongue is *not* in my cheek when I say that. But I also don't want to draw such a sharp line between male and female. I think there is a human who wants to emerge in all of us and who wants to be present. I know from my own work that within each of these faiths there is also a tension, and sometimes it's easier to bring interfaith groups together than it is to bring certain people within the same faith together. The striving to find the commonality is inherent in all of us, though, and I don't think you even have to be part of a religion to experience it. There is a humanistic side to people who claim no particular formal faith and who are filled with faith in the human and in the collective. If I attended a session like yours I'm not so sure I would have left. I think that as we grow we come to see that tension provides very useful information.

Speaker: How *do* we come together? We recognize differences that are based on religion, sex, lifestyle—all those things. It is difficult in our current climate to just have a different opinion than someone else, because it becomes so much more than what it was intended to be. So how do we come together and get information about another person's thinking, without it becoming much larger than you intended?

Mino: Great question. It's through the conditions you create. We are creating a safe, welcoming, warm container where everyone can share their thoughts about a topic. Then we add some practices such as generous listening, gentle speaking and a way of honoring differences without running away from them. Practitioners can facilitate and teach others how to do this. We could teach people to name the emotion, and not to personalize their difference. They have come to their views for a valid reason. Maybe if I tell them mine, they might reconsider how they came to it. Maybe they will see some distortions along the way, which they have just embraced without thinking about it.

Speaker: We are doing this in the Department of Corrections, and you did that in Manhattan. How much more advanced would this world be if we could also do this in the real world—if we could all sit down, come together and talk. You have accomplished so much. I'm glad I came to be part of this group today.

Speaker: In your case study you mentioned the ladies developed trust in one another. How important, if important at all, were critical thinking skills, because we know not everyone has access to those? Did they play a huge part?

Speaker: Trust—absolutely. In addition to listening and speaking, it is important to pause and reflect—and to suspend judgment, because most barriers come from judgment.

Speaker: I think some media channels have become alternative religions. Watching them is like attending a church, only people are attending Fox or CNN. I only thought of this the other day because of conversations with certain people. I realized that their passion and their excitement (about what they heard said by their favorite person, who they turn on at the same time each day or week) is just like hearing someone echo what their high priest or rabbi said.

Postscript

The author's reflections, written some months after the conference

At last year's conference I appreciated engaging with Academy members about my case study, *Women Weaving Peace*. Our reflections reminded us that we all feel the call for peace deeply, whether we are men or women. A nobler human being in us is wanting to be reborn, one that honors the values that light our hearts. I call it *Insaniyet*—an Urdu word that means "the state of humanness." These values can arise from our faith or simply our humanism that wishes the best for the individual and the collective, locally and globally. It inspires us to keep trying in our own different ways and not give up hope.

The assaults on hope are many. Even the first truly global pandemic could not stop or lessen the hate pandemic. A century of Western civilization wars (they were not World Wars unlike the Western narrative) did not temper our brutishness. Although these forces are not natural—the FOX News channels of this world have an agenda of hate, and they produce their counterparts on the other side.

As a Sufi, I then turn to myself, an insignificant being, that hopes that through small steps- one person at a time or a group at a time—some healing happens, and the chance of hate is reduced. I reduce my sight of line to what I can control and influence and leave the rest to natural forces. I ignore the fact that millions of brains receive streaming hate, while our tiny circles of hearts continue to touch each other.

In the end, I am honored to have had the opportunity to create an experiment that showed a beautiful path to peace, and to share that experiment with Academy members and learn from them. I continue to look for other pathways in my micro world.

Brussels in Dialogue: Connecting Strangers Around a Table

Elisabeth Razesberger

Context

The city of Brussels is multicultural and multilingual, with a population of around 1.2 million inhabitants originating from 184 different countries. Brussels hosts international organisations and the European Institutions. What happens elsewhere in the world is felt in Brussels and impacts the work and life of its population. This was particularly tangible in the aftermath of 9/11 when public opinion associated all Muslims directly with terrorism. The presence of armed forces in the European quarter of Brussels increased and the existing and perceived isolation of poor neighbourhoods with large Muslim populations deepened.

This situation called for local action. Given Brussels' compact size, geographical isolation is easily overcome and there is an abundant presence of institutional and social actors. One of them, the Foyer non-profit organisation, has facilitated and promoted the integration of immigrants since the Seventies. It is situated in Molenbeek, a traditional working-class district where many newly arrived migrants have settled. Its population struggles with poverty, unemployment and neglected infrastructure. Foyer held the first dialogue day in Brussels in 2007, inspired by *Nederland in Dialoog*, a dialogue project launched in 2002.

Aim

The *Brussels in Dialogue* initiative was designed to counter stereotypes and get the individual participants out of their usual neighbourhoods and into circles of strangers. These experiences were meant to help demystify the other and to overcome the fear of getting in contact with people outside one's comfort and safety zone. The dialogues offered opportunities to talk, to be listened to and to hear unfamiliar perspectives and experiences. Seeing the human face of the other helps to overcome stereotypes. The dialogues were a first step in promoting community building and active citizenship.

Foyer invited organisations working with specific audiences such as immigrants, women, young and old persons and marginalised people, to meet with people representing formal institutions, such as the police, politicians, diplomats, and many more. The partner organisations would bring their own public and provide volunteers to be trained as dialogue facilitators. The dialogues were also open for the general public.

Brussels in Dialogue included not only persons but also buildings: if possible, the dialogues were organised in uncommon locations which attract curiosity, such as the King's private waiting room at Brussels Central Station, churches, Embassy Buildings or museums. This was a way of helping participants discover new places and new people.

Method

The dialogues are facilitated following a set structure and format, with a new topic for every calendar year. The participants gather around a table, ideally 10-12 participants per table. The timeframe is two hours. Each dialogue moves through four separate phases and four speaking rounds. The first round is a round of presentation, using prompts or icebreaker questions. It can be spontaneous, like "take your bunch of keys and tell us something about one of the keys". Or participants can choose amongst a variety of small objects to tell a story or a memory. The second phase is for exchanging experiences about a specific topic, which is usually very wide, like *sharing, together, Made in Brussels*. In the third phase, participants talk about their dreams in relation to the topic, and in the last phase each participant thinks about what he or she can take away from the conversation. This might be a resolution or a concrete action plan. The dialogues are organised as one-off events.

The following guidelines are announced before the dialogue starts: *Listen to each other*, *talk about your own experiences* ('I perspective'), *share positive experiences*, *suspend judgement* and *give each other time*; a dialogue is not a debate.

The facilitator participates in the dialogue and is part of the process. He/she shares his/her own experiences. This is particularly important at the opening of the presentation circle to set a model and get the conversation going.

Outcomes

The dialogue tables evolved from a single dialogue day to a dialogue week. At its best moment, more than 100 dialogue tables were held all over Brussels. Over the years, partners have included a great variety of actors such as immigrant organisations, faith-based organisations, museums, the police, a teacher training college, embassies and international organisations. The partner organisations felt the dialogue tables helped to increase their own visibility and become more transparent. In later years, Foyer organised dialogue weeks for specific audiences, such as children or prison inmates. Since 2020, Foyer has moved on to offering dialogue on demand, accompanying dialogue processes for individual organisations. A highlight was the year 2013, when the Brussels public transport company offered to advertise *Brussels in Dialogue* on one of their tramways.

It is difficult to define measurable outcomes of one-off events. However, the effects of continued dialogue work by Foyer emerged when the situation got worse. The terrorist attacks in Paris (2015) and Brussels (2016) were planned and carried out by a group of men based in Molenbeek. Suddenly life in Brussels was again driven by fear, hostility and the securitisation of public life. During this time, people from Molenbeek stood up, calling for peace and collaboration. This can be credited to the dialogue work done and promoted by Foyer and its people. There are now active citizens taking the courage to participate, speak up and to stay in difficult conversations.

Learnings

This type of dialogue table, a facilitated conversation in four phases, is easy to set up. However, it contains all of the basic elements to start a successful dialogue. All voices are equally heard. There is suspension of judgement as well as transformative moments through self-awareness and listening.

Participants share insights, which are both deep and to the point, despite the spontaneous setting and the fact that they do not know each other. This opening up in front of strangers is remarkable. Based on a simple prompt, participants develop their own insights and explanations about societal change and what can be done about it. They leave a dialogue table with the feeling of having shared a moment of connection.

Conference Session Extracts
From the consideration of the case study with conference participants

Speaker: I have a question, Elisabeth. You talked about trust and mentioned that they didn't trust you. How did you develop trust in that very diverse group of individuals?

Elisabeth Razesberger: I clarified at the beginning that the session is confidential, and that people are free to say what they want to say. Everybody is invited to present himself, but for the next rounds I offer people the choice to say, "Pass," or to say, "I just want to listen".

Speaker: Elisabeth, you spoke about someone sharing why she chose a box to represent herself during a check-in process. Do you see the box as representing vulnerability?

Elisabeth: For me, the mock box was more a symbol for being locked into a situation. I asked after the closing round of that specific dialogue table, if anybody wanted to add a comment. Then a women asked if she could say something to the women who had chosen the box. I said, "Yes, feel free!" Then she addressed that woman and said, "You said you felt as if you had lived in a box all those years, but look at yourself, you are already out of that box!" I still have goosebumps because I thought, "This is something that dialogue can do, but maybe 200 hours of psychotherapy can't". This is the kind of wisdom this woman needs to access but she will never, ever, get near a psychotherapist. But if she knows that she's out of the box and other people have witnessed that she's out of the box, well, she will go ahead. I would say one third of the participants declared that they never ever talk with anybody except their husband and their mother.

Speaker: My question is, "Do you find it simple to find trust by dividing the group into smaller groups, just to share in a smaller group?" In my experience it's easier to do with three people than 30 people.

Elisabeth: I separate people into breakout rooms with pairs in my dialogue courses, which stretch over several weeks. But for this once-off dialogue table we stay together for the entire two hours.

Speaker: In the worker's union we use a concept called 'tell your story'. We ask what committed you to engage with your work, to tell your story. It is often deep and connected, and that lowers the barrier.

Speaker: I'm with the Virginia Department of Corrections, and we invited some Virginia state troopers (state police) to meet with a group of inmates who were about to return to society. It was the first time that many of these men had actually spoken to a police officer in anything other than an arrest or other bad situation. Their eyes were really opened to difference and how people see each other. It was really evident in that event. It was a larger group. I wouldn't necessarily call it a dialogue, but it was very similar in breaking down some barriers and stereotypes and just seeing a human face, people to people.

Speaker: I have a question about that moment where you recognized your own internal bias. I'd like to explore that with you just a little bit further. How do we become better at recognizing our own internal bias?

Elisabeth: Suspending the judgment? Do you know the example of *The Little Prince*, the story by Antoine de Saint-Exupéry? There's a scene in the book where a Turkish expert discovered an asteroid. He presents his discovery to the rest of the world but they don't trust or believe him, because he's wearing traditional Turkish trousers. Then he comes back a year later wearing a suit and tie and then they believe him. For me, this is a good way to represent a classical mistake based on stereotypical judgement and bias in action.

In other contexts, I give an example of 20 different people, and participants can choose two people with whom they will go on a train journey and share a compartment. I then let them explain why they chose these two people and not the others. You see very easily what your interests are, what your dislikes are - why you would not take this or that person - because you might think he, or she, would be too boring or too loud or too young.

Speaker: I'm also from the Department of Corrections in Virginia. As I listen to the comments, and certainly after reading your case study, I reflect on our situation in America, where we struggle with how history is taught. There are different perspectives about how we look at history. It makes me think of the title of the whole conference, *The World Needs Dialogue!* It just kind of brings it all home when you start talking about why I think one thing, and why it's important to me, and then getting into conversations with other people who have different thoughts. We're able to see each other's points of view through the dialogue process and still come out on the other side respecting one another. I appreciate this conversation because what we say means so much right now. It's making me wonder how we can have more conversations, which hopefully will change the way we think about one another in America, then we might find how to go forward and how to live in harmony and peace with one another.

Postscript

The author's reflections written some months after the conference

The project *Brussels in Dialogue*, hosted by the Foyer non-profit, was where I first discovered dialogue and where I learned to facilitate dialogue tables. It awakened my curiosity for dialogue, why we do it and how it works. Ever since, I have attended various trainings on dialogue facilitation and facilitated many dialogues.

Writing about the Brussels dialogue tables made me look back at what happened in those conversations and made me think yet again about what enables dialogue. It is surprising how complete and thorough the format of these dialogue tables is. While the structure remains so simple, the core elements of dialogue and dialogic practice are present: creating a safe space, finding one's voice, listening to oneself and others, suspending judgement and the often very palpable feeling of connection perceived among the participants. It leads directly into a dialogue experience.

It was very gratifying to share and present a trusted concept for dialogue at the AofPD conference. This simple format can easily be replicated everywhere. Talking about it to an audience scattered over many different countries offered a live experience of exporting the idea to a new public. My wish is to share these simple dialogue tools as widely as possible. They can be transported into new contexts wherever you want to bring people together.

The conference was an opportunity to explore how the Brussels experience resonates with a new audience. One person said, "Reading your case study, I can see why it works". That was a welcome confirmation that the idea is accessible. I hope many people will use it in their own work.

Revisiting the writing, the conference and the feedback, I discovered that the four phases of the dialogue tables represent four questions, which are so universal that they resonate with every audience wherever you are, Who am I? What is my experience? What are my dreams? What am I going to do?

Section Five

Putting Dialogue to Work for the Benefit of Society

A large society incorporates many local communities, cultures and jurisdictions. The scale and complexity of such a society makes it hard for individuals or organisations to influence the way in which it develops. It is evident all around the world, however, that where people have a sense of citizenship the society flourishes. The essential spirit of citizenship is that people want to contribute to the good of the whole, and they respect the diversity of ways in which others can express themselves for the benefit of the whole. This is where Dialogue is paramount. Dialogue inherently engenders a spirit of citizenship. It encourages people to listen to each other with respect, and to be authentic in explaining their own experience and understanding. The world does indeed need Dialogue! The four case studies about putting Dialogue to work for the benefit of society involve four very different examples of working with this same spirit of citizenship.

In a novel three-day Hero Outdoor Training **Rijk Smitskamp and Bernhard Holtrop** took homeless people and social workers as peers through a dialogic process of trust, challenge, learning and personal goals, aiming to impact the many social workers and vulnerable citizens in the Netherlands.

Loshnee Naidoo engaged the community for a company that brought renewable energy into an impoverished community in South Africa. Despite the inequality, through Dialogue those in the !Kheis community identified their own projects that were incorporated into the development plan.

Many of the economic problems in Sierra Leone result from the poor discourse between commerce and government. **Chukwu-Emeka Chikezie** is addressing this fragmented situation at a high governmental level by encouraging Public-Private Dialogue via a UK-funded development agency.

120 | Putting Dialogue to Work for the Benefit of Society

Peter Garrett recounts the first seven years of the project to establish international recognition for Dialogue as a professional practice for societal benefit. This book and its many case studies are an active tribute to the growing influence of the Academy of Professional Dialogue and its aspirations.

HOT Challenge – An Outdoor Development Programme for Dutch Homeless People

Rijk Smitskamp and Bernhard Holtrop

Situation

HVO-Querido is a homeless aid organisation in The Netherlands. With about 1350 employees it offers shelter, housing guidance and daytime activities to 4750 vulnerable citizens, including homeless and people with a psychiatric and/or addiction problems.

The homeless approach in the big cities in the Netherlands follows a pragmatic, procedural, problem-solving approach. This includes a focus on solving the problems and handling the 'nuisance' that homeless people create for the rest of society. The homeless often feel lost in the procedures of the many different authorities they have to deal with. They feel as though they are being treated like a number instead of as a human. Although it is the intention of HVO-Querido to provide a healing environment for the clients, there is in practice little space for taking care of the personal issues the homeless person faces, though these are at the root of the actual needs. Social workers are pragmatic, with a focus on fixing short-term problems. They are less focused on providing a safe and healing setting in which the clients can develop the self-esteem needed to fix their own problems. In order to provide effective help, social workers and we as facilitators also need to work on our own personal development.

Objectives

In our aim to make a difference in this situation, we have chosen three related objectives. First, provide a healing program for the homeless in which they can accept themselves and experience themselves in a social context and take personal steps. Second, invest in the trust relationship between the homeless and their personal social worker. And third, provide the organisation – specifically its management – a first-hand insight into the necessity and power of this approach, and connect it to their strategic goals. To do this we created a multiple-track approach. This included developing and then rolling out a transformational, dialogical personal development program in which clients and social workers participate side-by-side, in nature and away from old patterns and distractions. We also created awareness and goodwill among the managers and social workers about the power of experiential learning and dialogue in nature.

Method

To do this, we created the HOT ('Hero Outdoor Training') Challenge, a three-day, out-in-nature personal leadership program in which homeless people and their social workers participated as equals. Designed according to ancient rituals and dialogic work in the tradition of the Native Americans, the participants follow a careful process where activities (experiential learning) alternate with reflective and healing dialogues and rites of passage. In three days the participants experience and reflect on themselves and each other. In dialogues they help each other to come free of the ineffective surviving reflexes they encountered. The participant gains trust in him or herself and in the other participants. Moreover, they reconnect to nature and to a deeper sense of meaning.

The program contains a natural flow of activities and dialogues:

- Day One focuses on investing in group safety, trust and openness. It includes building a base camp, building rafts, cooking together and hosting a drum workshop in the evening.
- Day Two is more focused on facing individual challenges in this new social context, with breathwork, ice bathing and a sweat lodge. Each activity is preceded and followed by dialogues. All participants, homeless and social workers alike, reflect on themselves after having being confronted with the natural elements. They adopt dialogue and breathwork as their instruments for going inward, to cope with the external stressors they experience on a day-to-day basis.
- Day Three has participants share their insights and define their personal goals, which they bring home to the big city. After one month there is an integration peer group session where participants share about their lives, learnings and challenges.

We also focused on creating engagement in the organisation, up to the boardroom level. To do this we had a moviemaker make a short documentary of the first HOT Challenge for the HVO-Querido board. This resulted in an impressive short documentary titled "Hot Challenge" (available here: https://youtu.be/5rN0uz5EoWo – English subtitles will follow).

We asked the homeless, who were very enthusiastic about both the program and the documentary, to join us and even facilitate the dialogue with the board. We trained them for this.

This resulted in an impressive transformational dialogue session with the top 40 leaders of HVO-Querido. After a short ceremonial welcome we presented the documentary and hosted the dialogue among the top 40, facilitated by the participating homeless. Touched by the documentary and especially by the self-conscious homeless leading the dialogue, all present were unanimous about the value of the program.

Outcomes

The clients experienced new trust in themselves, others and life in a broader sense. Some moved to a new house, got a job and stayed abstinent from substances. The participants created new relationships in a positive and healthy way. The social workers gained deeper insights and developed talents in their role of supporting personal development.

Learnings

What surprised us:

- Clients and their social workers: After each HOT Challenge all were so touched and inspired that they motivated other clients and team members to participate in the Challenge.
- Clients: A strong brotherhood/sisterhood emerged among the homeless participants. Five years after the program, with their social workers gone, their friendship is still enormous. They support each other in their steps in life.
- Organization: The top 40 were deeply touched by the homeless facilitating the dialogues and seeing the documentary, which resulted in them adopting the program. (Now, however, we are facing a new challenge. Recently a new board has been installed. These new members don't have the history of this process, so lack the engagement.)
- Personal: We were personally confronted by the homeless in interactions. They communicate in an unfiltered way, and gave direct feedback if we failed to be authentic.

We also discovered that, at the client level, there is a big gap between how clients experience themselves in nature and how they engage back in the system in Amsterdam. Dialogue is the bridge between the two worlds, challenging social workers to really support the homeless in their mental development process.

Conference Session Extracts
From the consideration of the case study with conference participants

Rijk Smitskamp: [For my first homeless group outing] I had an idea. I wanted to take 12 people into nature for three days. But meanwhile we were back home having this Covid situation – we ended up in quarantine with four of us, but they were enthusiastic. Before I knew it, I was with 12 homeless people, and we were building rafts, making campfires, doing sweat lodges and having beautiful conversations around the campfire. Something different was happening from what I knew in Amsterdam during the normal work – we were having real conversations. It was not me helping somebody. We were equal. We were all having our own experiences, working together, being cold and drinking coffee to warm up again.

We were working around different challenges together. And you saw the smiles coming up, bit by bit. Even the social workers who work in the projects told me they were having such different conversations now. These boys from the streets were coming back to the shelter in Amsterdam with so much energy, everybody was like, what happened there? That was really the start of a whole new episode. My colleagues didn't really understand what was happening, so we did some team-training dialogues, and I asked Bernhard, "Can you help me with this, because I don't know how to do it!"

Bernhard Holtrop: We have had to do this work from the bottom up – and I've learned that it's a bigger struggle to inspire from the bottom up. We worked on it for about five years, and now our organization's board is convinced that dialogue should play an essential role in the development of the organization. It was hard, but it all started with this outdoor challenge. And we wanted to show a short video clip we did about the experience.

(After the video clip)

Bernhard: We made this documentary and then we showed it first to the homeless guys. They had the first right of refusal and they were very anti-enthusiastic. And then we said, "Okay, what do you want? We want more of this". They said okay. And then we said, "Well, then, we have to go to the board. Are you ready?" And they said yes. So we said, "If we train you, are you ready to facilitate the dialogue with the board?"

Five of them said yes. So we had a dialogue with the top 40 of the organization, the board members and the top senior management. They were facilitated by the homeless themselves.

That was a very impactful and touching moment with the board and the general management; they saw this group making such a huge step in only three days.

Speaker: Did you guys have dialogue about why these men ended up homeless, and also what the results were after this camping trip? What happened to them? Where did they go?

Speaker: It was a goosebump moment for me when I watched the movie – it reminded me of my own experiences during the pandemic. I have no idea about homelessness, how that feels. But know how loneliness feels. What was woven through this project was to reconnect people with themselves and then give them some tools to connect with others.

Bernhard: We interviewed participants of these programs afterward and asked, "What was the gain you got out of it?" They said that they felt human again, because in the big system of homelessness, in the big city, you have to pass through all kinds of gateways, all kind of conditions. You become a number. We brought them back into feeling the ability to respond instead of being dragged along in the system. We asked them, "What do you want – what do you need to bring back from the forest into the big city and into the homeless organization?" The answer was dialogue, and that's what we did. We brought dialogue back as one of the treasures from the outdoors into Amsterdam, because through dialogue they started to see each other as a peer group, as a sharing group on a frequent basis. We also started introducing dialogue to their social workers and with the social workers' team managers.

Rijk: Why did many start reconnecting with their families through this process? Because they felt inner strength. They were proud of themselves for going through this process and for helping other brothers. They had something they could go back to the families with. On one trip all of the guys were fathers. We asked them, "What do you guys want to do next with this?" A couple of them said, "One day we want to take our children with us out in nature". Some of them hadn't seen their children for years, and now they were so proud that they had the inner strength to step over their shame and pain to get in contact with their children again or talking to the moms.

Bernhard: What made us want to go into nature with a group of homeless people? Rijk and I are both nature lovers – we both were before we did programs, and we still are. We take people into nature to come home to themselves. We do nature quests, vision quests, these kind of programs. Rijk started to work with the homeless and I worked in a lot in troubled neighborhoods, so we said, "Let's join forces and let's do this as a healing program for the homeless". It proved to be a wonderful journey for them and for us.

Postscript

The authors' reflections, written some months after the conference

Insights on the programme itself

During the programme, participants gained many insights into themselves, and showed the ability to practice with new positive behaviours. After returning to the city some participants fell back into old destructive behaviours. After the programme they offered the feedback that they experienced a gap between the safe space in nature and the unsafe space back in the city. They weren't yet able to uphold their new perspectives without support.

Our next question was, How do we bring the essence of the outdoor program back to the city? We realized dialogue was this essence; and it could be done through follow-ups in peer-group sharing and in dialogue with their social workers and the organisation.

Insights on the organisational level

The organisation initially 'did not understand' the purpose of this programme; they were not yet able to understand where to place it within their working process.

Social workers found it challenging to deal with their clients in a dialogic way. This intuitive programme needed thorough embedding within the whole organisation.

We realized how much change and development is dependent on personal drive, interpersonal resonance and trust, and the important role dialogue can play in this bottom-up process. When bringing in unconventional 'knowledge' about healing and personal development, all stakeholders involved had to stand for it personally.

Could we have done it the other way around, through embedding it in the organization first?

We tried, but we think the answer is no. This is due to the fact that exactly during this phase a new board was installed, and the first focus of the new chairperson was on the economical side of the organization.

Our personal development
Rijk: It was easier for me to work with the clients and team managers than to connect with the board members. Looking back I've learned that the board members need just as much trust and safe space as the homeless people need in order to feel safe enough to open up and change perspectives.

Bernhard: Working with the clients was enormously valuable and sometimes confrontational. I learned with them to feel myself more, becoming more aware of what is happening inside of me. I learned to trust parking my analytical brain more and more. With their intuition they sensed me before I sensed myself and gave feedback that the trust was no longer there. This only could be re-instituted by coming back to myself and reconnecting to the other.

Community Engagement and Effective Socio-Economic Development

Loshnee Naidoo

Context

South Africa (SA) is a developing country with a population of 55.7 million, an unemployment rate of 34.4%, a poverty rate of 55.5% and a Gini index (a measure of income inequality) of 63 (100 = maximum inequality). The SA Government views socio-economic development (SED) as a key driver to address these dire social imbalances.

As a result, SED is a key component of government initiatives. Communities often see it as a panacea to poverty and addressing immediate needs, including housing, electricity, water, sanitation, healthcare and employment.

The private sector's interest in SED is evidenced at numerous levels. Because companies are compelled to comply with the Broad-Based Black Economic Empowerment (BBBEE) programme, which attempts to redress imbalances created under apartheid, companies that empower more Black people (e.g., through more SED spending) are rated higher on the BBBEE scorecard. This in turn gives them competitive advantages, especially in Government procurement. Companies can also benefit by offering specific training to communities, through SED programmes, ensuring they have access to the skilled workers they require. Developing local business to participate in the value chain reduces a company's cost of business. Finally, fostering a mutually beneficial relationship with the community is valuable for managing labour negotiations, unrest and recessions.

Aims/Objectives

The SA Department of Energy (DoE) commenced the Renewable Energy Independent Power Producer Programme in 2011. A mandatory component of securing a licence included the commitment to job creation, local content procurement and SED. ACWA, a Saudi owned energy and desalination company, was awarded the licence for the R5,5b (£0.27b / $367.6m USD) 50 megawatt CSP Bokpoort project, which included constructing and operating a renewable energy plant. A key deliverable was the SED programme with the !Kheis community surrounding the project site. ACWA's SED commitment amounted to R20m per year (£0.99m / $1.35m USD) over a period of 22 years.

Northern Cape, where the plant was constructed, is the largest province in SA in terms of land mass, but with the lowest population density. !Kheis is approximately 1,5 hours from Upington, with a population of 16,637 and unemployment rate of 29,7%, with the resultant poverty levels.

I was appointed to work on the community engagement process in the !Kheis community on behalf of ACWA.

Method

For effective community engagement it was imperative to become aware and respectful of the needs of the entire community in the planning, execution and feedback process. Understanding that the community differed in race, culture, class and gender, amongst other factors, was critical. All groupings needed to be treated, and seen to be treated, fairly and equally, via a transparent process. Inclusivity was critical.

Our work began with research about the !Kheis community to understand employment, travel and family constraints. This enabled us to determine where and when meetings should be convened, and to ensure all community members were informed of the meetings. We found most adults were employed a distance from their homes and, due to lack of transport, travelled by foot. This affected the time when the meetings could be held and led to sessions being hosted in the evenings, in each of the seven towns in the area. The community lacked access to newspapers or radio – hence notices were pasted onto shop doors as well as distributed at schools and via police units. These considerations ensured that the entire community were informed and were allowed the opportunity to participate in the sessions.

The culture and needs of the community were also factored into the facilitation of engagement sessions. The community needs took precedence over other stakeholders. The meetings were held in Afrikaans, the predominant language of the community.

Although an introduction to ACWA and the Bokpoort Project was important, the maximum amount of time was allotted for dialogue. This created a platform for the community to raise questions and concerns and engage with ACWA. The community was also requested to identify *their* critical needs. Inquiry focused on how a programme would address a need (and determining if it had been attempted previously), the results, the benefits and who would take responsibility for the programme. This allowed an in-depth understanding of the community as well as the ability to craft joint accountability and partnership for projects. Together we created an honest space for dialogue that ensured the management of expectations.

We maintained regular two-way communication after the engagement session. This process enabled the ongoing concerns of the community to be addressed in order to retain the trust fostered.

Outcomes

The success of the community engagement was that the SED projects *identified by the community* formed part of the SED plan, rather than projects identified by the commercial enterprise or government. The !Kheis Community benefitted directly from electrification of informal settlements, water reticulation (from a network of pipes), improvements to the quality of school education, access to computers and internet and bursaries. Small local businesses were able to provide services to the project, which brought employment and skills development opportunities.

ACWA and the DoE benefitted from reduction in labour unrest by skilling and employing from within the community; availability of cheaper inputs; and relevant skills. Socially they were able to manage expectations and perceptions of bias. As trust grew, vandalism fell.

ACWA won the Africa Utility Awards: Best Community Project 2015 and, due to the success, members of the !Kheis community were invited to Parliament to share their experiences.

Learnings

Considering the community's circumstances, such as lack of access to technology, and incorporating this into the engagement process established inclusivity and respect. Creating a space for dialogue between ACWA, the community and Government moved the situation from distrust to trust. This was enhanced by the constant feedback and availability to the community.

The communities have an extensive understanding of their needs and, in many instances, the needs of all parties dovetailed. For example in the Bokpoort Project, when the community requested employment opportunities the skills training matched the project needs, resulting in community employment. This in turn led to building of trust. Effective SED leads to a path out of poverty – and a path out of poverty leads to healthier communities, economies and societies.

Conference Session Extracts
From the consideration of the case study with conference participants

Speaker: I have a question. When did the project complete in terms of the initial setup and coming online?

Loshnee Naidoo: Are you talking about the renewable energy project, or you talking about the development project?

Speaker: Both. You went through the development process and then the company got established within the community, and now that project is online. What was that timeline like?

Loshnee: For the construction, it was a year and a half, and then post-that, it's a twenty-year operational phase. The way the economic development side works is that once you are in operations a portion of your revenue goes into community development. So for the entire twenty-year period they have to spend and they have to report back to government on what they're doing.

Speaker: I thought I heard you say that as you met with each small community you had to reach consensus on what projects they thought were most important, and you made sure that you did those. If there's 300 people in a room in a community, I guess there probably was some disagreement as to what they wanted done and was most important. How did you seek to get that consensus as to which projects to do?

Loshnee: Very true. Each community has its own dynamics and tensions. We had seven towns that were quite a distance from each other, so within each community we would say, "Give us your top projects". Then, based on the kind of impacts each project could have and its alignment with ACWA's vision, we'd say, "Okay, these are the projects that we need to look at in this period of time". There would be various ranking processes, but what we would always do is go back to community a few times to say, "Based on these criteria, this is what we're going to do, and these are the time periods that we'll follow as we roll out the different projects".

Speaker: Did this project create opportunity for additional dialogues? I'm thinking more like medical interventions; for example, you said there was a

	huge problem with alcoholism in that area. Things that were specific to energy are important, don't get me wrong, but I'm just wondering if the community in and of itself thought this was their biggest need.
Loshnee:	The biggest need being energy . . . ?
Speaker:	Yes, did they start off by thinking, "This is what we want to focus our resources on"? What was the process for having more dialogues around community issues?
Loshnee:	There was definitely a need for solar energy. I'm not sure if you saw some of those pictures. Many of the homes are reed homes and there are a great many windstorms. Reed homes with candles and storms means that many people have lost their homes and all their possessions. Solar was one of the things that they required. Other requirements were around addressing alcoholism and healthcare. So that was a project that was also introduced.
Speaker:	I like how you discussed getting people included, using a variety of inclusiveness tools to make sure that everyone who needed to be there was in the room and in the discussion. It sounds to me like there was a lot of preparation and planning, for example, making sure that you didn't do it at a timeframe when a certain TV show was on. You all took the time to think about the people and I'm hearing from you that you built a safe container. Good rapport was needed. My question is about how political parties were also invited to come as they were not provided the opportunity to address the people. How were you able to manage that?
Loshnee:	I identified all the sectors within the community that needed to be met with. In the local municipality structure, you have local ward counselors that are aligned to political parties. So I actually met with all the political parties from all towns and the ward counselor, and I explained to them who AKWA is, what we're trying to do and that we need to be seen as apolitical because of the long time period. My engagement with them was not disrespectful - it was, "I am honouring what you're trying to do, but you also need to understand where we are coming from". So they were invited and they were part of the audience. We gave voice to all the parties, and we treated all of them alike.

Speaker: Do you see this being implemented with dialogues in other projects similar to this, by other companies who are going into communities? I'm assuming, based on what you're saying, that dialogue played a big role in it. Have you shared that with the powers that be, to maybe incorporate that in future initiatives?

Loshnee: I have. Your organization (the Virginia Department of Corrections) is very dialogic, but the normal thing here is, "It's too much work and we don't have the time". Governments want quick turnaround solutions, and renewable energy companies are normally tracking the bottom line. So there's been lots of problems. Some energy companies are not honouring the commitments, some do a tick-box exercise. We're trying to get dialogue instilled as a culture, but it's quite difficult trying to get government to talk to private sector and to also to listen to development specialists.

Postscript
The author's reflections, written some months after the conference

On reflection, I realise that I learnt something on every step of the way from doing the original work to writing this postscript.

In economic development parlance, the work I conducted is referred to as stakeholder engagement. Engagement, or dialogue, of this magnitude was daunting and a challenge due to the size and diversity of the community; the national and local political complexities; the levels of poverty; the power brokers that arose; the potential disjunct between the needs of the community, that of government and that of the company; and, finally, my location as a development practitioner. I know that my skill, knowledge and expertise were tested and that I grew immensely as a practitioner and as an individual.

In writing the case study I was intrigued by the similarities of what I defined as stakeholder engagement to that of dialogic engagement. In analysing and capturing the work I had done I was able to imbibe some of the dialogic tenets which were new to me.

By engaging with the work with the participants I realised that contextualising the work for an audience external to South Africa was challenging. The discussion also allowed me to understand that engagements of a large magnitude were not always conducive for complex dialogues, as these proved to be.

With rereading my case study I was realised that I did not offer a strong enough critique of the work conducted. I also felt that the language style was too colloquial.

Reading the extract I realise that the questions and challenges raised were similar to those I had broached when I was conducting these engagements. This was interesting for two reasons. Firstly it highlighted the similarities between stakeholder engagement and dialogue, and secondly it showed that these comparable challenges exist in different parts of the world. Looking through the extract I also realised that I may have misunderstood certain questions and hence did not respond to them appropriately. I now have a deeper understanding of dialogic engagement and realise that some of these questions were couched in this arena and my responses were those of a development practitioner.

The journey from conducting the stakeholder engagements to working through the extract has been extremely enlightening as I now see how dialogic engagement could be an invaluable asset in my economic development toolkit.

Institutionalizing Public-Private Dialogue in Sierra Leone

Chukwu-Emeka Chikezie

Context

This case study presents the early stages of institutionalizing a culture and practice of public-private dialogue (PPD) in Sierra Leone, a small, poor country in West Africa. Over the last 15 years, the World Bank has promoted PPD as a critical instrument to improve the investment climate in developing countries (Herzberg & Wright, 2006). The plot twist to this conventional story is an attempt to blend elements of "Bohmian" dialogue practice as promoted by the Academy of Professional Dialogue Practitioners with this traditional approach to PPD. This is a work just beginning, and thus the story is conceptual at this stage.

Sierra Leone's investment climate is hostile towards business. It ranks 163 out of 190 countries in the World Bank's *Doing Business 2020* index. When government and business actors talk, it's usually because of problems caused by new government rules, introduced with little or no consultation with business. But business isn't organized to provide sound policy inputs to the government. There's low trust, fragmentation, and poor coordination.

Government, business, and donors all agree on a need for PPD, *but what space exists to infuse conventional PPD with flavors of Bohmian dialogue? Why is Bohmian dialogue even relevant in this context?*

First, the problems afflicting the investment climate in Sierra Leone are systemic, complex and interconnected. Fragmentation is embedded, pervasive and endemic, and exists between and among the government, private sector and donors. Sierra Leone's history has produced cleavages around ethnicity, gender, rural-urban dwelling and class. These fragmented identities interplay with Sierra Leone's politics. Memory and fragmented consciousness hamper progress. Fragmented consciousness can lead to counterproductive and divisive actions that compound problems. *How can we escape these traps and engage in more conscious, connected thinking to problem-solve?*

Does Generative Dialogue offer a way forward? Coherence can emerge from this. New meaning weaves together. There's both a science and an art to creating the enabling conditions for this emergent dialogue. First, get the whole system in the room (Weisbord & Janoff, 2007).

Second, help participants appreciate the interconnectivity and interdependence of their respective concerns as well as the common ground they share. With such recognition and resolution, systemic interventions to resolve underlying problems become feasible.

I work as a Team Leader for Invest Salone, a private sector development program funded by UK aid to boost investment into Sierra Leone and exports from it.

Aims and Objectives

We aim to contribute to Sierra Leone's inclusive economic development by promoting investments into Sierra Leone's productive sectors, and by export buyers of Sierra Leone's products and services, to boost economic diversification and transformation and to ultimately increase Sierra Leoneans' incomes and jobs.

Our objectives are to:

1. Build a culture of dialogue and collaboration between government and business leaders;
2. Tackle systemic barriers to investment through investment climate reforms;
3. Strengthen systems of tracking and accountability to drive reform implementation.

Methods

Invest Salone hopes to achieve its objectives by working with the government-designated agency, the National Investment Board (NIB), to institutionalize PPD in Sierra Leone.

There are several strands to this collaboration with the NIB:

1. Work at senior levels of the government of Sierra Leone (Presidency, Vice Presidency, Cabinet, agency heads) to promote a culture of public-private dialogue
2. Support enactment of primary legislation enshrining PPD, and PPD to precede introduction of laws, regulations, policies, procedures, and processes that impact business
3. Support formulations of PPD regulations, procedures, processes and practices across all tiers of government (central, local, chiefdom) in line with primary legislation
4. Support development of a PPD issues-and-actions tracker to monitor and effect resolution of agreed issues
5. Build human capacity to facilitate Bohmian-style dialogue and effect systems change across all levels of government and business
6. Support formulation of technical working groups to design and drive reforms identified through Dialogue

7. Generate public awareness and understanding about and support for PPD as a means of improving the investment climate leading to investment and export growth, jobs, and higher incomes
8. Support outreach to Parliament to deepen awareness and understanding of investment climate challenges and broaden support for reforms
9. Support outreach to and engagement with business membership organizations to strengthen their engagement with PPD processes
10. Monitor the PPD institutionalization process on an ongoing basis

Intended Outcomes

What will success look like from these efforts? First, having the President, Vice President, Cabinet members and senior business leaders model dialogic practices will be half the battle. In fact, we hope to see the culture of dialogue spread far beyond the PPD domain. Second, tangible movement on some of the vexing problems that hobble business in Sierra Leone would help to build trust in the process, system and individuals in charge and generate momentum for more change. Third, public awareness and support for this process will be crucial in sustaining the effort over the coming years.

Learnings

None of this has been or will be easy. Getting big men (Sierra Leone is male-dominated) to abandon their sacred space on the "high table" is hard. Nor do people want to give up their beloved monologues in favor of listening more. We have to frame dialogues in tangible ways, thus limiting space for Generative Dialogue. We cannot overlook the truism that every system is perfectly designed to deliver the results it does. To maintain the status quo, vested interests will try to thwart reforms. They are powerful and savvy. We also see that the absence of collective business action undermines progress. Companies use their patronage networks to get things done in Sierra Leone. Persuading them to work collaboratively with peers and competitors to improve the investment climate is a novel idea.

Nonetheless, the world needs dialogue—Sierra Leone certainly does—so we know we must try.

References
Herzberg, B., & Wright, A. (2006). *The PPD Handbook: A Toolkit For Business Environment Reformers*. Available at http://www.publicprivatedialogue.org/tools/PPDhandbook.pdf.
Weisbord, M. R., & Janoff, S. (2007). *Don't Just Do Something, Stand There!: Ten Principles for Leading Meetings that Matter*. San Francisco: Berrett-Koehler Publishers.

Conference Session Extracts

From the consideration of the case study with conference participants

Speaker: How far are you in this process? Have you just started, have you had any meetings so far?

Chukwu-Emeke (Chux): We have had meetings, but we are at the very early stages. To give you an example, we will have a facilitated dialogue tomorrow. Every year the government of Sierra Leone introduces a finance act, where it sets out the tax codes for the next financial year. We engaged the private sector across the board to find out what measures they would like government to introduce. We've now done that, and we've shared that information with senior people in government, and tomorrow we will have a meeting to talk about that. We have examples of what we would like to see, and we would like to achieve the institutionalization of that.

Speaker: Have you had any outcomes so far that you could use to encourage others to join suit?

Chux: Outcomes will come down the line, but what we have got are some commitments from government. For example, the president and his advisors would like to organize a presidential-level, public-private dialogue. Now that would be very significant in sending a signal that government wants to listen to the private sector and takes it seriously. That would definitely encourage other government departments and agencies to follow suit. It is a very fragmented process, however, because some government departments are still producing laws or bills with no interaction with the private sector.

Speaker: Are you in the stage of your dialogic development with them where you could bystand the inconsistencies you see happening with the private sector? Or would it be dangerous at this point to bystand?

Chux: Tomorrow we will just try to guide them. They've set up the meeting, so that's good, but we will try to guide them. "If you want this meeting to be a little bit more participatory, we suggest you do this, or you do that," and so on. Bystanding could be done at different levels. We could, for example, write an editorial for some of the national newspapers to encourage more of this reflection. A useful suggestion . . .

Speaker: Chux, how would they describe your role? A consultant? How much overlap is there with the way you see your role and how they see it? That defines the permission you have for certain interventions.

Chux: The minister of finance, as he was then, last year acknowledged that they did the budget but didn't have a proper dialogue with the private sector. He said he would like that to be done better, and on a more sustained institutionalized basis. So that was an opening for us. We said, "We can help you, sir," and we put together concept notes. Some people will see us as facilitators, which is how we would like to see ourselves. Others see us as an interfering nuisance because they're happy with the things the way they are. Others would see us as consultants who are there to do something for them, but the minute the consultant goes away, everything stops. We believe the facilitative role is key. There's a political economy here where coming up with policies that are contradictory or confusing means people have to seek some discretion or explanation from the policymakers, which gives them an advantage. Transparent policies and rules are not in everybody's interest.

Speaker: My understanding of a facilitator or a consultant, both, is that he has the power to define the process. The process is not defined by the big bosses. How is that seen by you and by the participants?

Chux: We absolutely *don't* have the power, and that's the constraint. I agree that normally when you are hired as a consultant or facilitator, you define the process. We have a lot of constraints and we have to be almost 'guerilla dialogic' in the way we do things.

Speaker: In our small-group session on this topic we were an excited all-female group, and we spoke a lot about the high table you mentioned. The phrase was not common for some of us. We wanted to learn about its structure and how challenging it would be for you to break it down, if it is viewed as a barrier.

Speaker: What's a high table? I am not familiar with that term.

Chux: At a banquet, there's always hierarchy with important people seated at the high table. The minister, boss or CEO sits at the head, and there an assumption that they will speak and most people are there to listen.

Speaker: To your earlier question, I would recommend starting by using the Dialogue practices yourself. So, first is you listen, listen to people in power and understand what they are trying to achieve. Give them the feeling they are well heard and respected, not only because of their position, but also because of the intention. If you put yourself in the service of them and the shaping of the process, you will be allowed to shape the process a little bit – and then you can do it more and more. At the same time, I would find a lower rank of team leaders or experts in those organizations you could work with. I would get permission to teach them, because then you have knowledge at another place in the system that you can use later on. I would do the two things in parallel.

Postscript
The author's reflections, written some months after the conference

Writing the paper was a useful exercise because it forced me to articulate a conceptualization of institutionalizing public-private dialogue (PPD) in the Sierra Leone context. Looking back a year later, I think the conceptualization of PPD institutionalization as multifaceted has proven correct. With hindsight, what I could have emphasized more was the anticipated nonlinearity of the process.

For instance, over the last year, the all-important, powerful, and influential Ministry of Finance has established its own private sector liaison unit, opening up a new front to pursue in our quest to institutionalize PPD. One conference seminar participant at the session where I presented the case study shared her experience of targeting midlevel officials as potential change agents to champion dialogue while their more senior bosses might be reluctant, disinterested or even hostile. These are precisely the level of officials for whom we have targeted to offer dialogue training over the year. Such officials (and individuals outside of government or public service) are often more influential than their titles suggest.

Over the last year, Sierra Leone's parliamentarians have passed a law bringing the National Investment Board (NIB) into existence with a mandate, among others, to "initiate, organize and lead all public-private dialogue relating to investment." On the one hand, this is a positive step toward institutionalizing PPD. On the other hand, it will be difficult for the NIB to garner the capacity needed to organize all the PPDs needed everywhere. More realistically, the NIB could track all the outcomes from PPDs relating to investment and ensure there is follow-through. Thus, a support program such as Invest Salone must be agile and constantly adapt to prevailing conditions to support PPD institutionalization.

Reflecting over the last year at a personal level, while we focus on "dialogue" as an act in the public space (PPD especially), we must remember the accompanying "inner work" (to paraphrase leading dialogue practitioner Bill Isaacs) needed for us to become dialogic and learn to "walk the talk." This is especially true as we've facilitated PPDs in markedly different settings and contexts but tried to remain true to the essence of dialogue as enabling the emergence of fresh perspectives and understanding, if we allow it.

The World Needs Dialogue! Dialogue for the Benefit of Society

Peter Garrett

Context

In 1984 a new kind of Dialogue was conceived by David and Saral Bohm, Don and Anna Factor and Peter and Jenny Garrett with 40 other participants gathered for a weekend in the English Cotswold Hills. Further private weekend Dialogues in Israel and Europe established why Dialogue is necessary and continued a deepening participatory enquiry into proprioceptive awareness. An adaption of the approach was later popularised by Peter Senge in his book *The Fifth Discipline*, and became well-known in business circles in the 1990s. This was enhanced by Bill Isaacs' book, *Dialogue and the Art of Thinking Together*. Further books were published by Linda Ellinor and Glenna Gerard, and by Nancy Dixon.

Two decades later the whole field of Dialogue was largely fragmented and competitive, with newer practitioners learning mostly from the few books available on the subject. There were no commonly accepted standards, and anyone could call themselves a Dialogue Practitioner. Peter Garret and Jane Ball, the principals of Dialogue Associates, a long-standing and successful consulting firm, realised that their impact was limited to what could be done by two people, and they would need to help others to do the work if they were to contribute more substantially to a meaningful impact on society.

Aims

An inaugural meeting was held in the Cotswolds to determine the value of forming an Academy of Professional Dialogue. It was attended by 10 people from the UK, USA, Sweden, Austria and Germany. People were surprised to discover the extent of Dialogue work being done by each other. For example, over 30,000 people had been trained in Dialogue skills in Sweden. The unanimous decision was that the Academy was needed to *inspire* people to use Dialogue, to *acknowledge* those who were already doing good work, to *inform* people how to work dialogically and to *develop* the whole field in areas such as social research.

Method

At a further meeting in 2016, Lars Åke-Almqvist (Sweden), Jane Ball (UK), Jim Herman (USA) and Peter Garrett (Chair) were appointed as Trustees to this new non-profit educational charity, along with a total of 10 Voting Members to create a framework for accountability. This International Board has met regularly ever since (with changing membership) and publishes minutes of all its monthly meetings. The first decisions were to accept national groupings that were formed with the same purpose and legal status as the International Academy, and to raise the flag by holding an international conference in 2018.

Under the title *The World Needs Dialogue!* 80 participants met at an English conference centre to launch the international initiative. To acknowledge the practitioners present, we asked 20 of them to write working papers about their Dialogue work that we could circulate beforehand and consider in more depth during the conference. We have continued this practice annually. The fourth one, *TWND! 4,* will be held online in 2021. We formed a publishing company, Dialogue Publications, to make these working papers and extracts from the conference widely available, to inspire and inform the public as well as acknowledging our working members.

A website and online platform were designed for the Academy internationally, and it has accumulated a substantial library as well as providing an online learning forum for members in the form of Practitioner Circles and Generative Dialogues. The membership has grown steadily in geographic breadth and slowly in numbers. We have around 130 members resident in Europe, North and South America, Africa and Asia. Many are active and participate regularly in the annual conferences and smaller meetings.

The Trustees appointed a subcommittee, the Professional Standards and Accreditation Board (PSAB), to develop criteria for the recognition and accreditation of competent Professional Dialogue Practitioners. To determine these criteria the PSAB held consultations in the form of monthly online meetings to which all members were invited, and a three-level model of 'Bringing Dialogue into the Room', 'Dialogic Intervention' and 'Whole System Dialogue'. The Integrated Dialogue Model has formed the framework for the emerging educational programme for the development of confident and competent Professional Dialogue Practitioners.

Outcomes

Our four *The World Needs Dialogue!* conferences have given the Academy an international profile, and the direct participation of close to 1,000 different participants. We have increased substantially the available literature about Professional Dialogue with 43 working papers published in three volumes, and a further two books by Marie-Ève Marchand and Peter Garrett. Our first accredited Organizational Member (the largest state agency in Virginia) has expanded our organisational working bench strength significantly. The Academy's accredited educational programme has just been launched publicly and we have designed a Learning Centre to enable participatory online learning. The aspiration is for Dialogue to be recognised internationally as a professional practice. This is an ambitious long-term journey for which we are laying the foundations.

Learnings

- There is an extraordinary personal commitment to Dialogue by those who have had a first-hand experience.
- There are very different levels of skill, experience and scope amongst the many people offering Dialogue services to others, from simple experiences and basic trainings to full whole-system architectural design and implementation.
- We have connected with lively Dialogue movements in Finland, Germany, the Netherlands, and elsewhere in Europe.
- We were surprised to find Dialogue work had reduced significantly in the USA, with many working papers from US practitioners being more historic than recent.
- We found the existing books on Dialogue were the primary resource for many practitioners, and that the Dialogos 'Leadership for Collective Intelligence' programme has had a significant impact on the field, along with the international work by Dialogue Associates.
- We discovered other attempts in the past to establish international organisations for Dialogue that did not succeed.
- Establishing the Academy as a professional body, rather than a network, has not been easy. There is still a tendency by some to promote (or defend) their reputation and status despite having limited experience of dialogic intervention and whole-system work.
- All growing organisations discover that the freedom to make decisions is dependent on accountability. The existing leadership will need to make space for this to become more evident within the dialogic context of the Academy.

Conference Session Extracts
From the consideration of the case study with conference participants

Speaker: Peter, this has been on my mind. We're in a very intense political period right now in Virginia and politics drives a lot of what we do administratively in terms of procedure, and what we look like as an agency. I'm wondering with the fragmentation that has developed because of politics, what are we going to look like as politics change and affect us moving forward?

Peter Garrett: There are real forces out there to manage. Your video on Tuesday is one great way of writing the story yourself, you know, because it was written in an extremely inclusive way.

Speaker: It was. That was an awesome video.

Peter: One thing is to write the story, rather than having other people write it.

Speaker: The election coming up in November could affect the department in different ways, but we've done a really good job of making Dialogue a business practice and embedding it in our culture. No matter the political affiliation, people will see how great what we're doing is, and how much Dialogue has helped Virginia. It's a business practice like the director said, and we'll just keep doing business as usual and keep moving forward. That's my hope anyway.

Speaker: I think if you put the right seeds in the right soil, then you'll have growth. I was in church in a meeting, and I saw everybody talking over everybody else. We were trying to make a decision about something, and it was just chaotic. I raised my hand and I said, "We need dialogue!" So, I gave the Dialogue Manual to my pastor. I said, "We need to teach this in the church!" I feel like if we have the right seeds and put it in the right soil, then it can continue to grow, because the world does need dialogue!

Speaker: Those of us that's been around for a few years have seen this Dialogue, how it has evolved. And for me, even with teaching the inmates over the last few months, how it has evolved from the beginning of this group to what it looked like on graduation day. There is something to be said about how this thing evolves.

Speaker: I graduated and got my Dialogue Practitioner certificate at the beginning of this month. I went home and I taught my older children and my high school children some of the things that I had been learning, I've also started teaching my grandchildren. I mean, even at one and two years old, if you teach them respect they tend to grow. I'm trying to plant my seeds early. Personally, I would like to see Dialogue taught in 10th, 11th, and 12th school grades for a week or two – to get them to express their feelings and to teach them the proper ways to do it. Then maybe they wouldn't have as much trouble as they do in high schools with fighting and disrespect and stuff like that. Maybe we wouldn't have as many people in the prison system if they would be trained properly.

Peter: I can't see how any administration could say, "Stop listening to each other", or "Stop respecting each other". The Dialogic Practices are too elemental for that. What do you think, as one of the longest-serving members of the staff? You've seen these things come and go, no doubt, over the decades.

Speaker: I have that. I would like I say that the Working Dialogue is really working. I'm intrigued with the Working Dialogue sessions, and we really have accomplished a lot through them. I like those sessions because we get a lot of good coming out of those particular sessions.

Speaker: To great success, many important dialogues have been conducted online over the course of the pandemic. As we think about regrowth, there's an opportunity for imagination in a new way of doing things.

Speaker: Through Covid coming in, I can be honest, I lost my passion for Dialogue, because everything else just overwhelmed me. So getting back into this, I feel it's reigniting my passion. I appreciate everybody's comments. I'm back rebuilding again now.

Speaker: I remember how uncomfortable I felt when we were sitting in the visitor room when you first introduced Dialogue. The trust that we have built since then with each other, and the openness and respect! If someone were to say quit dialogue, they would be on island by themself because that's our livelihood now. That's just how we communicate. It's not second nature to us, it's first nature, you know, it's the first thing we do. It amazes me how every day, how we just advance with it.

Speaker: I've got four kids ranging from 18 to nine, and we were all sitting around planning the vacation. My wife and I were explaining where we were going to go, and my 17-year-old daughter said, "Dad, can we dialogue about this?" My daughter wanted to have her voice heard!

Speaker: I brought my ears to the conference and my questions. The Virginia experience is very interesting for me. The big message is how in a closed system, in a tough area like prisons, you have achieved such a success to shift the culture of command and control to an open system. It helps me to find my direction!

Postscript

The author's reflections, written some months after the conference

The invitation to write this postscript is a welcome opportunity to pause and reflect. My case study begins seven years ago, with the conception of the Academy of Professional Dialogue in 2015. It has the simplicity and logic of a story seen retrospectively. At the time it was less obvious where we were heading and what was being achieved. It did, however, always feel significant. At the inaugural 2016 meeting, for example, when we appointed our first Trustees, Lars-Åke Almqvist declared "I will never forget this the rest of my life!"

As well as my case study consideration with conference participants, my book *A New Kind of Dialogue* (Dialogue Publications, 2021) was launched at the *TWND!4* conference. This is a fuller description of the journey over seven decades. In its 26 chapters, the Academy first appears in the penultimate chapter. Yet it could not have happened without the preceding 24 chapters of purposeful learning. Writing that book enabled me to see the significant roles played by many individuals, each adding essential threads to the fabric being woven. I have had the honour of working with some for much longer periods of time, including my business partner Jane Ball. She and our fellow Trustees Lars-Åke Almqvist, Jim Herman, Robert Sarly, Mark Seneschall, Timo Nevalainen, Nancy Dixon, Marcus Elam and Thomas Köttner have led the Academy to become an international professional organisation. We have made a great start!

What I enjoyed most about the conference consideration was how little reference was given to the roots of the Academy. The conversation hardly referred to the past, as I recall. It was all about the sustainability of the work and its long-term future. Participants were noting how Dialogue is now a business practice in their government state agency, how it is no longer second nature but first nature there, and how productive the Working Dialogues are. They enthused about the need for Dialogue in their schools, churches and their own families. I find this inspiring, and I long to see the Academy underwriting their urge to extend Dialogue into their worlds, as I have taken it into mine. It may take another seven years to establish the 'School of Dialogue' for professional organisational and social work. We will need resources – not so much finances, but the investment of integrity and passion. Fortunately, both are in evidence as we move into our next seven-year chapter.

PART TWO

SECTION 6

ENGAGING AND MANAGING THE COVID-19 PANDEMIC

Section Six

Putting Dialogue to Work During the Covid-19 Pandemic

The Covid-19 virus first impacted the world in early 2020. The pandemic turned things upside down in a matter of weeks. Attempts to contain the spread of the virus and to reduce deaths by isolation resulted in many adults being apart from their workplaces and children apart from their schools. Travel was significantly curtailed, reducing contact between family members and friends. Employers were severely stretched to provide ongoing services, and employees had the challenges of managing work and home life under significant constraints. Online 'Zoom' conversations largely replaced face-to-face communication as people tried to make sense of what was happening and worked out how to manage the pandemic. Many believed their lives would never be normal again. We have included an interesting set of six papers about the use of Dialogue in managing the pandemic. The initial three are more about making sense of things, whilst the latter three are more about actively accommodating the changes in working situations.

William Isaacs describes the powerful series of seven online dialogues he provided for a large group of leaders from all around the world to make sense at many different levels, from personal to planetary, of what was disrupting everyone's lives internationally in such a profound way.

Abigayel Bryce and Rebecca Cannara held their Intergroup Zoom Dialogues during the heights of the pandemic, providing a meeting space for isolated Americans. They supported difficult conversations about experiences beyond the pandemic, including racism and the conflictual US politics of the time.

More locally, but equally meaningfully, **Jennifer Kittrell and Virginia Pauls** (VADOC) had a dialogic, and first face-to-face reunion of the Williamsburg Probation and Parole staff (who had been working from home and largely isolated from one another for the previous year) to reform themselves as a team.

Jeremiah Fitz and Whitney Barton (VADOC) were charged with the risky challenge of reopening the prison's religious worship services that had been suspended a year earlier to reduce the spread of the virus. They worked with people from operations, treatment, legal, education and epidemiology.

The emergency declared for Covid-19 led to the suspension of random drug screening. A year later, **Tecora Davis and John Fedor** used Dialogue to successfully redesign, improve and reimplement the screening, despite increased drug usage and the necessity for social distancing in confined offices.

The huge challenge of tracking, responding and being seen to act upon the changing needs of 5,400 VADOC Correctional Officers, spread across 45 different locations, involved six Dialogue sessions with 90 randomly selected participants co-facilitated by **Matthew Whibley and Eric Fling.**

Seven-Series Dialogues

William Isaacs

Context

In April of 2020, a group of colleagues and I held a series of dialogues to try to make sense of the pandemic. As a result we set up a series of seven, 90-minute biweekly dialogues between April and July of 2020.

Aims

Our intention was to make a genuine space for conversation—a dialogue that allowed people to uncover the meaning they were making of the situation, and to listen collectively for what was emerging in an unprecedented way.

We did not seek to impose meaning on what we saw as a massive reset for the planet, but to catalyze an inquiry into it. As we put it in the invitation,

> *This cycle of seven dialogues is an opportunity for you to join in communion and connection with others. It will be a step-by-step exploration that will enable you to bring your questions about the current moment, to listen, and reflect. You will participate in a larger community of people focused on genuine collective inquiry and deep exploration. We will all be teachers and learners simultaneously… Each of us has some of the requisite experience and perspective; no one has all of it. We give each other permission to live more fully and operate in a way that transcends fear.*

Method

We invited our network, which consists of leaders all around the world—people who had studied with us or worked with us over many years—as well as a wider audience. We had the added challenge of running this virtually. We had never before run a dialogue online and had some doubts as to whether this was even possible. We discovered great advantages to virtual exchange because we could include people from all over the world who would otherwise never have connected.

Each layer and detail of the process we set up had meaning and significance to us as organizers. For instance, the preparation for each session followed a similar pattern. Our core group would meet in advance to reflect on themes we felt were moving, and to design the flow of the session. We saw ourselves as "holding the space," which meant that what emerged in and through us was important information about what was emerging through everyone.

We held a "loose-tight" model of design, one where we articulated what we sensed was the deeper, unstated potential moving in the group, the patterns and emotional themes that were showing themselves, and potential traps or polarizations that we were noticing. We also knew to suspend all of this, taking the stance that whatever needed to emerge would do so. Typically one person would facilitate.

Our preparation included identifying different thematic starting points, beginning with the idea of a great "reset," as the pandemic stopped almost all so-called normal activity. We examined the dilemmas of a "mirage," of seeing something that turns out not to be there. We reflected on the idea of disturbance, and how to hold space for it, and trace its origins to find the source of it. We also explored the problem of the relationship between dialogue and action.

We began and closed each session with music to set the tone. We began with improvisational piano music selected by a close colleague and friend who has worked with us for over two decades. We ended each session with an a cappella piece from three women called the Wailin' Jennys: a song called "One Voice," a piece that reiterated the qualities moving in the dialogues.

Each session began by inviting the participants to reflect quietly on a series of questions, followed by a ten- to fifteen-minute small-group reflective conversation. The questions we asked in the first session included: *What is being reset in you? What is the meaning you are making of this?* and *What could you let change, to make space for what is new?* The small-group conversation was followed by a larger-group dialogue that lasted about an hour.

We also invited a graphic artist to "scribe" the dialogue, capturing impressionistically the themes that people voiced. At the close of the session, we showed this and gave people a chance to make very brief comments and observations.

Outcomes

About 350 people signed up, and about 150 came to the first dialogue. Subsequent sessions had between 75 and 125 people each. We had wide regional representation—people came from South Asia, Central and Western Europe, Africa, South America, and North America.

Throughout this process there was a remarkable flow among the participants, and a quality of presence that was quite striking to everyone. People noted, for instance, that while at times we had 100 or more people online, no one ever interrupted anyone. People were genuine, thoughtful, direct, honest, and very open. There was a wide sense of inclusion of different voices from every continent. The feeling was one of a great witnessing and being together. No one sought to impose or instruct others.

As was evident in the notes from the final session, we found ourselves moving into an almost "primordial" inquiry, exploring questions like, "What does it mean to have a human life?" The dialogue evidently impacted people deeply. Said one participant, "How different my body feels and energy resonates when I come to these dialogues—Ah, that's right! I am connected, there is an energy field, a way that we humans can connect with each other. It's everything."

Learnings

Key learnings from this process include the following:

- It is possible to hold a powerful and authentic dialogue virtually, with people that do not know each other.
- One needs to set, communicate and facilitate a clear intention to have a *dialogue*, in order not to fall into serial monologues or debate.
- There are many ranges of experience with dialogue, and experience matters. Experienced participants supported less experienced ones.
- The detailed attention to the quality of the container matters enormously.

Conference Session Extracts
From the consideration of the case study with conference participants

Speaker: You mentioned a couple of times the importance of a core group that is really well prepared, because they are the carriers of the energy in the larger group. Is that right?

William Isaacs: That's correct. Well, they're the carriers of the holding environment in which something can unfold.

Speaker: Did you work on that event with four or five or 10 people beforehand? Or are the people that you used whoever showed up because they carry the spirit of dialogue in that circumstance?

William: No, the group that we work with is a core group that I've worked with on many different things for years. We met every other week for the dialogues. In the interim week we would meet and think about what we were hearing from the last cycle that's moving in us. Dialogue isn't just (this could sound mysterious, depending on the frame you have), the 90 minutes you have when everyone's together. The dialogue is the whole cycle from when we started to 14 weeks later when we ended. We very deliberately held it as a larger cycle of learning and listening.

When we met, we were like a proxy of the larger group. We weren't holding an event. We were inviting the world, in a subset of our friends and colleagues, in a 14-week cycle to contemplate and learn from each other on what was happening. So, what you hold in your consciousness is massively relevant to what happens. And again, this sounds mysterious, but it isn't, if you start to get used to it. If you're a parent, when are you done parenting? Do you make breakfast and say that "That's it?" Well, no, you're not just making breakfast, you're raising a boy, or girl. You get the idea.

Here is a question for you to consider: If you could initiate anything, how would you prepare the field? Who would you work with, what would your intention be and how would you prepare the space to have what you wanted to have happen, actually happen?

Speaker: You mentioned that all the principles don't really matter in a way. Then what is the essence of dialogue in your opinion?

William: The principles matter, but we didn't try to teach the principles. That's what I said. In other words, it wasn't pedagogical. Not "Here's the idea, now go do it." It was a direct drop into an experience. You have to have the experience yourself to drop them into it. This is the key. You have to be having an experience to invite people into it.

Speaker: I want to say one little story. I want to hear your opinion. A Chinese koan master was teaching one of his students because a bad guy, a very strong bad guy, is coming to fight. He cannot fight himself, so he needs to teach this student a very good form. Then after he taught him the form, he asked him, "Do you remember everything?" He replied, "I forgot everything already." The master said, "Great! Now you're ready to go."

William: Great. Exactly. Right. I agree with that. The principles, the conceptual material, the technique is the scaffolding. It's necessary—it's necessary, but it's not the thing. We're all trained to think that the way to work is to mentally try to control outcomes. That's how we've all been trained to get anything done. Fine, except for the small detail: that it isn't actually how anything really works. So there's a whole lot of unlearning to be done, to understand how to activate something that is actually very natural, but that we kind of mess up because we over-control it or over-structure it or overthink it. I think this is a subject for great consideration.

Speaker: There were absolute high points and there were also recoveries from speed bumps. It was being able to navigate those different terrains. So it was a delicate balance. For example, someone may have come online to prompt a topic, and that person spoke as if it was a lecture or a debate or a classroom. They hadn't quite moved into dialogic frame. We would do breakouts and we would return as a group, and the group would hold the intention of being dialogic, even if certain participants came without that level of awareness.

William: I think that's a really important point. There were several who went on a little too long, and there were a couple of places where a bunch of people were talking about politically energizing subjects like, "Are we all just a group of privileged people?" It wasn't all white people by the way: "are we just super privileged?" They throw bombs into the middle of the room, and in another context that might have created a big polarization, but it didn't here. It just fell into the ocean and got received. It was kind of interesting in that way. We didn't need to redirect it; the space was too big to allow that gritty energy to get too much traction.

How do you handle difficulty? What happens when a big fat disturbance shows up in the room? What do you do? You go, "Wonderful! It's exactly why we're having this conversation." Welcome. No defensiveness. It's received. Can you be bigger than whatever disturbance shows up?

Postscript
The author's reflections written some months after the conference

In retrospect, several insights stand out:

The dialogue series we ran during the pandemic emerged from a sense of curiosity, awe and opportunity at the immensity of the collective changes that struck simultaneously around the world. Things simply stopped, illuminating the tenuous and ephemeral nature of humanly invented patterns and structures. It raised the question, What else could just change? Everyone seemed to be having a shared experience of a state of separation from the familiar, while also reeling over its meaning and impact.

When any established pattern is shaken up, there is always an opening for dialogue. With a change of these proportions, the opportunity seemed historic and too great to pass up. We could sense this opening. Clarity about one's motives in setting a dialogue in motion is essential and sets the pattern of all that is to follow. Our motive was to engage in a clear, open flow around the world into what was happening, to make space for the questions and the answers to emerge from the whole.

Typically, one must work with a group for a while to get to the point where established structures can be called into question. That was already the shared starting point and made for a remarkable launchpad for inquiry. It also became clear that the quality of the space we held needed to protect this opening and keep agendas—our own and others'—from controlling the design and experience. One can see now by the pace at which memories fade that old habits reassert themselves. People quickly seek to come back to more settled and familiar ground.

These dialogues produced a sustained flow across the miles and among many people, making it very clear that this is possible, at scale, and even in virtual space. People were amazed at the quality of the connection and presence they felt through their screens. The success of this was a function of the willingness of the people to move with this energy and the sense that this moment really did not belong to any of us—that we were merely providing a space in which it could unfold.

Finally, the process had a clear rhythm, with dialogues held every two weeks for the first cycle and every month for the second, giving time for momentum to build and making clear that this was a cycle unfolding over months, not a discrete series of disconnected events.

Motive, protection, participation in a larger flow and an extended cycle over time were all key elements in the success of this process.

Intergroup Zoom Dialogues During Pandemic Times

Abigayel Bryce and Rebecca Cannara

Context

Between the fall of 2020 and summer of 2021, Universal Human Rights Initiative (UHRI) offered two free series of intergroup dialogues as a form of community-building during unprecedented times—the advent of both a worldwide health pandemic and a national reckoning of US racial oppression. This was situated in a time of extreme political polarization that left everyday conversations about these issues severely fraught.

Intergroup dialogue offered an antidote for some to join together during these times and create spaces that set aside debate and academic discussion, instead creating intentional spaces grounded in inclusion, listening, and validation of each other's experiences and perspectives.

These interactive dialogues promote communication tools that aid participants in engaging with people they might not otherwise feel connected to. We incorporate the research-based University of Michigan four-stage model of intergroup dialogue that promotes comfort through listening actively, self-reflecting on one's own experience, engaging in difficult conversations and exploring meaningful actions to take for oneself and for one's community.

4-Stage Model of Sustained Dialogue

INTERGROUP DIALOGUES: facilitated, open-ended conversations that center diverse experiences of participants using key communication tools and foster deeper engagement and understanding across differences

1. Introduction to intergroup dialogue through communication tools and guidelines, exploration of social identities, and community building.
2. Understanding intersectional perspectives to address barriers to inclusivity by reflecting on our roles within systemic inequalities.
3. Putting dialogue tools into practice by responding to and dialoguing about controversial and/or difficult "hot topic" issues.
4. Planning and taking action for interrupting oppressive behaviour and upholding social justice, exploring meaningful allyship.

Dialogues transform differences into stronger relationships that are essential for effective decision-making, taking a critical perspective, and promoting social justice through inclusion.

Aims

Since 2016, UHRI has been offering intergroup dialogues in community and school settings to help build bridges during times of increased polarization and hate crimes. The Covid-19 pandemic halted our usual in-person format, and we decided to offer weekly, Generative Dialogues on Zoom in partnership with Howard Crampton Jr., a dialogue facilitator based in California. These Generative Dialogues provided a welcoming space for people isolated during the heights of the pandemic to connect across the U.S. and beyond. However, given the history of countless deaths of people of color in the U.S. and the recent murder of George Floyd in May 2020 by police, UHRI adapted the intergroup dialogue format to offer free, online dialogues focused on issues of social justice.

Method

Each dialogue series consisted of 10 weekly sessions, each lasting two hours and facilitated by UHRI facilitators Francine Ortega and Rebecca Cannara. Participants registered via Google forms, sharing their contact information and information about what social identities they hold, their comfort level in participating in dialogues, what "hot topic" issues they might be interested in, and any accommodations facilitators could make for them. While 26 people registered, due to scheduling constraints, 13 people attended. The first series was held from October until December 2020. Six participants regularly attended, while some participants joined one or two sessions. The second series was held from April until June 2021 and was supported by a grant from the Whole Foods Market Community Giving program. Five participants regularly attended, while a sixth participant joined for only two sessions and left due to work schedule conflicts. Each group met for a total of 20 hours.

The majority of participants were white and female, which is a trend in participation that we have noticed since the murder of George Floyd. Prior to the summer of 2020, we often held dialogues with few if any white participants, although the majority have usually identified as female.

Outcomes

We had 13 total participants across the series. Pre-surveys were sent as registration forms. Post-surveys were sent in September 2021.

Pre-dialogue survey: When asked what expectations they had for the workshop series and what they would hope to gain, participant responses combined communication practice with anti-bias work. The most common responses involved improving one's communication and dialogue practice, especially with difficult conversations and dismantling internal biases and practicing critical reflection.

When asked about their comfort sharing personal beliefs and experiences in an open dialogue, most participants felt safe sharing, and expressed a commitment to listening. Some expressed the importance of group consensus, communication agreements, check-ins and icebreakers for connection.

When asked to suggest two or three hot-button, or controversial, issues that currently impact our communities, the majority suggested racism, white supremacy and tokenism, followed by politics, elections and voter suppression.

Post-dialogue survey: According to participants, the dialogues yielded common, positive experiences. When asked about their takeaways from the series, participants shared that they learned to notice their thoughts and feelings that emerge, acknowledged that they felt supported during and after difficult conversations, appreciated hearing different perspectives, forged deep interpersonal connections, and were provided the language and exercises to encourage such connection.

Through exposure to each other's identities, our participants also noticed shifts in attitudes, beliefs and assumptions while participating in the dialogues. Such shifts include an increased awareness of what it means to share common ground, broadened social perspectives, increased comfort in accepting differing opinions, deepened familiarity with preexisting beliefs and better observation skills. As one respondent noted, "I do not have to change my views to still care about others." This sentiment rings true to the intergroup dialogue ideal of exposure to new views while maintaining practices of inclusion and community-building.

Participation in these dialogues has influenced the actions, projects and other activities of respondents. They reported gains in comfort advocating for communication guidelines in varying spaces, confidence in dialogic best practices, continued interest in topics or anti-bias ethics introduced in dialogues and confidence in taking on facilitation roles.

Learnings

For the participants who joined either of the two series, the motivation to join ranged from a desire to build on their personal communication and facilitation practice to a need for critical reflection and personal understanding of internalized biases. They expressed a comfort in sharing about themselves and a desire to hold difficult conversations, mainly on racism and the polarized politics of the time. After the series completed, some participants expressed feeling supported by dialogue in difficult conversations, along with a raised awareness of their own experiences and those of other participants and practical takeaways of additional exercises to hold these conversations. An unexpected theme that stood out was a new or renewed appreciation for the power of community guidelines. According to the National Equity Project, the creation of such guidelines allows participants to determine what the "group needs from each other and commits to each other to feel safe, supported, open and trusting."

The responses, while only from a small number of participants, were overwhelmingly positive. This holds with our experience in facilitating intergroup dialogues. Even though everyone enters the dialogue space as strangers, the dialogue activities, languages, and tools are effective in community-building, transcending the dispersed physical locations we called in from, and building quick connections across a variety of identities.

References

University of Michigan model of intergroup dialogue described at https://igr.umich.edu/article/intergroup-relations-research

The National Equity Project https://www.nationalequityproject.org/tools/developing-community-agreements

Conference Session Extracts
From the consideration of the case study with conference participants

Speaker: What was the toughest subject that you broached during this time period?

Abigayel Bryce: The first one was Israel and Palestine. We had folks with both Jewish identity and Palestinian identity, and then we had folks who'd never spent any time thinking about Israel or Palestine ever. It was really powerful to make space for that. The second topic was abortion.

Rebecca Cannara: The question we really want you all to think about is your experience over the past two years, and what has affected your practice? Maybe emotional, practical, or maybe at your organization.

Speaker: Although we had different jobs and different lifestyles in different places, literally all of us experienced similar things. We passed through similar thoughts, feelings and emotions, and that's something important to consider and realize.

Speaker: In our group it was very good to hear people get a little personal and share their experiences because each one of us dealt with different things outside of work as well. It affected people in more ways than one. It was very good to hear that they were still able to manage and cope with things. We had one person with a sister that is over in Japan and because of new technology they were able to communicate more. Sometimes things are moving at a fast pace, but the pandemic slowed a lot of things down for us. We have more time with our loved ones, which we wouldn't normally get in a fast-paced working environment.

Speaker: The pandemic pushed our agency more towards the technology base in our day-to-day operations.

Rebecca: Are you saying that with a smiley face or an unhappy face, or somewhere in between?

Speaker: For me, it was a necessary thing, and I was glad to see it happen. I have been with the department for a pretty long time. When I started we didn't even have a computer, I had a typewriter! Moving forward to where we're at now, some of the things that we have added have been a benefit to the department.

Rebecca: I certainly relate to that. We had to go on Zoom, and we had to figure it out, and it opened the world. It literally opened the world to us. It was a challenge at first and then it was a benefit.

Speaker: We started off with a barrier and then we had amazing growth and challenges, which we still face as a department. We can see how far we have come over the years in accepting people's differences and different opinions.

Speaker: Three of us talked together and we serve very similar roles. It was good to hear how heartfelt it was and that we shared a lot of the same struggles through this pandemic, with an increase in workload and a greater need to pay attention to detail. It was good to hear that others feel the same way I feel.

Speaker: Yeah, it was nice to be validated. I talk a lot about the importance of experiential learning. Sometimes we put too much emphasis on holding programs and creating curricula when the most meaningful learning happens through experience. Holding dialogue circles, holding restorative circles and creating space for people to engage with the work and to feel the power of the work.

Speaker: I'm currently incarcerated and I've been incarcerated for over 13 years now. Over the past four years, I have been in professional development and dealing with restorative justice. The deputy warden (who is now the warden) and the warden (who is now the commissioner) were part of this process of contracting with the Restorative Justice Institute to bring in new ideas. We are trying a grassroots movement starting at the resident level, but we've been beating our head against the wall for four years now. Over the past year, I have been cultivating a relationship with a dialogue facilitator and coach, and she has helped facilitate the potential of building a partnership with the Virginia Department of Corrections to look at the feasibility of introducing dialogic practices into our whole department.

My warden is actually here, somewhere, today and the warden and deputy are also going to be at tomorrow's session to really start looking at the possibility of this. For me, the hot button topic is any engagement that I have with staff or administration. If I didn't have respect and credibility with the resident population, any interaction I have could cause conflict. Residents, line staff, middle management, administration, upper administration, I deal with all of them. What it does is create spaces to engage with conversations that start to tear down this "us versus them" mentality, and to realize that we need to work together to create a system that works, and that makes people better and improves community safety. I'm really glad that you directly tackled the need to address hot-button issues. I really appreciate that about your work.

Rebecca: Thank you! I'm so appreciating you right now. It is an outstanding and amazing example of tearing down the "us and them" mentality. You're going to become a role model for so many people to find dialogue in this way.

Postscript

The authors' reflections, written some months after the conference

Offering intergroup dialogues (IGD) felt urgent and necessary during the height of a global pandemic and racial reckoning in the U.S. So often when it comes to making sense of large events and movements, we may over-intellectualize or feel mired in emotions. As an organization, we believe that embodied learning with educational components supports the kind of intentional environment necessary to bridging social divides. Taking time to review the feedback from our participants was extremely meaningful. It validated our intuition that people needed ways to connect over difficult subjects, and that they valued the interpersonal connections made with people they had never met before. It also offered up some pleasant surprises about IGD features that were meaningful to participants: check-ins and check-outs and community agreements.

We learned from the conference participants that intergroup connections offered in IGD are also needed at a global level. Rereading the case study offered us a gentle reminder to lean into the basics of IGD, that they really help to shape a braver, more vulnerable space. People continue to tell us that they don't have conversations like this in their social circles. We ask readers to imagine what might prompt participants to say things like, "I do not have to change my views to still care about others." These "aha moments" represent significant moments that occur between individuals. We continue to offer post-dialogue surveys that aim to capture such moments, but many happen quietly and over time in the duration of a series.

As we reviewed the excerpts from the conference presentation, we were reminded how a quick breakout room interaction, or pair share, can allow people to feel validated by and find common ground with someone they may never connect with in "the real world." We truly appreciated the validation for leaning into hot topic issues, as that is where the value of IGD can really be felt and where change can emerge.

Covid Check-Up: Coming Back Together

Jennifer Kittrell and Virginia Pauls

Situation

Like all of the Virginia Department of Corrections (VADOC), by May of 2121 District 34 (Williamsburg Probation and Parole) staff had been figuring out how to effectively work to protect the community, meet probationers' needs, and balance very different lives at home for just over a year since the Covid-19 state of emergency had been declared. Children were just returning to classrooms after being homeschooled and staff were hoping to find ways to safely bring probationers into the office for screening and to check in with them in person.

Aims

Chief Virginia Pauls wanted to check in with the staff on how they are doing with managing work and adjusting to changes. The interaction would be a dialogue, and the first time the staff had all been together since March 2020. In planning the session, the Chief and the Dialogue Practitioner discussed having a Working Dialogue, but in the end felt this could be an opportunity to use the practices of dialogue to listen to one another and to come to a shared understanding, rather than trying to agree on any solutions. As such, the dialogue was facilitated solely by Deputy Chief Probation Officer Jennifer Kittrell, who is the Dialogue Practitioner for the District.

Method

District 34 leadership held a staff appreciation luncheon and then all the staff sat socially distanced. Some wore masks, including the two staff members who were not vaccinated. We offered a check-in and then asked the staff to share what they felt had been difficult to adjust to since the pandemic started and what (if any) positive changes they could see in the work we are doing in the "new normal." Staff listened respectfully to one another. Some noted that while changes were positive for some staff, those same changes increased the stress of others. The discussion lasted about two hours and ended with an affirmative check-out.

Outcomes

Overall, we heard that the staff has adjusted well to telework and managing a work-life balance. As one Probation Officer said, "It was nice to telework with children doing school virtually and, although stressful, to be there for them and adjust my hours." Another said, "I am thankful I could work at home while we were so worried about the pandemic, and being exposed." Still another noted, "Our staff really has come together as a team. When some of us are in the office we help the people at home and it rotates depending on coverage." A few participants made comments about the collaboration between our leadership and the Courts, including, "Our staff really came together with the court, especially when JK covered the dockets while Covid was high." "York Circuit heard us and did not subpoena staff from other districts," said another. "The courts and the jails let us do virtual and phone interviews for pre-sentence reports." Staff missed seeing everyone, but were grateful to have the telework options. They reported feeling more caught up, due to the ability to work with fewer interruptions on telework days. Staff seemed to appreciate the opportunity to be heard and to listen to one another.

Learnings

District 34 staff are doing well with their work-life balance at this point in the pandemic. They recognize ongoing uncertainty, but appreciate their coworkers and are grateful to VADOC to be able to telework, so they can be there for their own families during this time. Further, staff are grateful to VADOC for providing them with the technology to creatively but safely remain in contact with probationers and continue to try to work with them to move them forward despite all the ways life had been on hold during the pandemic.

Holding this dialogue helped staff reconnect with each other and offered structure to the conversations surrounding coming back together. One Probation Officer offered a reflection: "It was nice to have the in-person contact in real time, to feel the comradery and to laugh together. It can be difficult on Zoom. We feel like a team again."

Conference Session Extracts
From the consideration of the case study with conference participants

Virginia Pauls: Folks really felt it was a matter of survival, if they had to do the work to get a paycheck they had to get creative in how they did it. They also had to change the way they did business, not only at work, but at home also. I was very surprised because it usually takes a long time for such a transition but not with this group, they did it almost immediately. We would call and say, "This person is out, who's covering court?" only to find out it was already arranged.

We have four courts to cover and folks also have multiple court dates every month. Some have three court dates a week so there is a lot to manage. I thought Because of the high numbers I thought telework would never be an option, but the team approached things really well. What surprised me was when people started to share their experiences and what worked for some folks about telework was very difficult for others. For example, a lot of folks did not like being at home. We learned that they preferred to be in the office because they missed the structure and were stressed by the interruptions at home. On the other hand, some folks could catch up when they worked at home because there were less interruptions. I realized despite my assumption that everybody loved telework and wanted it to continue there was a handful of people who preferred not to.

Speaker: I really don't like working at home because I miss being around my peers. Our lead secretary also needed to be at the office every day because she was brand new and had to learn from peers. I always believe your co-workers are your greatest teachers and I think there was a lack of appreciation for the different scenarios and situations that people were encountering throughout the past year.

Speaker: We had a similar situation, but one of the main things that came out of this new normal was the utilization of technology. We still had to maintain and sustain public safety and we had to do so it from home, and because of this we found out that technology worked well. We also found out that we received better quality work from many people working from home because they had less interruptions. It was mostly a win-win, especially with people who had family members or needed to commute from further away.

Speaker: I come from the probation and parole world, and I joined this session because I knew you created a lot of setups and arrangements in your environment that we didn't have to put in place in ours. However, because we have custody and control 24/7 here, we had to add more layers, more structure and more things to do onto the facility side. It really added a lot of additional strain and restrictions on staff, as well as create extra job duties. I wanted to see how you were able to prioritize your tasks while being away from your work site and how you were able carry out your role. We might come from opposites worlds but I really appreciate how you were able to move in a new direction and remain effective. On the facility side, we have a more structured routine with a lot of headed duties and a lot of stress. But we were there, day to day, with each other and I think the pressure galvanized us together.

Virgina: One thing that came out of the probation officer's dialogue was their surprise at how well the technology worked and how in-depth phone conversations could be. Folks also tended to feel more comfortable in their own space and would reveal more about what was really going on with them.

Speaker: I think a lot of the officers were able to enhance their skill-level in technology. Some folks had never had a meeting on zoom, and now it's second nature to them.

Speaker: We have three offices in our district, so we had to have many conversations and many dialogues with each office. Because we serve multiple courts we also had to find out what was needed for people from each office to telework and work around court schedules. I thought it was kind of ironic that although people initially requested telework, and were allowed to do it two days per month, once telework was increased to many more days they found out they preferred to be in the office.

Virgina: It may have surprised them that they were missing the collaboration and teamwork.

Postscript

The authors' reflections written some months after the conference

We recently received extracts from the case study session we hosted at the World Needs Dialogue! Conference in 2021. Reading the comments took us back to the beginning of the process, and we reflected on the journey we have traversed together since the Covid pandemic hit Virginia in March 2020. President Biden recently announced that the pandemic is transitioning to an endemic condition, and this made us aware of how our business practices also seem permanently changed.

We held the Covid Check-Up dialogue thinking that this was the beginning of life in the office returning to a prepandemic "normal." Within the dialogue we realized the ways the pandemic had actually improved services and communications with our probationers and enhanced our work. There were certainly setbacks and inconveniences, but we do not think anyone realized how many positive changes would occur. We hoped at the time of the dialogue that we could hold onto some of the technological improvements and flexibility in schedules that benefitted the team.

Sharing the experience at the 2021 conference helped us connect with colleagues from our organization and others who had experienced many of the same transitions, struggles and celebrations we did at Williamsburg Virginia Probation and Parole. They too had to rely on technology they had never tried, meet the expectations of outside agencies who were unaware of the challenges and be creative in problem-solving. They too had found surprising results.

Now in reflecting 18 months later, a year since the World Needs Dialogue! 2021 conference, we are pleased that we continue to utilize the technology and are able to offer employees some flexibility in their schedules, although not as much as we have originally hoped. We hope that we take these lessons of thinking outside the box into the next challenge we face and remember that change is constant and will always provide opportunities alongside the difficulties.

Covid-19 vs. Religious Services at the Virginia Department of Corrections

Jermiah "Jerry" Fitz and Whitney Barton

Situation

In March of 2020, Virginia governor Ralph Northam declared a State of Emergency for the state, based upon the spread of the Covid-19 virus that was affecting Virginians, and of course many millions around the world. As the virus continued to spread, those who were in congregate settings such as nursing homes and correctional facilities were identified as more susceptible because of the close proximity in which individuals in these settings lived. The Virginia Department of Corrections (VADOC) has over 40 prisons and an additional six Community Corrections Alternative Programs (CCAPs), all of which are congregate settings.

The executive leadership of the agency acted immediately in response to the spread of the virus and essentially shut down activities that could promote the contamination of the inmates, staff and contractors with the virus. One of these activities was religious services. From a Federal rights perspective, inmates have the right to practice their religion in a correctional setting, which includes worship services. From an operations perspective, religious services offer an opportunity for expression, reflection and, for many, the opportunity for individuals to attach to something that is much bigger than themselves. This leads to more structured, well-mannered inmates. Unfortunately, because of Covid, these in-person services came to a stop in March of 2020, as outside clergy were not permitted to enter facilities and the movement of inmates was stopped in hopes of slowing the spread of the virus.

As the spread of the virus became more contained and as positivity rates were declining in the spring of 2021, the need to plan for the re-start of religious services in prisons and CCAPs became even more important. The need to do this in a safe, practical and, most importantly, beneficial way for both staff and inmates increased. This would include a plan that would take into account all of the relevant voices that could provide feedback on how VADOC should move forward.

Objectives

The process of coming together to discuss and design a plan for the restarting of religious services was the aim of the Working Dialogue we conducted. The outcome of the Dialogue would serve as the blueprint for guidance from the Chief of Corrections Operations that would give direction to the facilities and CCAPs on how to safely re-start religious services.

Method

Initially a group of staff members from across the agency met—not in a Working Dialogue, but rather to identify all the voices needed to accurately cover all the facets of this discussion. This group was made up of regional office staff, leadership from the prisons and headquarters staff. At the conclusion of this meeting it was decided that there was a need for a representative from the Health Services Unit, as well as counselors from the prisons, in addition to those who were represented at this meeting. The Dialogue and Business Practices Administrator was contacted to assist in facilitating the Working Dialogue. After agreeing to facilitate, the Dialogue Administrator, along with the Dialogue sponsor, planned the process of how to complete the session.

The following positions were invited to participate in the Working Dialogue:

- Assistant Wardens: 3
- Epidemiologist: 1
- Teacher: 1
- Regional Manager: 1
- Counselor Managers: 2
- Lieutenant: 1
- Office of the Attorney General Representative: 1
- Regional Administrators (Facility): 3
- Project Manager-Operations: 1
- Regional Operations Officer: 1
- Operations Support Staff: 4

The group met in July of 2021 for two hours. This was the only meeting of this group. The group had a robust discussion on the current situation throughout the agency, the legal ramifications of not holding religious services and how to proceed in the best way in order to keep all staff and inmates safe.

We took a wide range of factors into consideration during the Dialogue. These included the following:

- Vaccination rates of the inmate population
- Success of official visitors coming back inside the facilities
- Duration of individual religious services
- Equal access to in-person worship services for inmates with disabilities
- Current status of vaccine reporting within facilities and access to this information through the agency's information system
- Ensuring equal access to services
- Access for non-English-speaking inmates
- Whether one service per week for each religion could be obtained
- Staffing concerns

Outcomes

The Working Dialogue achieved its desired results. The group was able to pull together suggestions for a draft memorandum that was forwarded to the Chief of Corrections Operations for review and approval. Also, a template was designed for the use by the staff at each facility. This template served as a reminder of the items to consider as each facility utilized the guidance given from the Working Dialogue in order to adjust to their specific facility's environment. This included, for example, the number of inmates, space considerations, vaccination rates and other factors. The date of August 1, 2021 was designated for facilities to restart religious services, if they were prepared to do so.

Learnings

While it was another example of the interconnectivity of the divisions of the VADOC (and not a complete surprise), this Working Dialogue demonstrated how the agency was brought together as it responded to the Covid-19 virus. In looking at the participants of the Working Dialogue, all three divisions were represented (Operations, Administration, Programs) and each shared their voice. The common goal of devising a plan that would keep both staff and inmates safe, while also allowing for the right to worship, was the focus of the group—and it was another opportunity for the agency to show how resilient it is in the face of adversity.

Conference Session Extracts
From the consideration of the case study with conference participants

Jerry Fitz: Even before Covid, we experienced a lot of challenges in responding to individuals wanting to practice their religion, and then Covid was tossed in on top of it all. There is a huge need, so it is good to hear that once the guidance was put in place facilities were having Working Dialogues, and that people were looking at it from a dialogic perspective to make it work for their specific facility. The guidance from headquarters suggested starting when you are ready to begin rather than giving a hard and fast date.

Speaker: Prior to the pandemic, operations seemed to be running as normal but when the pandemic hit, we had a lot of issues as requests were coming in about not allowing inmates to attend religious services. As the treatment department we were also assigned other jobs, but we were able to get together and have a dialogue. It was a very small Working Dialogue; I believe we just had the assistant warden and the treatment team, and I private messaged in the chat. We just talked about it, and we just tried to figure out the best option. We came up with the idea of reaching out to the clergy and seeing if there were some digital files or books that they could send that would allow for self-study.

Then we enabled them to get into the day room, obviously six feet apart and two or three at a time, over different time slots. This allowed them to practice their religion and also do it with their peers. I think it ran smoothly although initially it was very chaotic because they were very frustrated and not understanding where we were coming from because they didn't believe that Covid was a thing. They assumed we were trying to lock them down for no reason. But we gained more resources as we really reached out and asked, "Hey, have you guys got some booklets or something?" They were willing to send them to us with no issue. Then they just kind of kept on revolving, which was a good system for us because we didn't have the space to put them somewhere where they could be six feet apart and do it digitally. We couldn't do it. The fact that we reached out and we got together as a treatment team to think about a solution was a great job by us as a facility, and as a whole.

Jerry: Do you want to comment on the fact that they, that the way they were able to get together in dialogue? I'll let you handle that one with Whitney.

Whitney Barton: Dialogue is really designed to be used proactively. We may need to use it reactively, but it's something that we can also use on the front end. It sounds like you all did that, and that is outstanding. Because you had already done the work upfront you were probably able to transition into the statewide resumption of services more easily through those recommendations.

Speaker: In assembling your room for the Working Dialogue for this particular topic, was any thought given to having somebody from the chaplain services or a formerly incarcerated person be a part of that room also to get a different perspective?

Jerry: Well, I would tell you Morris was a huge part of this Working Dialogue as well as Michelle. In terms of chaplain services, throughout the entire pandemic, Melissa and Bernie have been talking to different faith leaders to figure out ways to allow them in. As everybody mentioned we really tried to allow them different opportunities to continue in some form, whether it be DVDs or virtual platforms to continue with providing services. One thing that was very impressive was that I had the opportunity to be on a call with a couple of religious leaders as well as Melissa and Bernie. It was very interesting to find out how much they really took ownership of their piece in helping. They wanted to be able to come back in, but they were also very nervous about coming in and being there in person. The conversation was very interesting because all they fundamentally wanted was to make sure that our inmate population had what they needed, and I thought that was extremely important. It made me remember that the Department of Corrections is bigger than just our staff and our inmates and our supervisors. Rather, we have a whole network of stakeholders who want to see our population do better. So, yes, definitely the chaplain services were involved in those conversations. We did not talk about having a returning citizen or having someone who'd been formally incarcerated join that conversation, but it is an interesting concept. I think we drilled down and tried to get as close to staff who have direct access on a daily basis, but maybe as we go forward that is a voice that needs to be at the table.

Whitney: It will be coming soon because we're introducing dialogue skills to our inmate population so that they are learning the same skills in engaging because I certainly see opportunities where they should be at the table when changes are made to have a voice.

Postscript

The authors' reflections written some months after the conference

As I look back on it, the journey that brought us to the drafting of our case study was somewhat like a thrill ride at an amusement park. In the beginning stages of the Covid-19 pandemic, we knew that we were in for a serious, perhaps very tumultuous process of understanding how the operations at the Virginia Department of Corrections would continue, but at the same time we were concerned about our own personal safety. Looking back in retrospect, the use of dialogue gave us a sense of direction as we navigated the many twist and turns presented by the pandemic.

During the "World Needs Dialogue" conference, it was refreshing to share our story with so many participants from across the world and learn that many of the challenges that we faced were the same as others. It is my hope that those who heard our story understand how important it was to have the skill of dialogue to bring calm to chaos and give all those who needed to hear how input from all relevant voices can be used to bring about change. The idea of "leadership" not making all of the decisions in an agency as large as the Virginia Department of Corrections can be a foreign concept to many, but our sharing during the conference also allowed participants to hear that it is not the job of leadership to make all of the decisions, but it is the job of leadership to have the correct voices in the room and, just as importantly, ensuring those people that their voices matter.

Moving from the panic state in 2020 when the pandemic was just moving across the world until now, I have realized the process we used to work on our issues professionally, are the same processes that can be used personally and in other areas of our lives. The use of dialogic practices: suspension, voice, respect and listening are concepts that can not only help at VADOC, but truly can help the world, if only given a chance.

What's Your Color? Restarting a Random Drug Screening Program

Tecora Davis and John Fedor, Jr.

Situation

In March 2020, the governor of the Commonwealth of Virginia declared a state of emergency due to the Covid-19 Coronavirus. Newly implemented contact and social distancing restrictions caused the District 20 random drug screening program, known as color code, to be suspended.

Drug screenings, which are a necessary and impactful tool used most frequently during the term of supervision, were being administered only when they were court ordered or when there was a public safety issue.

In February 2021 the District 20 Probation and Parole District was faced with reimplementing the random drug screening color code program with new procedures and social distancing mandates. The physical layout of the District 20 Probation and Parole Office presented a logistical challenge due to the limited size of and space for the staff. This, along with increasing concerns of opiate and methamphetamine use and overdoses, set the stage for drastic changes to the random drug screening program in the District.

Objective

The objective was to successfully reconstitute the District 20 drug screening color code program and then bring it back online, while making the required adjustments in order to meet the Covid-19 protocols and procedures that already were in place. This would ensure effective public and employee safety.

The aim and anticipated outcome were to create a plan to start the District 20 drug screening color code program. This was to be followed up with a flexible and dynamic Implementation Memorandum outlining the new/modified program.

Method

It was determined that the most effective method to obtain this goal would come from a Working Dialogue. Prior to the set-up for this, the need for the drug screening reimplementation was discussed with the management team. The set-up participants included the Chief Probation and Parole Officer, the Deputy Chief Probation and Parole Officer-Dialogue Practitioner, the Senior Probation and Parole Officer-Team Leader, and the Office Services Specialist. The team decided that the dialogic input of all line and support staff would be required to solve this issue and to effectively carry out the Working Dialogue.

The initial District 20 Working Dialogue occurred in March of 2021. It included six staff and one dialogue practitioner. Subsequent follow-up Working Dialogue sessions occurred later in March and in early April. After implementation, the team conducted the final follow-up and recap session.

Outcomes

The group identified required changes, along with associated tasks that were needed in order to effectively implement those changes. These tasks were assigned to participants via various flash committees (temporary groups assigned to complete a task), and appropriate deadlines were set. Upon completion of the tasks and goals the committee members reported back to the core group. The flash committees were then disbanded and participants returned to the core group.

Tasks included updating color code forms, updating colors, and integrating and eliciting assistance from District 20 interns to develop a spreadsheet for assignment. Other actions included developing a schedule, creating a log note template, updating the auto attendant for the phone line message, and assigning identified probationers in color code. Finally, they created the tasks of developing the screening and cleaning process, including information to be posted in lab; color code frequency and times schedule; colors assigned; and implementation timeline.

The much-improved and Covid-compliant District 20 drug screening program was successfully reimplemented as scheduled. All associated tasks were completed and staff reported increased personal safety and satisfaction with new procedures and lab construction and set-up.

Learnings

It is absolutely vital to have all the necessary voices involved in the Working Dialogue process. This ensures that all perspectives and critical details are provided and considered.

Involvement of all parties also creates critical buy-in and investment, as well as commitment to the process by all of those involved. It also increases the chances of long-term success.

Of note, opposition to the process, when suspended judgment is utilized, plays a crucial role in decision-making when conducting Working Dialogues—in particular, when making operational decisions or establishing procedures. Bystanding, or offering an unbiased viewpoint, can also provide critical perspectives, knowledge and information that is indispensable for successful implementation of the issue at hand.

Conference Session Extracts

From the consideration of the case study with conference participants

John Fedor: An important thing about the gates is that sometimes you need to stop and shut the Working Dialogue down. It doesn't happen often, but I remember getting to an eight or nine on a gate and when I looked around the room I could see that many were fatigued by the conversation. If you get to a stage of being fatigued with the problem, it may be time to stop at that gate and come back later, or it may even be time to shut the whole dialogue down. We told everybody go back to what they were doing and come back only when they were refreshed and ready to hit it again.

Speaker: I want to follow up with what you just said. We recently did a Working Dialogue here and we didn't make it through one of the gates. We realized that it was time to shut things down and we will probably revisit it later, but we needed to think more about it. We thought the Working Dialogue was something that staff wanted, but once we got into the session it took on a life of its own and went in a different direction. So we backed off of that one. It is nice that you can pick up the Working Dialogue again and move forward with it at a later time.

Speaker: I want to add to that, because I was actually in that Working Dialogue. I'm not a DP [dialogue practitioner] but I could recognize that the Working Dialogue was not going in a good direction because, at that point, tensions were getting a little high, and we were really not going to get anywhere. So it was good that the DP was able to recognize that and make the decision to stop and rather come back at a later time, because when tensions are high people kind of shut down and going on is not going to be effective at that point.

Speaker: As a DP it is critical that you have that kind of support from your management team as well, though. Rather than your leadership being focused on checking a box and saying, "I've got this done," they are interested in listening to the voices, and trusting the DP to be effective in the roles that we are serving. I think that's critical. I also think that the gates and the accountability pieces that come along with a Working Dialogue are part of what is responsible for obtaining so much more buy-in. When staff sees the evidence that their voices are being heard and contributing to the changes that we see, you can put an action plan in place that everybody can take ownership of and feel good about.

Speaker: What's your advice on when you get to a point that you need to stop? Do you pull the management out of the room before you make that final decision?

Tecora Davis: It depends on the situation. Sometimes I'll go ahead and take a break so we can have a quick discussion with management so I can give them my feedback. I have done a Working Dialogue that took most of the day and it was not going in a good direction. So when we took our last break, I came together with management and we decided that it was time to take the information we had and for management to decide later whether or not we needed to reconvene on that particular situation. As a DP you have to be aware of the room and read the individuals who are participating.

Speaker: You also have to pay attention to people's body language, which says way more than they are willing to say, and this is an indication that you might not have authentic voices in the room. Sometimes it is an indication that we need to work on something else because people are not feeling safe enough to really give their input, and what they are not saying is probably the input that is desperately needed. So I will say, as DP, it is not a role to be taken lightly. It has to be something that you really believe in and have some level of passion for because it takes skill, and it is a skill that you only acquire after being involved in Working Dialogues for a long time.

John: As a leader I allow, and I watch. If I see people are not participating, I don't try to call them out; rather I try to encourage them. But if it looks like we've hit frustration central and it's not going, I'll call it off so we can regroup and figure out what do we need to do so as not to have this breakdown. I know our team is one that will typically speak out, they are not afraid because they know there is not going to be any retribution. They really do. So when they are not speaking out we know there is a real problem, and then it is up to us to figure out what is wrong with the process.

Postscript

The authors' reflections written some months after the conference

Tecora: Doing the work is a productive way to bring together many different perspectives, thoughts and ideas to develop a plan or solutions to achieve the identified goals. Doing the work is a rewarding process as a dialogue practitioner. Witnessing the results of the work as the plans and solutions to the identified goal are put into action is the ultimate reward.

John: I agree the process is extremely rewarding, productive and gratifying. In the end it is very gratifying to see the positive outcomes of teamwork, fellowship and productive work. From a supervisor standpoint the District 20 team, the agency and the Commonwealth are the benefactors of some really great work and problem-solving.

Tecora: The process of capturing the work on paper offers an opportunity to examine the work that has taken place as well as the results of the process. Writing the paper offered an opportunity to memorialize the work.

John: Writing the paper helped me to step back and look at the process from a strategic viewpoint. It was also very helpful to research and critique the process to see if it needed to be updated or improved. There was also the satisfaction of being a part of and seeing a really great process at work.

Tecora: The vigorous thinking that occurred during the Working Dialogue was regenerated while sharing the process and outcomes with the conference participants.

John: This is something we don't often get to do, and it was great having the perspective of those from the outside. It was an opportunity to think outside the box and look at things that would otherwise not be seen or considered by our team. It is always a pleasure interacting with your peers and receiving a fresh perspective. One tip: bring your suspended judgment skill set, as you may need it.

Tecora: One of the most profound realizations that was revealed through this process is the importance of understanding and valuing different perspectives and how limiting perspectives can sabotage a process or result in diminished outcomes. This process helped bring further and deeper understanding of suspension. The use of suspension can and is a key element in the Working Dialogue process and continues to be a key element while revisiting the process and sharing with others.

John: I follow Tecora on this one—well said.

Operations Dialogue in Pandemic Conditions

Matthew Whibley and Eric Fling

Situation

During the Covid-19 pandemic, organizations around the world have had to reassess their business processes; the Virginia Department of Corrections (VADOC) is no exception. It has become expedient to check on staff to make sure they have the resources and guidance needed to do their jobs. To this end, VADOC Operations adjusted Dialogue to elevate the voices of staff, supporting their well-being and meaningful work by focusing on front- and back-end steps outside of the sessions themselves. This was done in anticipation that issues or opportunities beyond the control or authority of the participants, at their units, could be raised. Follow-up would require attention at the regional, division or agency level.

Objectives

The intent was to provide a cycle of meaningful Dialogue for Correctional Officers (COs), the most prominent role within the agency and, for the sake of accountability, to ensure that comments lead to follow-through in tangible ways. The process combined the facilitation expertise of Dialogue Practitioners with qualitative data analysis methods to identify trustworthy opportunities for actionable initiatives at the regional and divisional levels. In this case, the interest of the Chief of Corrections Operations was to understand *What is going well?* and *What can we improve upon?* to support the work of the COs.

Method

Front-end steps included a randomized, purposive sampling process to ensure representative demographic representation of the entire CO population. The 90-CO sample represented every facility and mirrored the age, race, gender and tenure characteristics of the VADOC's 5,400 COs across 45 locations. Six sessions allowed for representation by both a.m. and p.m. shifts and various categories of regular post assignments. Due to the constraints of the pandemic the sessions took place in the Google Meet virtual environment, with great success in providing audio and visual connection for participants.

Dialogue Practitioners (DPs) lent their expertise and insights to the design of the Dialogue sessions. Organized into three roles, teams of DPs facilitated, transcribed or assisted participants with technical difficulties that arose during each session. Each DP focused on doing their part to strengthen the fidelity of the session for participants and to ensure that rich data came out. Sessions lasted an hour and a half and had between 12 and 20 participants. Four sessions were scheduled during day shift hours and two during night shift hours.

Outcomes

These Operations Dialogues began with the end in mind. Over the course of some earlier Dialogue cycles, staff members expressed a desire to know what might come out of the Dialogues. Satisfying this question was the design goal. Summary reports were supplemented with filterable workbooks containing all comments and organized by key, manageable support themes. The workbooks also allowed a user to key in on specific information from a Dialogue such as the prompt, region or element of an analysis framework to see all related comments. The summary report informed management with an agenda of 13 topic areas, spanning divisions and functions across the agency. The strength of the Operations Dialogues was twofold. First, the purposive sampling process ensured that bias was eliminated from participant section. Second, the multirole teams of DPs ensured that facilitation of the virtual Dialogue went smoothly. These two elements hold great promise. Another future area of attention would be to consider how participants can join, semi-anonymously, by phone or via computer with their camera off, and the impact on the safe container.

Learnings

The Operations Dialogues emphasized co-creation in formation of the Dialogue environment and follow-through by Operations management. The purposive sampling process enhanced staff representation in Dialogues and ensured that all the right voices were in the room. Collaboration with DPs before the Dialogue improved support for staff participating in a new virtual environment. The analysis and reporting process ensured that Operations management was able to quickly identify areas for action. DPs will share the summary report and schedule a virtual Open House to which the original participants will be invited to come and share their thoughts about the experience. These elements lent themselves to a virtuous cycle that enhanced the Dialogue experience for participants, DPs and management.

A serendipitous gain from these Operations Dialogues was an enhanced appreciation of duties that are performed in different areas within Operations. This was the first time that Dialogue Practitioners were able to work closely with the data analysis team, and vice versa, in a collaborative effort. This opportunity was invaluable in gaining a deeper appreciation of specialized Practitioners' ability to align and accomplish a shared goal.

Conference Session Extracts
From the consideration of the case study with conference participants

Speaker: We talked about having to roll through the resistance and how the Dialogue Practitioners were able to handle those folks who came in with resistance because Peter and Jane taught us how to bring resistance into a group and into the conversation by saying: "It's ok to oppose, but you have to do it respectfully."

Speaker: We also talked about the importance of Dialogue Practitioners coming in when there has been a contentious subject or issue or a really heated dialogue. When this happens it can be useful to follow up with a Working Dialogue and have a Dialogue Practitioner who was not involved the first time to run the show as a more neutral outsider.

Speaker: I want to follow what was just said about the importanc e of our Dialogue Practitioners, especially when we're holding a Working Dialogue. Sometimes when you're holding a Working Dialogue on one subject it can tend to go to another subject and the Dialogue Practitioner reels it back in to the subject at hand, to make the Working Dialogue flow and go through all the steps or gates.

Eric Fling: I'll just add something from my experience to also keep in mind. Dialogue does not always have to be reactive. In fact, it can help to be proactive and to eliminate things from happening rather than reacting to things that have already happened.

Speaker: You're right, Eric. This is a lesson I learned in the beginning because when a person is resistant and your norm is to react, that's not good. It can be such an awkward feeling when someone shifts your atmosphere, so as a Dialogue Practitioner you need to know how to flow through that. Absolutely.

Speaker: As a leader it can be really hard to let people voice what they need to, but the biggest thing that I have learned from dialogue is that you have to let it happen. Even if it is not in line with your perspective—it could be the complete opposite of what you think is the right thing—you still have to hear it and you have to make space for it to be voiced and to let them feel heard. It is the same thing we do with our probationers: we let them vent and get out what they need to and then we know where everyone stands, and we can move forward.

Speaker:	I am a student from Finland, and I study BBA at Proakatemia. You might recall Timo, who presented yesterday, he is one of my coaches. In our school we study entrepreneurship and team leadership, and we do our studies through working sessions that are held as dialogues within our own teams and our Dialogue Practitioners, who are also our coaches. They always tell us to just let the dialogue flow and to let everything come, allowing whatever people say, even when it might not go as you would wish. What I understand is that no matter how interesting the topic might be it is really important for the facilitator to stay on top of the discussion. In our team, if we just let the discussion flow freely and everybody say what they feel, we kind of lose the talent of argumentation, and it becomes all about how I feel and what I think, and the red dot of the whole discussion is kind of lost at that moment. These are great words everybody.
Eric:	You are making a great point, and my add for Dialogue Practitioners would be to balance the need to stay true to the topic with the need of an individual to expound, expand and voice their experience. At times, allowing them voice, to some degree, allows for a more authentic voice to come out. The more somebody typically talks the more comfortable they become and the more genuine they become, particularly on a virtual platform. So it's a fine balance staying with the topic versus letting them speak. But when you find that balance and you are able to fine tune it, you get great information while staying on course.
Speaker:	Absolutely. Eric, it's a slippery slope when a person's voice is cut off.
Speaker:	When the pandemic hit and we were doing virtual dialogues, I felt like people were more comfortable opposing than how I previously experienced them in person. It was like they were more hesitant to speak in person, but virtually we had some good dialogues in our district. People were just more open and more willing to speak. That was the difference I saw with virtual dialogues as opposed to in-person dialogues.
Matthew Whibley:	One of the greatest benefits that I have seen come out of these new virtual dialogues is the much lower barrier to entry and engagement. We needed to get 90 Correctional Officers from all over the state and 90 Dialogue Practitioner to all these different locations. I don't even know

how we would've done it before the pandemic, but we were able to conduct six sessions within two weeks, pretty much back-to-back, and then turn in a report. It was all possible because the sessions were done virtually. We will need thoughtful reflection to select what type of dialogue we do in the future, whether it's in person or virtual, but there will be times where virtual dialogue might be the best choice. Not always though.

Postscript
The authors' reflections written some months after the conference

Reflecting back on the Correctional Officer (CO) Dialogues, this was the first time the Department of Corrections (DOC) utilized a virtual platform to hold dialogues of this magnitude. We knew there would be some challenges, from technological and logistics challenges to staff engagement and authenticity, during a virtual meeting. We also knew at the development stage of this process that we wanted to come full circle and provide clear, transparent responses and follow-through on voiced concerns throughout all six dialogue sessions. This was a cognizant decision that would make this statewide dialogue different and meaningful.

Through this experience, we learned that it is not only possible but advantageous to hold such dialogues virtually. Due to the vast geographical distances between participants, virtual meetings were realistically the only way to conduct these dialogues in such a short time frame. We also learned a lot from listening to the voices of the COs. They were authentic, respectful and spoke with purpose and conviction. Our data analysis team was able to collect everything said and compile it into a report. The report and its findings were shared with the participants and contained answers, resolutions or a plan of action for all the comments captured during the six dialogues. This approach was so successful that the Department has since conducted mirror dialogue sessions with 90 probation officers across the state.

As we reflect on writing the case study and our facilitation session during the conference, we noted that many participants shared comments about the importance of authentic voice. The use of authentic voice is the bedrock of Dialogue; without it we are only groups of people moving wind with our mouths. During the dialogues with CO's and during our session at the conference we all benefitted from the insights shared through authentic communication. In many ways the pandemic forced us all to reckon with authenticity as we accepted the fragility of our own experience. It was through shared experiences that we have been able to manage these conditions both internal and external.

In summary, we have proven to ourselves that our pre-pandemic culture of dialogue in-person is not always the best solution. In-person dialogue sessions are very valuable—some may even say priceless. However, there are barriers to in-person dialogues that are removed with virtual dialogues while simultaneously opening up a whole new realm of possibilities and opportunities. This format has allowed leadership to hear the voices of many, and to take appropriate action and respond accordingly, therefore building trust, comradery and empowering those who authentically and respectfully use their voice regardless of the platform.

PART THREE

SECTIONS 7 TO 9

Section Seven

Putting Dialogue to Work for Inmates and Probationers

The most common measure of success of the criminal justice system is recidivism. In this regard the Virginia Department of Corrections is remarkably effective, having the lowest rate of any state-wide corrections agency in the USA. This is the result of many factors including leadership vision and planning; management procedures and practices; and financial budgeting and resourcing. Another unique factor is the incorporation of Professional Dialogue to enable intelligent, rigorous and widespread participation in devolved decision making. Organisational change requires time when (as the largest state employer in Virginia) it involves around 12,000 staff and a high turn-over of employees. It took seven years to embed Professional Dialogue into the organisational culture. Now the organisation is extending the methodology to those in the agency's care, the tens of thousands of incarcerated inmates and probationers in the community. This is not only for the well-being of the many prisons and community centres, but also for the benefit of society since incarcerated offenders are released back into the community and, along with probationers, they interact with everyone in society. We have four case studies that are directly related to putting Dialogue to work for these inmates and probationers.

Before receiving vaccines, VADOC lost over 50 inmates and some members of staff, yet still there was a resistance to vaccination. To discover why, **Whitney Barton and Carrie West-Bailey** held Dialogues in five prisons, with inmates who a) wanted b) resisted vaccination and c) had suffered Covid-19.

Tessie Lam and Brandon B Daisy led a Working Dialogue to prepare a joint bid for funds to improve substance use disorder capacity in Virginia, so that inmates and their supervisees could be better connected with recovery resources. It led the district to completely re-evaluate their effectiveness.

Indian Creek Correctional Center is the only Cognitive Therapeutic Community for males in Virginia. When it was decided to introduce Dialogue Skills to the inmates there, **John Walrath and Wardenia Lassiter** co-facilitated the sessions – and they were startled by the response and the outcomes.

Joseph Owen, Dianne Motley and Eric Holloman used the Working Dialogue methodology to enable all staff to participate or be represented in the designing of a new incentive plan for Brunswick Community Corrections Alternative Program. Every voice contributed to the successful outcome.

Vaccinated: To Be or Not to Be . . .

Whitney Barton and Carrie West-Bailey

Situation

In early 2021, after having dealt with the effects of the Covid-19 pandemic for over 10 months, the Virginia Department of Corrections (VADOC) finally began receiving vaccines. Up until the availability of the vaccines, VADOC had experienced the loss of over 50 inmates due to the virus. In addition, the Department lost one of its most prominent leaders of more than 40 years, Warden Earl Barksdale. As a priority group, Virginia's inmates had access to the vaccine early. In January 2021 VADOC set out with a goal to provide as many vaccinations as possible to help protect inmates and staff. Despite intensive efforts to support and encourage vaccine acceptance, the Department experienced a high level of resistance and vaccine hesitancy among the inmate population, resulting in many refusing to be vaccinated.

Objectives

To understand the thinking behind resistance to the vaccine, and to provide the inmate population with a voice, the Dialogue Unit set out to engage inmates in Dialogue related to the vaccine. During this process, we hoped to learn from the inmates what they needed and what we could do as a Department to enhance their comfort levels with the vaccine. We knew that personal stories and testimony were having a huge impact on people's perspectives related to the virus and the vaccine. Through Dialogue, we wanted to provide a safe place where this could be done.

Method

As part of the Department's vaccination efforts, the Research Unit was collecting data on a daily basis for inmates receiving, refusing, or being placed on a waitlist for vaccines. Using this data, we were able to identify the sites with the lowest vaccination acceptance and highest refusal rates. The set-up process for these Dialogue sessions involved us collaborating with the Wardens, Superintendents and Chiefs of Security to identify inmates who would participate. To create a meaningful Dialogue, we requested a diverse group of inmates that included individuals who had been vaccinated, refused vaccination, or experienced the Covid virus. The five facilities below were identified as sites with the highest need:

- Central Virginia Correctional Unit 13—Low-security/female
- Lawrenceville Correctional Center—Privatized Medium-security/male
- Baskerville Correctional Center—Low-security/male
- Nottoway Correctional Center—Medium-security/male
- Appalachian Community Corrections Alternative Program (CCAP)—Community facility/male

Each Dialogue session was limited to 10 inmates. This limit was set not only in an effort to maintain pandemic safety protocols, but also to assist in creating the right level of engagement.

Outcomes

In April, the first Dialogue session took place at Central Virginia Correctional Unit 13. Attending the Dialogue were the Superintendent, Chief of Security, Operations Manager and the Health Authority. Prior to beginning the Dialogue, we provided an explanation and demonstration of the Dialogic Actions and Practices. This allowed the inmates to understand the fundamentals of how we would be engaging as a group. We were amazed at how well they received the information shared, and they were amazed that the executive leadership was just as engaged in wanting to hear their voices. This successfully helped us to develop a safe container.

During our Dialogue the inmates shared their experience of having Covid, their fears of needles and shots, of not having enough information about the long-lasting effects of the vaccine, and their concerns about the risks of the vaccination. There was also open sharing from leadership about why facility activity had to be limited until vaccination rates were achieved to develop herd immunity. The Health Authority provided invaluable information that eased some concerns and helped address misinformation about the vaccine. Questions were answered, stories were shared, authentic voices were used, and tears were shed. As the Dialogue came to a close, four out of five unvaccinated inmates participating verbally committed to receiving the vaccine. One individual wrote:

> *I fully enjoyed how comfortable the DOC women were that performed the Dialogue. Personal experiences were shared from these ladies along with other staff members that were present, and facts about Covid-19 were presented. I am now signed up for the vaccination shot. With the facts and*

the personal stories of all that were there, I became open and convinced that the vaccine is safe. Also with the Dialogue being done in groups of 10, it was more personal as not everyone was speaking over one another. I believe if more of these Dialogues were done that more offenders would be apt to want the vaccine. I am happier today to know that my voice was heard and that my thoughts and opinions were valued by DOC staff. I feel now that I can move forward with this vaccine and with trusting more in staff here at CVCU #13.

This same process was used at all five sites and the information that was shared inspired inmates to sign up to get vaccinated.

Learnings

There are so many things we learned during this process! The first thing learned is that Dialogue is needed in all things that we do. So many times we talk about people and make decisions for them, thinking we know what's best, failing to get their input. Simply giving people a voice can be empowering for change. We learned how vital it was to include the community we serve to get the most tangible solutions and outcomes. Shared experiences allow us to remember that we are all human. We learned that inmates are receptive to Dialogue, want to learn more about the skills and want more Dialogues with staff. We acknowledged that inmates can assist in our goal of lasting public safety by educating their family and friends on the vaccinations. Last but not least, we recognize that Covid has affected our staff, inmates, the community and the world, and through Dialogue we can effectively impact the field!

Conference Session Extracts
From the consideration of the case study with conference participants

Carrie West-Bailey: At the very beginning of Covid-19 we identified some losses. We lost numerous inmates and also a great leader in the department, a warden, Mr. Earl Barksdale. He modeled our healing environment, being a dialogue practitioner and a mentor to a lot of people. He really impacted most of everyone's lives well.

As soon as the Covid-19 vaccinations became available the Department of Corrections played a role that surpassed so many other organizations through offering Covid-19 vaccinations to both inmates and staff. We noticed that there was some reluctance to vaccinations and, being a dialogic corporate culture, we knew we needed to hear the voices and understand what some of the challenges and reluctances were about.

So, we set out to have dialogues at different locations with the highest refusals for vaccinations, to find out what their thinking was and what challenges they saw.

Whitney Barton: There were several key things as far as setting up this dialogue. As Carrie mentioned, we not only wanted people in the room who had refused the vaccine, but we wanted to hear all perspectives for the diversity of voices. Carrie and I tried hard to make this more of an inquiry into where people were at in their thoughts. Wherever they were at in that moment, we wanted to invite them to share that. So that's why we very intentionally chose all the different inmate groupings to be included, as well as include the leadership and the staff from the site and, as always in Virginia, we set up in a circle.

Carrie: Can I just add something? One of the big parts impacting the inmates is hearing from their peers. A lot of times when you listen to someone from a hierarchy position, you're less ready to receive the information because you feel as if you're being told to do it. But it was the sharing of peers' information that shifted the whole dialogue—it was the most impactful.

Speaker: Is your measure of success that more people got vaccinated? I am hearing that your measure of success was, at least, giving everybody a voice so they could just share their concerns and make the paradigm change possibly. I suppose what I'm sitting with is that I am also noting that your measure of success is that more people were vaccinated, so then clearly there's bias, an internal bias, and clearly there's an agenda. And maybe I'm just making a case for the other side, asking, is there really a case for the other side, in your view, or not a genuine case?

Whitney: I want to respond to you—one of the dynamics is that Carrie and I both went into the session, which is one of the reasons we covered suspension and respect at the beginning of the session. We did not want to impose or put any biases into the situation and, yes, the department did have an overall agenda to see if we could impact vaccination rates through this measure or tool, because, as you know, we use dialogue in our department a lot as an intervention tool.

But as facilitators Carrie and I went in without any bias, or we worked very hard to do so. We know we all have biases but setting the ground rules for engagement by introducing respect and suspension means you really have to let go of your biases, to be open to other people and to reinforce that throughout. We did not impose information into the dialogue because we were facilitators and we recognized the role and the little bit of authority it gives you, even without us really trying to have authority.

What happened is that it was through their own stories, which they started sharing with one another, that their perspectives changed.

So, I would say the first measure of success was that we were able to effectively engage them, so they felt safe to share their stories. That was really the number one priority.

As to an outcome, we did see that it impacted vaccination rates, that more people received vaccinations, but that was not a result of us as the facilitators. It was a result of them sharing their own stories. We had one inmate say, in response to someone saying, "I don't know the long term of what they're putting in my arm, you know I don't have very valid arguments," which we acknowledged throughout the dialogue. He responded, "You know, I understand that perspective, but I've been a heroin user my whole life and I never thought twice about what I was putting into my body."

Postscript

The authors' reflections written some months after the conference

The work written about in this case study represented a turning point in our pandemic efforts. It was meaningful to be in dialogue with and alongside the population we served, on something we were all facing together as one. The pandemic connected us across all divides and provided a great opportunity to share our stories with one another. The differences between staff, supervisors and inmates didn't matter, and we were very intentional in ensuring the participants were mixed. No matter what the impact was on vaccination rates or acceptance, we knew it would be a success if we were able to effectively create an atmosphere where it felt safe for individuals to share.

We used a collaborative process to write this case study. Reflecting back on the work we had done was a rewarding experience. While writing the case study, we were given an opportunity to think more about whether the goal of our work was to advocate for a particular position or to inquire with individuals about their own. This consideration further solidified that the significance of our work was the experiences being shared and the evolving perspectives—a deep inquiry.

Sharing the case study at the conference offered another opportunity to expand on perspectives regarding the topic, which again connected everyone across the world. It was refreshing to receive positive feedback and learn from others how we could continue improving our dialogic processes. It's always empowering when people take such a keen interest in the work that you do. It reminds us that learning and development is continual, especially as a practitioner of dialogue. We are deeply honored to have been able to contribute in this way.

Connecting Probationers to Substance Abuse Disorder and Recovery Services

Tessie N. Lam and Brandon B. Daisy

Situation

Sometimes an opportunity presents itself to stand back and take a look at what we are doing and how well we are managing. Such a situation arose when our Community Corrections District #11 Probation and Parole unit was invited to participate with the Department of Medical Assistance (DMAS) on a Support Act Planning Grant. The grant is designed to support DMAS's work to increase substance use disorder (SUD) provider capacity in the State of Virginia and assist the efforts of the Virginia Department of Corrections (VADOC) to connect inmates and supervisees to SUD and recovery services. Our District was requested to provide information on community corrections for the planning grant, and to serve as a pilot if DMAS were to be awarded an implementation grant. It should be noted that since 2013 this District, located in the Northern Shenandoah Valley in Virginia, has experienced a serious heroin and fentanyl epidemic.

Objectives

District #11's objective was to provide a snapshot of the District's operations pertaining to re-entry efforts within VADOC and the local regional jails. Furthermore, the District was to identify the availability of community resources for substance abuse and co-occurring disorders (multiple medical or mental health issues), as well as homelessness in the geographical communities within the District. In order to achieve an accurate snapshot, we conducted a Working Dialogue, utilizing a SWOT (Strengths, Weaknesses, Opportunities and Threats) Analysis for District #11 Probation and Parole's re-entry practices and SUD or co-occurring resources available to supervisees.

Method

In March of 2021 we prepared for a Working Dialogue by reviewing the current situation and determining team members who should participate in the Dialogue. Several Management Team members were invited to attend the Working Dialogue.

Prior to the Dialogue, all participants were provided information about the DMAS Implementation Grant, District #11's role in the grant process and a SWOT Analysis template. Each participant was requested to prepare for the Working Dialogue by reviewing the District's re-entry efforts with VADOC/Regional Jails and identifying gaps in community services for SUD and supervisees.

A few days later, Deputy Chief Daisy facilitated a virtual Working Dialogue. During the Dialogue, each participant was allowed to identify areas of strengths, weaknesses, opportunities and threats involving the VADOC/District 11's re-entry practices and programming. We applied the strengths and weaknesses sections of the SWOT analysis to help determine what our Current Situations were for the Working Dialogue. The opportunities and threats sections of the SWOT analysis were used to determine our desired outcomes. We applied the outlined strengths and weaknesses into the Changes Required section of the Dialogue. The District later presented to DMAS the changes we felt needed to be made and what current efforts could be strengthened to improve our re-entry services.

Outcomes

Re-Entry Strengths: Cognitive Programming; Community Release Planning; "Making It on Community Supervision" Programming; Re-Entry Fairs; utilization of the COMPAS (Correctional Offender Management Profiling for Alternative Sanctions) system of Risks/Needs Assessment to identify risk factors and criminogenic needs. Also, preparation of Mental Health Assessments; appointments scheduled with local the Community Services Board (CSB) for mental-health follow-up; psychotropic medications provided to inmates upon release and prescriptions sent to the probation District; and completing applications for Medicaid (Medical Insurance) or Disability Benefits and the Virginia Department of Motor Vehicles.

Community Resource Strengths: Intensive SA out-patient services for certain jurisdictions by the CSB; Medical Assistant Treatment; formation of the Northern Shenandoah Valley Substance Abuse Coalition; a felony drug court; a VADOC Mental Health Clinician assigned to District #11; and Valley Health System (Hospital) investment in recovery education and Peer Recovery Programs.

Re-Entry Weaknesses: Delays in securing mental health and substance abuse (MH/SA) treatment with the CSB; regional jails' inability to provide psychotropic medications and follow-up mental health services prior to an inmate's release; limited bed space in the local Community Residential Program; an increase of homelessness due to a lack of affordable housing; and limited programs, especially for violent or sex offenders.

Community Resource Weaknesses: No medical detox unit; no affordable residential treatment; a re-entry system of care due to limited case management in the regional jails; lack of treatment programs accepting Medicaid; lengthy referral processes and waiting lists for clients with Medicaid; costly Oxford Houses that have inconsistent sobriety policies; lack of Medication Assisted Treatment (MAT) in the regional jails and Emergency Departments; and lack of public transportation in rural areas of the District.

Re-Entry Opportunities: Increasing re-entry efforts in the local regional jails to ensure MH/SA services are arranged prior to an inmate's release; allowing the District's mental health clinician to interview inmates at the regional jails that have probation to identify possible mental health needs prior to release; and addressing homelessness by establishing additional Community Residential Programs.

Community Resource Opportunities: two rural localities are pursuing Felony Drug Court dockets and one community is securing a Mental Health Docket in the General District Court level to reduce serious mental health cases from reaching the felony Courts.

Community Threats: Continued overdoses and deaths related to opioid addiction; future pandemics affecting services; introduction of new synthetic drugs; reduced funding; and prolonged waiting periods for SA/MH and homelessness programs.

Learnings

Overall, the District felt confident that re-entry services offered for VADOC inmates released to the community are effective. Areas of concern included release planning and effective case management in the Regional Jail settings, lack of a Detox Center and long waiting lists to receive treatment for SUD and co-occurring disorders in the community. One positive result of the SWOT Analysis was Health Management Associates and DMAS inviting the Northwestern Regional Jail to participate in the implementation grant and their willingness to contact other community stakeholders.

HMA and DMAS have arranged a virtual session in November 2021 to gather key cross-sector stakeholders (more than 30 public safety and health invitees from the Northern Shenandoah Valley area) to review information gathered about the issues impacting people with SUD in the Criminal Justice System.

Conference Session Extracts

From the consideration of the case study with conference participants

Brandon Daisy: We put those areas as our current situation that we moved on to what our desired outcomes were for each of the three areas: re-entry from the state prison level; re-entry from the local jail level; and people being referred to us straight from the court. We were able to draw from the 'opportunity' and 'threat' sections of the SWOT analysis to incorporate that into what our desired outcomes would be. Then we decided what realistic outcomes could be possible if we were awarded the grant, and what changes would be needed to make those outcomes a possibility. And these were put to DMAS (Dept of Medical Assistance Services) at a subsequent meeting.

Tessie Lam: We had three meetings with DMAS and we discussed all the information on November 3 this year. Members of the District 11 management team will be participating in a virtual summit with DMAS officials, and they have invited 30 public safety and health agencies to review information about issues, impacting people who suffer from the substance abuse disorder in our area of the criminal justice system. We're excited about the potential of participating in the grant with DMAS, and we hope that we can improve our re-entry services in our regional jails, as well as improve treatment services in the local area to address serious substance abuse. We hope to reduce recidivism, but also that we can impact and reduce the amount of drug overdoses and deaths that our area has experience due to the opioid epidemic.

Speaker: When will you hear about the grant?

Tessie: We're hoping to learn more next week. DMAS were very open minded, and they listened to all of our ideas and suggestions. We reached out to numerous people and agencies, especially the regional jails, so we had a great collaboration and we're keeping our fingers crossed that they're going to get the grant.

Speaker: In our conversation we thought it would be helpful if people knew what resources exactly were available in the jurisdictions where their probationers were being released to.

Brandon: I know there is a resource guide, and I know a re-entry specialist has to renew it every or second year, but I'm not sure where that is listed.

Speaker: Maybe put into that who offers all the different programs.

Tessie: We provided them with a detailed list of the agencies, plus they already had a pretty good idea of what we had in the area, especially the Winchester and Frederick County area, because they are the largest areas. But they were not as familiar as to what was available beyond that.

Speaker: In our area, we have a problem with heroin and meth, but we are very fortunate that our CSB [Community Service Board] has written grants and received grant money to provide us with discharge planners. We have discharge planners in each of our sub areas in our district to provide re-entry services. I noticed in your paper, you talked about your re-entry weaknesses. A strength that we have is that discharge planners connect re-entry individuals with mental health services and substance abuse services. If individuals had services with them before then they will continue to use them but if they never had services, they could at least connect with new services, and they work prior to being released with the probation officers. Our probation officers here try to work hand-in-hand with the discharge planners to try to get individuals on the right foot to be released. As I said in our group, our CSB are proactive in helping us with detox and things like that when we need that. I don't know if your CSB has grant options for discharge planners but those really are helpful to have in place.

Tessie: I appreciate the feedback. To be honest, our CSB is not really strong in certain aspects. They do provide intensive outpatient treatment for our drug court and the district has also been asked to work on a planning session with our CSB, on the governor's initiative, to see where we have gaps in services. I will bring this idea up as I think it's really good. Do these discharge planners work directly in the jails or are they just a part of the CSB in which they're referred to people coming from court, as well as people coming from the jail?

Speaker: They're employed with the local CSB and it's my understanding that the CSBs worked with the jail on securing a place for them to have office space in the jail and they can talk with the inmates as needed.

Speaker: I'm not sure if any of the CSBs in your area have started looking at the fentanyl strips as a part of harm reduction? We are embarking on that conversation, but more importantly, my comment was to thank you and your team at the district for taking this on.

Speaker: Alexandria also did a SWOT analysis and then a Working Dialogue. Ours focused more on growth and development. We asked questions such as, "Where are we as a district? What are the strengths, weaknesses, opportunities and threats for ourselves and our community stakeholders? How do we grow?" And then we did another Working Dialogue on succession planning, and we'll create an written document for the succession plan.

Postscript
The authors' reflections written some months after the conference

The Winchester Probation & Parole District was honored that our case study, "Connecting Probationers to Substance Abuse Disorder and Recovery Services," was presented during the 2021 Dialogue conference. Prior to preparing the case study, Peter Garrett met with members of the Virginia Department of Corrections and provided guidance in how to prepare these studies. Following this meeting, Tessie Lam and Brandon Daisy thoroughly reviewed the District's Working Dialogue notes and the SWOT Analysis and information, which was provided to the Department of Medical Assistance Services (DMAS) for the purpose of a grant study. During this review, Brandon and Tessie examined the strengths and weaknesses in recovery services offered to probationers in the probation district. Additionally, we reflected on the District's desired and realistic outcomes if a grant was awarded through DMAS. This information was gathered collectively and was placed in the case study. The case study was submitted for editing and ideas and suggestions were also provided by Peter Garrett to improve the final study.

For the final presentation, Tessie and Brandon selected portions of the case study to focus upon during the time frame allowed. On the day of the presentation Tessie and Brandon were honored that numerous participants selected the District's case study. Following the presentation participants were placed in groups to discuss the study, and when they returned several participants provided ideas and suggestions to improve the study as well as improve the desired outcome. One participant reflected that it would have been helpful to have a list of available resources in the local area outlined in the study. Tessie and Brandon reported the District provides a resource guide of all local services to probationers who are in need of substance abuse services as well as other services. Finally, one participant encouraged the District to work collaboratively with the local Community Services Board in securing grant funding for discharge planners, who work directly with the local regional jails. The suggestion of discharge planners was eventually provided to DMAS.

In closing, Tessie and Brandon found that District's Working Dialogue and participation with DMAS in a grant study to be an informative and rewarding experience. The case study also prompted the District to focus on realistic substance abuse services that could best serve our probationers and reduce overall recidivism in the local community.

Dialogue Training for Inmates Dialogue— Encouraging Pro-Social Behavior

John F. Walrath and Wardenia Lassiter

Situation

Indian Creek Correctional Center is the only Cognitive Therapeutic Community for male inmates in the Virginia Department of Corrections (VADOC). The mission of the facility focuses on substance abuse, with the majority of the inmates being enrolled by court order. As part of the ongoing enhancement of the use of pro-social behavior and cognitive skills, the opportunity to introduce Dialogue Skills Training to inmates made perfect sense. By developing these skills, inmates can better communicate and share their authentic voice with both staff and other inmates while actively listening to those around them.

Objectives

Due to the ongoing Covid-19 pandemic and the guidance provided by the Centers for Disease Control, Virginia Department of Health and the Virginia Department of Corrections, our objective at Indian Creek was to select a small group of cohorted inmates (inmates assigned to the same dorm) to participate in the Skills Training. We determined that the dorm designated as HU-4B was a great place to start for several reasons: 1) HU-4B has the highest inmate vaccination rate against Covid. 2) Inmates assigned to HU-4B provided an opportunity to select the most diverse group for this undertaking (race, age, sexual orientation, etc.). 3) HU-4B houses inmates have, for the most part, completed the phases of the Cognitive Therapeutic Community and are now focusing on learning the re-entry skills that can assist them as they transition out of prison and into our communities.

Method

In May of 2021, after selecting HU-4B as our participating dorm, we hung up a flyer in the dorm offering the Inmate Dialogue Skills Training to begin in June. The group would meet once per week for 1.5 hours, with the training lasting a total of 12 weeks. The Dialogue Practitioner assigned to lead this Dialogue Skills Training was Captain Wardenia Lassiter. Her Assistant Dialogue Practitioner was Unit Manager Pamela Wood. Participating inmates ranged in age from 21 years to 64 years, with seven black inmates and four white inmates, which is very close to the demographic percentages of the inmate population at Indian Creek Correctional Center.

Outcomes

In attendance at the first Dialogue Skills Training session were the Warden, Assistant Warden and Statewide EBP Manager. If the inmates were not wearing identifiable clothing, it would be easy to think this training was being delivered to staff, because the inmates displayed the same initial reactions seen during staff training sessions. The inmate participants were apprehensive and nervous, giving very short answers and being cautious not to divulge too much information about themselves; they weren't using their authentic voice. This was not at all unexpected, as you will often see the same apprehensiveness among staff in the beginning of Dialogue Skills Training, which is delivered using the Dialogic Circle. Initially, the inmates separated themselves by race and further separated themselves by age.

The Dialogue Practitioners did a fantastic job of keeping the inmates focused and engaged. As the Weekly Dialogue Skills Training for Inmates sessions continued, these barriers were broken down. Inmates no longer segregated themselves. They had formed a bond as part of the process through role playing and opening up to the group while learning social skills. In June of 2021, a Swedish television crew came to Indian Creek to film a Dialogue Skills for Inmates session as well as interview inmates and staff for a Swedish news program. Staff that work in HU-4B have reported witnessing these participating inmates share their experiences with other inmates that have not yet had the opportunity to attend and urging them to sign up when they can.

Learnings

The world needs Dialogue! Inmates are open to learning skills that will not only assist them with their daily life in prison but can minimize the barriers they encounter during their transition into society. As apprehension gave way to anticipation in the sessions, it was clear that this first class of inmates were appreciative. Comments made during the training included "Best program I have ever been a part of," "I can't believe you-all took the time to teach us these skills," and "During the weekly training sessions, I forgot I was in prison." Our graduation ceremony is scheduled for October, and Director Clarke is scheduled to attend and give remarks. We have already selected the names for our next Dialogue Skills Training for Inmates and we have scheduled their first session.

Sharing that perspective, you could see others have that "Aha moment," like, "Oh, wow!" You could see the impact of that.

Conference Session Extracts

From the consideration of the case study with conference participants

Speaker: You talked about the initial things that inmates wanted when they entered in. Did they ever develop to the point where they saw some benefits for their re-entry? And if so, what did they say about it?

Wardenia Lassiter: Absolutely, they did. For some it was looking at their interaction with their significant other first while they started talking to their wives about their children. They saw a difference in those interactions, and that was an eye opener for them at that point.

Speaker: My biggest question is, How much resistance did you get from staff and how did you deal with it?

Speaker: Based on my role and on doing trainings, and meeting with Dialogue Practitioners at the pilot sites, I didn't see a lot of resistance from staff. Did staff *not* believe it was going to work? Yeah. Realistically you are going to have challenging communication issues, no matter what role you're in. There were some challenges with inmates who participated in the program, and we had some behavioral issues come out during the trainings. I believe this goes back to what we talked about in the earlier sessions about becoming a Dialogic Organization.

Speaker: I think the staff was surprised to see the use of dialogue by the inmates. We would have inmates come back and they didn't realize that we were being taught this and they were surprised. It was really good to see that the challenge we faced most with inmates was that they thought they had everything they need. Kind of, "Gimme the book, let me read the book. Yeah. I'm, I'm good to go." But once they got through the sessions and they realized the importance and the use of dialogic practices, actions and modes they were wowed by it.

They were very excited to see everything come together, and it made a lot more sense to them. One of the main challenges was a lack of knowledge about the program itself. I think it is important when you set up for something like this, and you're picking your individuals, that you are thorough in explaining what the dialogue skills training program for inmates is about. They should not just sign a sheet and say, "Hey, I wanna volunteer for this and hopefully get some fried chicken out of it for graduation, you know?" It is important that we explain exactly what this program is, what it means and what it can do for them. That's the most important thing. We should provide a thorough explanation to them before they sign up for this.

Speaker: The main resistance was from the inmates. When I was part of a couple of meetings in the beginning, the guys were very resistant and rude and closed down. They didn't want to participate. You know, a lot of inmates are always looking for something external, not only in terms of incentives but also in terms of us giving them something external, which they feel can help them on the outside. They are not really thinking of anything cognitive. But halfway through the dialogue they all realize the benefit of the skill as a cognitive tool that enables them to communicate with people.

We had one guy who didn't want to do it at all, and he sat there and by the time we got to the second or the third session he was all in. He was a very angry inmate but once he actually engaged and could see the benefit of how things changed, even his mentality about his own anger, and he saw how it helped him to deal with his own situation, he bought into the rest of the training. By the end, they were all telling us, "We tried it in the community on this guy, and it actually works." When it got to the end of the graduation you could see the transformation for all of them.

Speaker: We had an inmate that was leaving the week after and we made sure that we had the graduation so that he could participate. He came to me the day we had the graduation and he was excited. He wanted to continue and assist the probation office that he was going to by using his dialogue skills and by having the dialogues at his probation office. When they can come to you and tell you what their benefit could be you know that there has been some progress. In addition to that when you hear a reflection from one of your participants who said, "You know what, when I came to the first two, three sessions, I thought this was not for me. I thought we were going to develop something and then it felt like it wasn't going anywhere, but by the end we all learned and we all helped while we progressed."

It just changed my whole perspective about having communication, even in a prison setting. When you hear complaints, then you can challenge them to create check-ins. We had a youth ask this check-in question: "When I'm released and I am faced with the same opportunity to commit a crime, what will I do differently?" When you hear a young man ask that, you can just feel the paradigm shift within each person.

Postscript

The authors' reflections written some months after the conference

When Director Harold Clark first introduced VADOC employees to the idea of thinking and talking together more effectively, it was rumored that this was going to be another short-lived idea. However, as time went on many VADOC employees began to see real changes in not only their work encounters but their personal lives through using the Dialogue Skills acquired.

Indian Creek Correctional Center was selected to be a pilot site to coordinate a Dialogue Skills training for inmates. Many questions were asked, and comments were expressed by VADOC employees. Nevertheless, the inmate selection process was started by the Chief of Housing and Programs along with the Dialogue Practitioners (DPs) because Covid-19 positive cases were continuing to decrease. The Housing Unit selected housed some veteran inmates and some Youthful Offenders. The ten inmate participants relayed during the ceremony, as well as after, that their criminal and addictive thinking had been interrupted. As the training continued the DPs observe how the focus changed with the inmates' attention from, "What I can get out of this" to, "This dialogue will change my relationship for the better." As the time began drawing to a close, motives gradually shifted from individual gain to the collective group advantages. Currently all but two of the graduates have been released to Community Corrections.

I realize that throughout this process it is critical that a variety and diverse number of the inmate participants comprise the group. Having such diversity will reveal different characteristics and all the ways that people are different, which simulates "real" encounters and produces a productive learning experience.

Being a facilitator of this pilot inmate dialogue skills training has stimulated learning and development with my own extended family. Recently my husband's family was attempting to figure out what our family reunion could look like after the Covid-19 years of not having a family reunion. I facilitated a Working Dialogue, and the family reunion was well organized as well as fun. Other than professionally, it continues to amaze me when I facilitate a Dialogue Skills Training to new employees who think the training is a waste of time—until a "lightbulb" comes on and by check-out time there is thunderous applause.

Progressive Reinforcement Through the Use of Incentives

Joseph P. Owen, Dianne Motley and Eric Holloman

Situation

The Brunswick Community Corrections Alternative Program (CCAP) is a secure, residential facility that was created as an alternative sentencing option, for the Circuit Courts in Virginia, to utilize for adult males in need of an Intensive Substance Abuse Program. The facility opened in January of 2020. The program provides a sentencing option for judicial consideration in lieu of an individual serving an active term of incarceration in a local jail or state institution. The curriculum is based on evidence-based practices and is set up to prioritize individuals who pose the greatest risk. It matches each individual with the appropriate programs and services to enhance a successful re-entry into community upon program completion. Our program and services are directed toward positive and measureable outcomes.

The staff at Brunswick CCAP have learned together by talking, listening and thinking together. This has allowed us to develop new meaning together and to help people find common understanding and purpose. The implementation of the Dialogue initiative has emerged into a practice that supports strong, safe containers and continues to exemplify avenues for progressive, impactful and long-lasting change in our facility. Learning Teams have regenerated the use of Dialogue, strengthening comprehension and promoting frequent and fluent use of the Dialogic Skills across the board. Check-ins and check-outs are routinely used in all meetings. Genuine voices improve the quality of our decisions. Regular use of the Dialogue Skills has promoted staff interaction in a respectful, supportive and caring manner. We have respectfully agreed and disagreed with one another, learned to appreciate diversity and accommodate our differences. Applying one move, follow, oppose or bystand at a time continues to impact the functionality of our conversations. Authentic voices, effective listening, respect and the practical application of suspension adds quality to our daily communication.

We have incorporated Working Dialogue at our facility to demonstrate the application of our skills and the impact Dialogue has in our workplace. We utilized a Working Dialogue to develop an incentive program for our population, which would affirm pro-social behavior and provide clear benchmarks for individual achievement as well as for the entire community of residents.

Objective

It was imperative that a variety of voices were heard during the development of our incentive plan for Brunswick CCAP. Information and insight were needed from various departments within the facility in order to create an effective plan. Staff were challenged to develop an incentive-based framework that offers recognition for both individual and collective positive behavior displayed while individuals participated in our program. It was also important to create opportunities for probationers to obtain incentive-based rewards related to positive adjustment, which would motivate participants to conform to program rules and would reduce staff interventions.

Method

In April of 2021, a selected group of staff were invited to participate in a Working Dialogue focusing on a new incentive plan for Brunswick CCAP. This effort would require the attention and input of all departments within the facility. Three separate Dialogues were held with the staff. A collaboration of two Working Dialogues and one follow-up session, held over eight weeks, resulted in a detailed plan to recognize and celebrate progressive, positive behavior. Meetings ranged from one to two hours. An average of eight attendees attended each meeting, with two Dialogue Practitioners leading the group. During this process we shared creative ideas as well as gaining increased understanding of what happens, how and why. We envisaged the benefits of having inclusive and progressive, positive reinforcement. We shared differences and similarities. We defined the best options to take us from start to finish. Finally, we reviewed all shared suggestions, acknowledged all who worked so diligently to develop our new plan and coached forward to ensure compliance with the established plan of action.

Outcomes

After completion of our Working Dialogue, staff felt that their voices were heard. They expressed that the process was safe, respectful and ethical. Dialogic Skills (actions, practices and leading energies) were present, promoting the opportunity for an appropriate action plan. We were able to change things for the better in our workplace. We were able to identify positive progressive change with new options through the help of those impacted. We were able to identify shared values. We developed new ways of working together to move our facility forward. We developed a collective plan which benefits all involved. Incentives were identified that would have the largest impact on our population, such as the ability to purchase food items, send pictures and video messages to family and friends and the ability to participate in special functions such as movies and talent shows held at the facility. Incentives were grouped and offered in tiers labeled Bronze, Silver, Gold and Star Performer, based on requirements that individuals remained infraction free over specified timeframes. Both individual and group incentives were put in place in the various tiers to provide peer motivation. The parts of the incentive plan that have been implemented have generated excitement for our participants and motivated many of them to comply more consistently with facility rules. We have celebrated their successes both individually and as a group. As more of the incentives are introduced, staff will monitor the impact that is being generated and meet to revise practices as needed to maximize the effectiveness of the program.

Learnings

By going through the process of a Working Dialogue, staff at Brunswick CCAP learned that we can come together, brainstorm, use our authentic voices and establish a collective plan to benefit both staff and probationers. Our ability to put our Dialogue skills to work increases comradery, demonstrates inclusiveness and models exemplary teamwork. Staff also learned that we all lead in some capacity, whether it's through Visionary, Citizen, Performance or Wisdom energy—perhaps a little of each—depending on the situation and time.

Conference Session Extracts
From the consideration of the case study with conference participants

Speaker: I've got a question, based on your Working Dialogue. Which gate did you feel like it was the most difficult to get out of the current situation?

Dianne Motley: Although we are a new facility, our staff were not new to dialogue and some people were already introduced to the concept, so there was not a struggle with either. Normally in a Working Dialogue you get people to talk about what they would like to see. I would say the first phase was getting people prepared and talking about the goals that we were trying to reach. After those were identified the rest flowed pretty smoothly during the two times that we met, and it was really great to come together for the follow-up and acknowledge the goals of the process. I would say the initial phase, the initial gate, was the gate that we probably had more issues with. But overall because people were already familiar with the process we didn't really get stuck. It was really an awesome Working Dialogue, I don't want to boast and say we didn't have any issues at all, but it went pretty smooth.

Joseph Owen: I'll follow what Ms. Motley said. We waited till we have been operating for about three or four months, during which we had new intakes coming in and learning from those experiences. Identifying the current situation and getting new staff comfortable with each other was therefore the biggest obstacle, but, like Miss Motley said, with everybody coming from a shared background with a foundation in dialogue, we were able to navigate through that pretty easily. We also had a topic that everyone was interested in and that was key.

Speaker: One of the things you mentioned was including the wants of offenders. Did you actually have them in the Working Dialogue and, if you did, how did you include them?

Joseph: Great question. They were not in our first three dialogues, which were developed by staff, because at that point people were coming in and going out fairly quickly because of the pandemic. So we only had secondhand information from the people who dealt with the population such as the probation officers who worked in the case management aspect, the spectrum substance abuse counsels who were working individually with them and security staff who were dealing with them day to day. Now that our population is going through the training the next layer is to bring them into the circle.

Eric Holloman: I would also add that we are at an advantage at our facility because it is a smaller facility. Most of the security staff, all the probation officers, work very closely together, and I'm one of the probation officers at the facility. So I was able to directly observe how it was impacting the probationers in our program.

Speaker: I was looking through the screens to see who here is not from the DOC [Department of Corrections] and wondering what incentives mean to them.

Speaker: I was wondering what the top three incentives for this dialogue were.

Joseph: Food and being able to reach out to their families were the top two, and then casual dress-down day was a third option that really appealed to people. Those are the incentives in our environment here in corrections. Then again, if you are developing an incentive plan you have to look at your target population and what is important to them. You can take the framework we used here and apply it to any situation with any group you're working with, though. We had a larger benefit from dialogue because it is a new facility with the new staff. We were able to bond together and build stronger relationships of trust as well as communicating and hearing all the voices present at the table and passing on what came out of the dialogue to our other staff who then also got excited about the process. The shared meaning of developing something that could be impactful to the population that we serve really energized our staff too. In a way that was a big benefit of the dialogue process, bringing people together to have their voices heard towards the common mission or goal of creating each incentive.

Speaker: Are any of the other CCAPs [Community Corrections Alternative Programs] in the state modeling your program?

Joseph: Yes. We have periodic steering committees where the CCAP groups meet together, and the information has been passed on to each one of those. CCAP are also developing their incentive plans to impact their population.

Speaker: I had an experience several years back where, as a unit manager, I did not have the right people in the process when developing incentives. The incentive plan was not going well because the incentives we came up with were not what the inmates were interested in obtaining. I now realize whether it is inmates or staff it seems that food is a big motivating factor, and in some female facilities we are actually paying money to wear jeans on Fridays. Some people outside of an institution might think that is insane, but if you're never allowed to wear them it is an incentive that definitely works and use the money to raise funds. So really looking at who your target is and knowing your target is important.

Postscript

The authors' reflections written some months after the conference

The decision to do the work described in our case study, "Progressive Reinforcement Through the Use of Incentives," was based on a need identified within our work environment as well as the means that were available to achieve the desired outcome. Topics for dialogues are chosen at Brunswick Community Corrections Alternative Program based on information obtained from our staff regarding issues that need clarity or solutions. The format of a dialogue serves as a perfect framework to address and solve issues pertinent to all those involved—as the necessary voices can be engaged and consensus reached on solutions that everyone feels committed to, because of their involvement in the process. Ideas and input are also derived from those most invested in having a better process in place moving forward. Clarity is obtained during all stages of the process as the current situation is defined and specific steps are outlined to move towards a shared solution. The work described in the case study not only provided the desired outcome of an incentive plan for our population of probationers, but it was also a driving force to increase trust and authentic communication among those who worked together to develop the plan.

The development of the case study was a collaborative effort by all three authors. Shared input allowed us to highlight the dynamics from the overall journey we wanted to share with our audience. Carefully selected details were included to reinforce that the process to obtain the finished product ended up being just as important as the actual incentive plan that was developed. Staff were able to take time to utilize the steps of the dialogic process and felt validated. They felt empowered to use their voice and be part of a process that produced outcomes that would benefit both staff and the program participants. This served as a catalyst to give individuals confidence that they were part of something larger than themselves. All of these positive outcomes provided a sense of excitement and accomplishment as the case study was shared with our colleagues at the conference as well as those that will read the paper moving forward.

Section Eight

Putting Dialogue to Work for Security

Temporary public safety is achieved by physically containing offenders for a set period of time to prevent them doing harm to others. Inevitably that means prisons hold a concentration of convicted people who require a different regime from those in the community. A secure environment is fundamental for the good running of any prison. The safety and well-being of all who work and live in a prison is a basic requirement. This is a cornerstone of every good correctional system. If staff members or inmates feel unsafe, it influences the decisions they make and affects their willingness to be open with others. It engenders a fragmented society where people tend to communicate only with those they know, and to withdraw their respect for others. This erodes people's health and sense of well-being. When staff members feel insecure it impacts their careers, and when offenders feel insecure, services like counselling and treatment are significantly less effective. We have five case studies that address the complexity of maintaining or re-establishing a secure environment in prisons in the Virginia Department of Corrections.

Sharon Burgess facilitated Dialogues with all the related staff about a situation where gang members had taken control of the showers and non-gang inmates were fighting back. They realised that a lack of procedures, inadequate staff presence and too few telephones all contributed to the situation.

When the synthetic drug 'spice' appeared and inmates began overdosing, **Crystal Butler** facilitated a Working Dialogue to prevent contraband entering prisons state-wide. Over 50 staff members met to understand the issues, and to define new policy and procedures affecting staff, inmates and visitors.

Troy Adams facilitated a Dialogue with everyone involved in a poorly functioning gate pass system that each day allowed or prevented offenders to leave the secure facility to work in the community. Legal constraints, changes determined by probation and tracking issues all had to be realigned.

In a mental health facility where high and low security risk inmates are co-located, the control of contraband through the kitchen is challenging. **Vickie Williams, James Brown and Michelle Galyean** co-facilitated a diverse Working Dialogue that altered procedures, staffing and uniform changing.

When critical security incidents or riots occur, locally trained Special Response Teams are available for rapid response. **Mahala Carter-Moore, Dianne Motley and Tammy Williams** used a dialogic approach to reactivate the morale and voluntary membership recruitment of their facility's SRT.

Ending Gang Control of Telephones and Showers

Sharon S Burgess

Situation

Facility personnel across the Virginia Department of Corrections (VADOC) began noticing a rise in inmate disturbances. The lead cause indicated that the telephones and showers were being monopolized by the gangs, specifically the Bloods. Their ability to be subtle with their activities caused staff to be unaware of the frustration that had reached a boiling point among the inmates who had no gang affiliation. The non-gang inmate population grew tired of the situation and began fighting back, bringing attention to what once was a well-laid-out plan orchestrated by the gang members. Action from leadership was imperative at this time as the safety of inmates and staff had become jeopardized.

Objectives

Leadership approached this situation by utilizing Working Dialogue to get all the voices in the room to construct a realistic approach that would control the usage of the phones, kiosks and showers. In search of a feasible plan that would be accessible throughout the State, the strategizing commenced. The end goal would include protecting all inmates from being extorted or attacked for utilizing phone and shower privileges during the appropriate times, and restoring safety and order in our prison facilities.

Method

Regional Operations Chief Gregory L. Holloway spearheaded the Working Dialogue and selected me to facilitate the process. I had a major role in setting the energy in the room with positivity and implementing the knowledge gained from my extensive dialogue training on how to monitor the necessary components needed for the dialogue.

The reminder of the dialogic actions and practices would be the notification to the participants of their role in maintaining our safe container.

The dialogic actions (move, follow, oppose and bystand), when used properly, allow the conversation to be functional. The practices (voice, listening, respect and suspension) enhance the quality of the conversation. The practices are paramount for having an atmosphere in which people feel comfortable using their authentic voice. The participants would include Unit Heads, Assistant Unit Heads, Unit Managers, Corrections Officers, Intel Staff, Security Staff and Staff from Headquarters. Global Tel Link (GTL) phone services and JPay kiosk payment management representatives were added to the conversation during the second meeting. They were from facilities that were currently experiencing this problem with the gangs. The participants welcomed and appreciated being a part of this Working Dialogue. As the group reflected on the current situation, it was highlighted that there was currently no process or strategy for staff to control the showers and phones and that specific policies, standards and procedures were needed. More training and programs were necessary for staff awareness. The shortage of phones and kiosks would also need to be addressed. Inmates were being extorted and having to pay to gang members to make calls.

This meeting also revealed that inmates had too much idle time. The inadequate staff presence on the floor in the housing units was also highlighted during this dialogue, and it was unveiled that there was some sort of unspoken rule within the dorms surrounding the showers that indicated when certain offenders entered no one else would. The facilities were in dire need of managing the gang behavior and so the process began. Leadership held two Working Dialogue sessions lasting approximately two hours each, and reached a carefully designed plan for David Robinson, Chief Corrections of Operations to review.

Outcomes

The proposed changes required would have a statewide impact. The success of this mission would include a diversified team of staff members working together. Unit Heads would be responsible for communicating to the inmate population the consequences they would face if they did not cease controlling the telephones. GTL phone service was on standby to assist the facilities as they addressed the situation. The need for more telephones was already being acted upon. Intel staff, responsible for security intelligence, were braced to initiate their duties once the gang members were identified. A plan for training staff was ready to be launched.

While the main focus was on the phones, JPay stood ready to assist with the kiosks. This well-discussed and thought-out proposal would provide hope for inmates who relied on conversations with loved ones. The connection was instrumental in having a family link to help them deal with prison life and to avoid a possible hardship on the relationship once they return home and to the community. It also provided safety within the facilities and assisted staff with maintaining a healing environment.

Success reigned with this Working Dialogue. Mr. Robinson approved of the participants' set of required changes to the current situation. As a result of the completed action items by participants, the facilities gained a better handle on the situation, with the gangs no longer controlling the telephones. The incidents declined. Staff were better able to recognize the signs of gang control in the housing units.

Learnings

Following the dialogue process it was obvious that the right people were definitely in the room and all the dialogic actions and practices were flowing throughout what now had become a safe container. The atmosphere in the dialogues was welcoming for individuals to share their authentic views. The group was able to create new meaning from talking and thinking together, and they successfully reached a tangible resolution to what had become an unwanted, unsafe situation inside the facilities. Surprisingly, the dialogic performance energies (vision, citizen, wisdom and performance) balanced the conversation remarkably. In many of the Working Dialogues that I have facilitated, I find the dominant energy of performance resonates in this atmosphere because a great number of leaders and Corrections employees know best how to get the job done to improve a situation. My passion for dialogue and a knowing from previous dialogues facilitated that it really does work were once again proven as a result of this Working Dialogue. The participants were able to pass each review section after the three phases involved in the dialogue process and they enjoyed the Department's Business Practice during this Dialogue.

Conference Session Extracts

From the consideration of the case study with conference participants

Speaker: I wanted to know what role *Global Tell* played in all of this, and I also don't think the case study said what the end result was. What other types of things did you all implement?

Speaker: I'll feel into that question real quick. One of the core things *Global Tell* offered was their ability to control the turning phones on and off. They could also determine who the frequent users were, when a phone was used and what phone was used. Also, they can restrict the use of phones if a warden or superintendent decides, *okay, now I'm at a situation where I need to manage the use of the phones*. Before we did any of this a memorandum went out to the inmate population, letting them know that we know phones are being controlled and abused by gang members, particularly the bloods. This gave the warden and the superintendent the ability to restrict use without too much pushback once they detected a problem. I do want to reiterate; we alerted the inmate population and the wardens before restrictions occurred through a memorandum stating why phone users will be restricted and that a whole dormitory or a whole housing unit will be shut down if it is deemed necessary.

Speaker: I speak for the community side of the house as I do not have much knowledge of the institutional side. Were you able to relocate those gang members who were controlling the showers or the phones to other facilities?

Speaker: Let me bring in a warden or superintendent that may have utilized that action. Is there a warden or superintendent who want to jump in to field the question? Feel free.

Speaker: Good afternoon, I am a warden. When I first arrived, we had an issue. I received a lot of requests from the inmate population that the phones were being run and manipulated by gang members. I then got together with the Intel department. We restricted the telephone calls to five telephone calls a day. Intel was able to identify some of the offenders and once Covid lifted we were able to transfer them. We all know the challenges of working inside the facilities right now with limited recreation and limited programs, especially in a dormitory, and the inmates are in there all day. Being able to restrict telephone calls, giving inmates five telephone calls, alleviated some of the gang fights we had, especially in the evening times, as well as helping create a smoother operation.

Speaker: What helped us out is that our decisions were supported when we imposed sanctions. Sometimes we had to move guys and sometimes we didn't, but we had an open conversation and we let the inmate population know what was going on. We addressed it. Sometimes it worked, sometimes it didn't, but it was appreciated from all levels that we had support with the phones and the showers.

Speaker: We had some similar situations, but they occurred in different settings. I'm quite thankful that we had this discussion because even though I don't hear about issues with our showers here, conversation has occurred regarding the phones. I now have an awareness that I should look closer at the shower situation because even though it's not being stated it does not mean that it is not happening.

Speaker: We talked in our group about how widespread the issue was, it wasn't just a high security thing. It goes from a field unit where things could be manipulated all the way up to high security.

Speaker: The awareness is great, but the one thing that I will share is that it at least started groundwork somewhere, so with an ongoing issue we at least have a baseline to start with. Then we can improve on all the different things that we have already learned. Hopefully moving forward, we can make our systems better as far as trying to control it.

Speaker: Yes. the report-outs were great. I listened very closely to what you have all shared. I'm going to go back and send the original memorandum to all involved and I will put it on the next agenda so we can put visibility back on it. Not that we had lost it, but it will be good to reset the button, to go through it again and to bring in new staff. To revisit this sensitive area and to keep moving forward.

One last thing that I will say about the phones and showers, I have to be honest and I'm probably being a little bit unpolished about what I'm going to say, but I'm going to say it. Those phones and those showers do not belong to any gang, they belong to VADOC. Every inmate that lives in that housing unit or that dormitory should have free access, within our schedule, to shower and to use phones. I'm adamant about that.

Postscript

The author's reflections written some months after the conference

I was honored to be selected by Regional Administrator Gregory Holloway to facilitate an important Working Dialogue relevant to our case study, "Ending Gang Control of Telephone and Showers," in 2016. It was a department-wide concern and I was hopeful that this Working Dialogue would be beneficial for the entire state. The outcome did provide guidance for all facilities, which provided a safer environment with fewer incidents related to this subject matter. Writing the paper from this Working Dialogue allowed me to revisit the process that occurred with the appropriate voices that were in the room. It was an engaging experience. The room was filled with leaders who were problem solvers. I had the opportunity to slow the process down to ensure the fidelity of this process occurred.

The ability to present the dialogic process of dealing with gang control of telephones and showers at our prisons in Virginia was an opportunity to allow attendees to have a better understanding of how dialogue may be used to combat challenges in the workplace. It proved the availability to conquer present-day challenges. This paper represents a Working Dialogue which generated an action plan and allowed staff and others to see that the Department of Corrections has a business practice available to make our environments safer, thus increasing the belief in dialogue for any who doubted that dialogue works.

I utilize dialogue skills personally and professionally, and I believe that if you provide safe spaces for individual authentic voices to be heard and to use the dialogic practices, the possibility of developing a better home, workplace and world just might exist.

Enhancing Security Procedures to Prevent Contraband

Crystal Butler

Situation

The number one goal for the Virginia Department of Corrections (VADOC) is long-term public safety. As in any other prison system, the VADOC is always looking to enhance its safety and security procedures to fulfill this goal. Looking at the visitation policies and procedures statewide, it was found that the common theme was contraband breaching the secured perimeter. Concerns statewide rose when inmate overdoses increased, prison infractions for contraband grew and concern for the new synthetic "spice" drug appeared. Inmates and visitors were exchanging contraband through candy and chip bags from the vending machines, and it was being sent through the mail taped behind pictures, stamps, etc. Also, contraband was hidden in body cavities of the visitors, while newer drugs such as suboxone strips were harder to detect. Long visitation hours offered a bigger window to pass contraband. There was clearly a need to address inconsistencies in interpreting the visitation policies and create more strict security procedures.

Objectives

Regional Operations Chief Greg Holloway sent out the direction for this Working Dialogue and tasked each unit with gathering staff from varying ranks to participate. Staff were gathered from the East, Central and West regions of the state, from Correctional Officers to Wardens, and placed in one room to identify the holes in the VADOC's procedures for perimeter security, and what is needed to improve them.

Method

In 2016, a Working Dialogue was conducted at the VADOC's Academy for Staff Development in Crozier, Virginia. There were approximately 50 staff members that participated in this Working Dialogue—to date, one of the largest held in the VADOC. Due to the size of the Working Dialogue and the need to complete it within the eight-hour workday, the 50+ staff members were broken into random groups and sent to separate rooms to conduct each phase of the Working Dialogue. This also helped to ensure authentic voices were spoken in the groups, and that everyone was given the opportunity to contribute. Two Dialogue Practitioners were sent to each room to conduct each phase. After completion of each phase, all participants were brought back together in one room, where the hard work began for the Dialogue Practitioners. With such a large group of participants, there were walls and walls of flip charts to decipher. One Practitioner walked the participants back through each phase of the Working Dialogue by combining similar topics on each flip chart. This also allowed the participants to see everyone's answers and to give anyone the opportunity to add or explain their answers on the flip charts. This Working Dialogue lasted the full eight hours.

Outcomes

You can only imagine the multitude of solutions this group came up with; after all, they are doing the work every day. New policy and procedural changes were recommended and implemented statewide. A few of the changes include:

Visitation: Vending machine items were cut back drastically, to only include snacks. Hot meals were no longer a choice. Visitation hours were cut back to enforce the one-hour maximum for visitation, and all inmates were now required to change their clothes and wear state-issued jumpsuits. A centralized bathroom was also designated for all inmates to use during visitation.

Mail: All regular mail was now to be copied and sent to the inmates. No original envelopes, pictures or letters were sent into the facility.

Other: Increased signage was placed in all front entry areas to show visitors the possible repercussions of bringing in contraband. X-ray machines and body scanners were to be placed at every facility (still in progress).

Learnings

Safety and Security is *everyone's* job in the VADOC, and everyone was very passionate about the process to enhance safety and security statewide. Staff were excited to be a part of a major process that would (and did) impact and change policies and procedures statewide. The Working Dialogue process proved that there is value in the line staff's voices and implementation of their ideas proved a great success. The staff that participated also learned that every section of the prison plays a part in the visitation process, and engaging staff and inmates increases security.

The Dialogue Practitioners learned how to navigate a large group through a Working Dialogue, and the importance of narrowing down the flip charts for a greater understanding and cohesiveness amongst the group. Also, breaking down the 50+ staff members allowed staff to be more authentic with their voices and put in the work needed to address this serious topic.

Conference Session Extracts
From the consideration of the case study with conference participants

Speaker: For me, one of most interesting aspects of this case study is the far-reaching effects that dialogue can have within an organization. I'll be honest with you: at the start of my career I would never have thought preventing contraband and dialogue would be related in any way.

Speaker: I do not know if the changes we have seen were the result of a Working Dialogue. A lot of times decisions are also being made and put in place from the top so we can't really know. And although there were some great changes made through that Working Dialogue, we still have some contraband problems. So we are looking forward to the next Working Dialogue and the next change to be implemented.

Speaker: You hit it right on the spot and, yes, we still are looking for ways going forward, because it has not been totally resolved. I don't know if it ever will be. We will strive to eliminate it, but it is part of a process that we have to keep redefining, and we need to keep moving forward with the most updated systems and technology to move us forward.

A few months ago, we talked about how the Working Dialogue process really did put us in a better place with regards to preventing contraband entering the secure perimeter. Another spinoff that I believe is going to assist us going forward is that we now do schedule visitations so we know who is coming and when they are coming. It gave us some significant information once we had that in place, and, of course, that was due to the pandemic. On the other hand, I believe that because we think as a dialogic organization, the recommendation would have come up even if we did not go into a pandemic.

Speaker: One of my concerns was that all of this was done in five hours, and that a lot of changes took place. I mean, it is awesome to get it done, and get it right. But we are a small facility. I would just be concerned about the impact of making the changes in the mailroom. It would need a lot of extra manpower to do all those copies of the mail, and it is only myself, a P14 and one other person to assist with the mail. It takes a lot of additional time to do all of the copying of the letters and envelopes, and all of that. So I was just wondering if that was ever brought up at the dialogue?

Speaker: It wasn't brought up in the dialogue, but there was a conversation raising exactly what you just said. I will revisit to see where we are now, and if it is still a direction that the department would go in. We were looking at an outside vendor to handle that process. It was strong conversation, but I will definitely look into where we are and I will let you know.

Speaker: I am a medical secretary and I manage the inmate account. I do all of the purchasing and I oversee the mailroom, so I often run out of time to do things. We only just recently started training a P14 in all the new mailroom facilities that have been implemented, and, in the meantime, we still have to do this and it takes a lot of extra time to process the mail. I was just wondering if that was even considered when the pilot was created, and don't get me wrong, it's a wonderful change because we were having issues with things coming in.

Speaker: Somewhat the concern going forward is about what people are forced to do if they are still trying to get drugs in. To the speaker's point, our frontline now is that mailroom and we are seeing many magazines, books and legal mail coming in, and that where they're trying to get it in.

Crystal Butler: You make a great point. This was done years ago and we're still seeing the effects of it. Times do change, which is why it is so important to follow up and complete the data and say, "Okay we've done this, is it still working?" That is where the evidence-based research comes in, which needs to be done constantly. We are facing a new era, so we need to ask, How do we move forward?

Speaker: Glad to hear you've got this. I'm glad that you are continuing because this a continuing problem. Once you stop one way, they are creative enough to find another way to get it in. There are so many ways that they keep trying to get drugs and weapons and cell phones in, it's a never-ending problem.

Speaker: One thing that we proved through this Working Dialogue is that we were able to take control of our security procedures, and now I feel like the ball is in our court. We can now focus more heavily on investigations and intelligence, and that is how we are staying ahead of it right now. We will always have issues with contraband coming in, but I feel like it's more manageable now because we have one large portion of it under control through the way we are doing visitation, so now we can focus our efforts on having good intelligence and investigation practices.

Postscript

The author's reflections written some months after the conference

Being asked to be a facilitator in a major statewide Working Dialogue that would directly impact the Virginia Department of Corrections (VADOC) policies and procedures was very rewarding and exciting. The process of the Working Dialogue was well organized and allowed me to see how to manage large groups through the process with fidelity. Following the Working Dialogue, major changes impacted every facility in the Commonwealth of Virginia, and many changes we would later find out would need to be re-evaluated. This was discovered through submitting the paper to the Academy of Professional Dialogue and allowing a platform for others to discuss the process.

Transparency has been one major benefit in integrating Dialogue and Working Dialogues in the VADOC. We pride ourselves on being a learning organization and this process has proven us to be just that. The Working Dialogue on Preventing Contraband was completed several years ago, so to see the continued impact and be able to reflect on what was done and what is still needed was a great experience. I learned that collaboration, reflection and including an outside view on the work creates a better understanding and generates more sound practices in our field of work.

Having participants in "The World Needs Dialogue!" 2021 conference inquire about the process and the changes that came out of the Working Dialogue provided more opportunities for the department to grow and shift the focus of the changes implemented to the new challenges we currently have. Many of the participants brought out issues that the Working Dialogue caused for certain employees, and without this platform to reflect on we would have never understood or known that impact.

Personally and professionally, being in the process increased my understanding and desire for inclusion in decision-making processes. It deepened my skill as a practitioner and as an employee to better understand the necessity of follow-up, which directly leads to evidence-based practices. We are in the business of helping people be better and we accomplish this by the inclusiveness of Dialogue, which allows for us to all learn from each other and our experiences.

Working Dialogue: Managing Gate Pass Cards

Troy "Eddie" Adams

Situation

The Virginia Department of Corrections (VADOC) operates the Appalachian Community Corrections Alternative Program (ACCAP). ACCAP is defined as an evidence-based alternative to prison for nonviolent offenders who have been convicted of a felony. ACCAP provides a structured, healing environment where participants can receive help designed to address criminal thinking, substance abuse disorders, and educational and vocational needs. Participants in ACCAP are given the opportunity to participate in work functions which award them community service hours that can be applied to their court costs and fines at minimum wage rates. Many of these work functions are performed in the community.

Upon arrival at ACCAP, all participants receive a red identification card that indicates they cannot go outside the secure perimeter of the facility to participate in work details. Participants' criminal histories are evaluated by their assigned Probation Officer to determine their eligibility to participate in outside work details. Those deemed eligible to participate in outside crews receive a blue ID after five weeks. If the participant has been charged with any type of escape, or if they abscond or attempt to bring contraband into a jail or prison, the participant will keep their red ID until a 90-day adjustment period has been satisfied, when they are instructed to put in a request to be reevaluated by their assigned Probation Officer. If they have made a positive adjustment to ACCAP and had no behavioral issues, the Probation Officer recommends that the Superintendent issue them a blue ID. If a participant has been charged with crimes against a minor or sexually explicit charges, they will only be allowed to work at VADOC-owned facilities to prevent them from having contact with the public. These participants keep a red ID for the duration of their time at ACCAP.

Objectives

There were several problems associated with this system. Since the Probation Officers kept the offender files, it was difficult for security staff to keep up with the dates when participants reached the five-week mark to change their card status to blue. In addition, many participants do not want to be assigned to work details, so they would never request to be reevaluated or they would simply say that they had lost their ID card. Another problem was that participants placed on restrictive status had the opportunity to work outside facility grounds at other VADOC facilities, but they had red cards just like participants who could not go outside the fence.

Therefore, many of these participants were never picked for work crews because the officers only saw the red ID, and there was no obvious distinction between the cards. It began to get hard to assemble work crews because many participants who were eligible to participate in outside work detail still had a red ID even after their 30-day transition period or after their 90-day restriction status.

Method

The Superintendent requested that a Working Dialogue be conducted to find a possible solution. This Dialogue included the Superintendent, Major, Senior Probation Officer, Probation Officers, a Lieutenant, two Sergeants, and a Secretary to take notes. The first part of the Dialogue focused on the current situation, while the second was aimed at the desired outcome. ACCAP needed a process in which the participants' ID cards would be changed from red to blue upon the participants' fifth week in the program—a system that does not leave it up to the participant to request their status /card color change. Also, a better way was needed to identify participants who were only permitted to work outside at VADOC facilities and assurance that a restricted participant would never be allowed outside the secure perimeter.

During the part of the Dialogue focusing on the desired outcome, the Lieutenant presented new information currently unknown to the majority of the group: not only do the participants have ID cards in their possession, but also the facility keeps an identical ID at the front gate for tracking. The system that was being used at that time did not allow the ID cards to be any color other than blue or red; however, the ID cards at the gate *could* be another color. Therefore, in order to differentiate between participants who cannot work outside the gate and those who are restricted to work at VADOC facilities, it was decided that the front-gate ID for those that can work outside VADOC facilities would be changed to green.

Outcome

Further recommendations included designing a new form for the Probation Officers to evaluate the participants' work eligibility. This form would consist of the recommended work status initially made by the Probation Officer, and a place for the Superintendent to approve or disapprove this recommendation. A section was added for a review for the participants not allowed to participate in community work for 10 weeks. After the 10 weeks, the Senior Probation Officer would present these forms to ACCAP staff and the Superintendent for review to determine if the participant would now be eligible to participate in outside work details. During this time, the Superintendent would complete the review process with the approval or non approval signature.

Probation Officers can then send out the five-week date for each group when they arrive, and the Major can schedule a reminder with the team to ensure that card statuses are reviewed and that necessary color changes are made. Policy would be revised to include the condition that any participant who loses their ID would be charged two dollars for a replacement. In addition, any participant receiving a major infraction would no longer be allowed to participate in work crews for the duration of their loss of privileges status. A label beside their name at the front gate would temporarily identify these participants. Staff was given approximately one month to make designated changes.

Learnings

This Working Dialogue enabled ACCAP staff to obtain a better understanding of the value of addressing procedures that are ineffective or that are nonproductive by utilizing Dialogue. The successful outcome of this Working Dialogue was very encouraging and has given everyone involved the confidence to voice concerns and address future problems through the use of Dialogue.

Conference Session Extracts
From the consideration of the case study with conference participants

Speaker: I never thought about having a dialogue about the gate passes—I never bothered to ask if this process really worked. This case study has prompted me to now ask, Is our gate pass system working? Maybe there is something we can do differently; maybe the process can be changed.

Speaker: One of the things that sometimes I still struggle with is that employees will come to me and say, "Well, I didn't have a voice in this decision." I am trying to explain to them that there are lots of things that we can use dialogue for but there are times that we can't use dialogue.

Speaker: I love to hear the dissenting voice. The person has reasons for their dissent and you can learn a lot. You might need to take a breath, take a step back and say, "Let me rethink this." Often people who disagree have the best ideas. Yes, it's hard to not just say, "Do this or do that." But we get a better flow and better buy-in when we make people part of the process.

Speaker: A benefit from Working Dialogues that continues to amaze me is how that we end up fixing things we didn't even know needed fixing until we did the work in dialogue. A big thing that came out of this dialogue is that the form we had was really outdated. So we figured out we needed a new form, and we decided how to make a form. Now we have a form that is much better. It has places for all the supervisors to sign, so instead of two forms we are using only one. It is something that we really didn't intend to happen, but now we have got a much better form.

Speaker: From the security side, the one thing that I liked about the case study is how, when you need a quick reference, you can look at the color and you automatically know you don't have to go back and look through folders or a spreadsheet. Looking at the card color is just so much easier and it makes it easy for the officers.

Speaker: It goes back to that old saying, "Work smarter, not harder." It makes it so much easier for your when it is as simple as looking and seeing the color and having your answer right there, rather than turning through a book.

Speaker: A lot of times for a Working Dialogue to work you have to have the unit head put their ego aside. It's a lot easier to have a Working Dialogue when a unit head or a supervisor can do those things.

Speaker: For me it speaks to trust. So I do try to be that listening ear. I try to suspend judgment and I want to listen to what people have to say, but sometimes there is no room for discussion. It is what it is. People want to have a voice but also that takes trust. Sometimes you just need to trust that your people know their jobs, and to let them do their jobs, knowing that they are not going to put anybody in harm's way. That kind of trust is a big thing too.

Speaker: When we did the Working Dialogue, we went through a lot of trouble to carefully select those we felt needed to be in the room to make some changes. Another thing that went really well with this particular Working Dialogue was staff involvement. We had a lot of suggestions and, although we ended up not using all of them, we did end up using a lot of them; the staff had a lot of good solutions. The benefit of giving everybody a voice is that although the superintendent might have some ideas and the rest of us might have some ideas, when you get everyone in a room together, we just have access to so much more information.

Speaker: Everybody participated really well, and everybody shared their voice. It helped us to find out more and also have more good things come out of the sessions. Another thing that we found out was how, when a participant here gets charged, he really wasn't eligible to go out on work crews because of that charge. But because there were problems with communications between the staff, we would send out an email but not everybody read their email, and there was a chance the guy might be able to go out on a work crew. This Working Dialogue helped us to figure out, "Hey, we need a policy or a procedure to help us know who is has a charge against them, which means they cannot work somewhere," and now we have a way to mark it so that everybody knows it at a glance.

Postscript
The author's reflections written some months after the conference

When utilized correctly, Working Dialogues have been an effective means of solving problems encountered by staff within the Virginia Department of Corrections. Therefore, when security staff presented a problem they were having organizing probationer work crews at the Appalachian Community Corrections Alternative Program (ACCAP) a Working Dialogue was scheduled to address this issue.

An important part of planning this Working Dialogue was ensuring that the appropriate people were included in the process. We knew that many employees at ACCAP had good ideas about making this process smoother who had never had the opportunity to voice their thoughts. This Working Dialogue also needed to include people who could make the changes needed for these ideas to become a reality. Therefore, the selection process was a deliberate one.

This Working Dialogue was successful because the people involved were willing to participate and voice ideas. There was a lot of feedback concerning problems involving the process of issuing gate passes that had never been made known to supervisors at ACCAP. This additional feedback resulted in a new form being created to improve the entire process of requesting and restricting gate passes. As a result, the process of orchestrating outside work crews became better.

When assigned the task of writing about and explaining this case study, we knew that many readers would not understand the meaning of gate passes at ACCAP or the process of Working Dialogues. Therefore, it was understood that during this presentation the process of assembling probationer work crews at ACCAP would need to be explained and the Working Dialogue process would need to be outlined so that readers not trained in dialogue would understand it.

When presenting this case study, it was found that when introduced to the Working Dialogue process, readers were quick to understand and value the concept. Once the gate pass issue was explained, they also began to see the benefits of this Working Dialogue. The importance of everyone having a voice and voices being heard was valued by the readers. It was emphasized by the readers that this study enforced how important it is for leaders to set their egos aside and to suspend judgment in order to allow employees the opportunity to offer solutions to problems. Better communication is what makes great Working Dialogues and better communication is what was needed to solve the problem regarding gate passes at ACCAP.

Cooking up Ideas to Revamp Kitchen Worker Hours

Vickie Williams, James Brown and Michelle Galyean

Situation

Marion Correctional Treatment Center (MCTC) is the state mental health facility for adult males. MCTC houses a maximum of 191 mental health inmates of varying security levels and up to 180 Cadre inmates, our minimum-security workforce. There are inherent challenges in having two diverse populations, such as controlling contraband, ensuring facility operations are maintained, controlling movement and allowing breaks for kitchen staff. The scheduling for kitchen workers affects multiple departments in the institution, including security, counselor programs and food service.

Objectives

Our aim with the Working Dialogue was to provide a process for everyone to use their authentic voices and work toward a solution that would benefit all. It was important to have representatives from all departments that manage different aspects of the kitchen and their inmate workers. Everyone needed to be available to provide input from their perspective and experience. Their commitment toward a collaborative solution was vital to the success of the Dialogue.

Our objectives primarily began with providing a secure process that was best for the institution. We needed a better search process to include consistent strip searches before and after kitchen workers report to work. There is a high potential for contraband to enter and leave the rest of the facility through the kitchen. This contraband could involve stealing food, which adversely affects food costs, or tools and equipment that could potentially be used as weapons.

Monitoring inmate movement is also necessary to provide a safe and secure environment. Kitchen worker hours needed to be updated on the Master Pass for accuracy and consistency. Work hours needed to be scrutinized for efficiency and to ensure critical sanitation and high quality of meals.

Method

Participants included Shift Commander, Kitchen Supervisor, Cadre Lieutenant, Institutional Program Manager (job par) and Treatment Secretary. Participants met in September of 2019 for three hours. The facilitator began by encouraging all staff to use their authentic voices and share their perspective. The Dialogic Practices were reviewed at the beginning of the process to expedite a higher-quality engagement. The practitioner also explained the process of the phases of a Working Dialogue and the importance of the gates, or stages, prior to the Dialogue's inception.

The check-in was purposely chosen to create an atmosphere where participants would be comfortable sharing. The practitioner chose a "round" format and posed the check-in, *What was your favorite Halloween costume growing up?* This allowed everyone to engage on a relaxed level and increased the energy in the room.

In explaining the gates, the practitioner reinforced that passing through the gates means a commitment from each individual that they are ready to move forward to the next phase. Participants had to verbally give their input on each gate before moving forward to the next.

During each phase "parking lots" were used to record ideas that were relevant to future phases. This allowed for expression of ideas, rather than suppressing them entirely. Then, the practitioner retrieved this information at the appropriate time, letting the participants know that their input was valued while still maintaining the fidelity of the Dialogue.

The checkout summarized everyone's reflection on the process: *Tell us one word to describe how you feel about this Working Dialogue.* The concise instructions challenged participants to convey their thoughts without adding a lot of time to the lengthy process of a Working Dialogue. Overall, participants expressed optimism and appreciation for the process.

The follow-through phase was conducted in November of 2019. This date was agreed upon during the Working Dialogue to allow for all deadlines to be completed. The Unit Head, Major, Chief of Housing, Administrative Captain and Food Service Director participated. All tasks had been completed and positive feedback was received.

Outcomes

During the Changes Required phase, tasks were assigned to participants for completion, along with deadlines. This adds a level of accountability to move the solutions forward. The Kitchen Supervisor agreed to reduce the number of kitchen workers and to revise their schedules on the Master Pass. The Cadre Lieutenant and the Shift Commander were assigned the task of moving the strip search room and ensuring that all Kitchen Whites were assigned and collected out of that area. Expectations were placed for a security supervisor to oversee the strip search process for compliance. The Cadre Lieutenant was assigned the task of developing a memo for all staff and the inmate population outlining the new procedure.

Learnings

This was MCTC's first Working Dialogue; therefore, participants experienced a small learning curve. There was a need for periodic redirection to stay on the current phase and not jump quickly to solutions. The Dialogue Practitioner used her skills to create mutual respect between herself and all participants, effectively shifting the environment to one of productivity and inclusivity. Explaining the process at the onset, particularly developing an understanding of the gates, is crucial. This experience validated the need to have key persons in the Dialogue that can contribute toward a solution mutually beneficial for all. If this commitment is not obtained, the progress and momentum gained from the Dialogue may stall as changes are implemented.

Staff initially were distrustful of the process but became more open as the process unfolded. All input during the phases was documented on flip charts with no names attached. This provided the necessary transparency to establish the safe container, which is critical in this process. All in all, this was a remarkable initial Working Dialogue which set the tone and confidence for future Dialogues in our institution.

Conference Session Extracts
From the consideration of the case study with conference participants

Vickie Williams: Working dialogues should take either a proactive or a reactive approach in response to a situation. This example was a reactive one because emotions were already running high. There was already movement on this, and it was creating a conflict. There is a great deal of energy in conflict. The dialogue practitioner's role is to redirect that energy into a productive channel, to help people be able to work together and to generate solutions. Not all conflict is bad but if it's allowed to fester and no action is taken to redirect it, it can be destructive. If it's redirected, it can be productive.

Another important thought is that the warden didn't have to make the decisions in this. He could, he's capable of setting the direction and making them do it, but through the dialogue they came up with their own way. It was within policy and their practices and stuff were right. At the end of the day, they don't have to go to the warden's office all the time. They can answer their own questions a lot better.

Speaker: I echo what was just said. I have a lot of faith in the team here. Early on, I knew that they knew what the answers were, and that once they got into the same room they could come up with a solution that both parties could live with. Instead of me saying, "This is how we're going to do it," and putting in place command and control, they figured it out and made it work. Then, instead of being part of the problem, they became the solution, and there has been very little negative feedback because they came up with the solutions themselves.

Michelle Galyean: When we first started the dialogue there were all these alliances and I could feel the room was divided, but then we looked at everyone's expectations around the follow-through. We had two security supervisors and two officers expected to conduct the strip searches, and then the kitchen manager said, "We'll assist with escort monitoring, let us help you, we know you are sometimes short on security." They started helping each other and we became more of a team. So it works.

Speaker: I realized we don't have to solve this problem. It was very refreshing for me to hear how you all tackled this issue, and it has given me great ideas on how to get all those voices in the room and talk about how we can make it work.

Vickie: Thank you, I appreciate that feedback from you. I think people who participate in dialogues that have a lot of supervisors in them are often real heavy on performance energy. They have built their careers on making and implementing decisions pretty quickly and of their own accord. That is how they have been promoted and became successful. Now we ask them to sit down in a room with other supervisors and with line staff. We ask them to take their time and slow things down so they can look at a situation from many different angles. Because sometimes the person who likes to fix things are not aware of the ripple effect and impact it can have on others. When you solve it in the short term it may create more work because you didn't anticipate the ripple effect it will have. But by slowing it down a little bit and taking a dialogic approach you may actually save time. This is definitely something that we've learned through doing Working Dialogues.

Speaker: I've been a part of a couple of Working Dialogues, so I know when you first come in everybody is in their own little bubble and everybody has a point they want to make. They are just waiting to see what the other person says before they voice their opinion. But when you give them time and the opportunity to come up with a solution, they tend to stick to it a little bit better.

Speaker: Coming up with a solution is a great thing to do but being able to stick to that solution is something else. Sometimes we'll try things for a little bit and then we will revert back, so I was kind of excited to hear that you have been doing it for three years.

Vickie: Thank you for that. You know even if you come up with solutions in Working Dialogues, through getting everybody in place and agreeing on what needs to be done, when you start to implement the solution there are always things that you didn't anticipate. It is great that we sustained this for three years but we did not just come up with the way we're doing things and then everybody went and did their own thing. There were ongoing discussions, ongoing reinforcements of what the solution was, and some more tweaks along the way. Still, I think that first having a mutual understanding of what was best for the institution allowed people to be open for follow up discussions. It made people more approachable to have some conversations and to making sure the solution is working for everybody.

Postscript
The authors' reflections written some months after the conference

Marion Correctional Treatment Center held its first Working Dialogue when we scheduled "Cooking up Ideas to Revamp Kitchen Worker Hours." This was an effort to address long-standing concerns between kitchen staff, inmate workers and security staff. Facilitators and administration identified participants during the set-up phase. Anyone who would be impacted by the process was invited to participate. This was an important first step in the eventual success of the dialogue.

At the onset of the Dialogue, Ms. Galyean, the lead facilitator, reviewed the differences between dialogue and Working Dialogue, with particular emphasis on the gates. This was important for the participants to understand, as they had not seen this process previously. As the dialogue progressed, participants were able to trust the process and used their authentic voices to work collectively toward a solution.

We learned through this process that the use of Dialogic Practices is of vital importance. Because participants have a vested interest in the outcome of the process, they can become quite passionate about protecting their assigned areas. It is important that they suspend and listen to others so that they can all work toward a common goal and resolution. The Dialogue Practitioner must be skilled at redirecting without offending and demonstrate patience while participants learn to work with each other, rather than against. By contrast, another learning for the facilitator is to become comfortable with silence while participants gather their thoughts. The practitioner must wait and not rush the process by offering ideas or solutions. Those involved will more readily accept and move forward with solutions together if they have generated those solutions themselves.

Always Ready, Always There: Special Response Team Recruitment

Mahala Carter-Moore, Dianne Motley and Tammy Williams

Situation

Special Response Teams (SRT) provide the Virginia Department of Corrections (VADOC) with specially trained and equipped teams available for a rapid response to VADOC critical incidents at their local facility or other VADOC units. SRT members are also utilized for missions determined to be high-risk, such as riots and disturbances, and to provide support for other security operations throughout the Department. Over the past few years, membership had significantly decreased at the Deerfield Correctional Complex (DFCC), impacting regional and statewide totals. This created concern regarding the team's ability to respond effectively to critical incidents within the Department.

Objectives

The need was to assist members and management to develop strategies to increase the strength of the SRT. The Deerfield Correctional Complex uses dialogue practices to solve day-to-day operational challenges and/ concerns, so a Working Dialogue was conducted on the recruitment and retention of SRT members. The main objectives were to: share ideas on how to increase membership at the facility level; gain support and buy-in from all supervisors; ensure members were assigned throughout the facility on all shifts and breaks; have supervisors be a part of the recruitment process; have staff view SRT in a positive light; offer additional training outside the quarterly training; and not have physical requirements viewed as a barrier.

Method

Participants in the Working Dialogue, "How to Strengthen the Special Response Team at DFCC," consisted of a diverse group of staff including current SRT members, institutional training instructors and facility leadership. We defined the current situation, desired outcomes and then the changes required. The agreed current situation was: SRT numbers were low; feedback from watch commanders was sometimes viewed as negative; not having enough hands-on training; and the physical training was sometimes a barrier for new recruits. Attention was given to the modes of talking and thinking together and there was no debate. Instead, skillful conversations led to the desired outcomes. These included increased SRT membership, gaining apparent support from all supervisors and additional training.

The conversation flowed and participants appeared excited and appreciative of the opportunity to dialogue. There was genuine and sustained interest in being recruiters for the SRT. An obvious sense of camaraderie was present. Of course staff were more willing to implement some changes than others, but the desired changes were welcomed by all of the participants. Indeed, the proposed changes inspired the participants to meet after the Working Dialogue to propose a plan for additional training for SRT members. Sharing of ideas and explaining intent reduced opposition and promoted a functional conversation, with several additional follow-up conversations held about creating flyers, making videos and meeting with all supervisors.

SRT members dialogued with supervisors and line staff to promote the importance and benefits of the Special Response Team membership and to answer questions and inquiries. Current SRT members raised the Security Department Leadership's awareness that their recruitment could be even more effective if they more readily shared the facility and team's vision. Security Department Leadership supported this initiative and voiced the need for improved communication from SRT leadership. As a result, more frequent dialogues occurred as well as more engagement, support and collaboration between the Departments, with active and ongoing recruitment of SRT members on all shifts and breaks at the Complex. There were regular SRT Commander and Assistant Commander dialogues with SRT members, and Shift Commanders regularly spoke about recruitment during musters and staff briefings. Flyers and posters were used, and efforts were incorporated into Employee Appreciation Events. Additional quarterly recruitment/awareness exercises were held, with the SRT Commander supported by the Warden and Chief of Security to offer voluntary "work out" days to prepare potential members for the physical training of SRT members.

Outcomes

Deerfield's Special Response Team ultimately reassured staff that the institution can be safely managed during any unforeseen event. Education of all staff remains ongoing, highlighting the importance of the Special Response Team to the facility, Region and Agency. Recruitment and Retention methods are ongoing. The current DFCC SRT Commander, who also serves as the Regional Assistant Commander, has stated there has been a significant increase in new staff expressing their desire to become members of the SRT. The current team is creating videos to use for training and educational purposes at the facility level.

As result of the Working Dialogue we all achieved positive results. SRT membership increased nearly 50% (8 members to 15 members). Staff have expressed their appreciation for the SRT through recognition incentives within the Department. As a result, there has been a noted increase in the morale of current team members and increased confidence in the team's ability to respond to critical incidents.

Learnings

Since the Working Dialogue, DFCC SRT has been called upon to respond to several critical regional incidents within the Department. More specifically, a high-volatile incident occurred at a facility, and DFCC SRT was activated to respond. Once the team arrived at that facility, the DFCC Team Commander was notified that DFCC SRT would take the lead in the response. Recently, the team was activated to conduct a special midnight security operation at another facility, and that facility did not use their own SRT; the DFCC SRT was relied on to complete the assignment.

One of the greatest lessons learned from this Dialogue was that having an adequate number of certified, willing and able SRT members gives peace of mind that the institution can be managed effectively in an unforeseen emergency or disturbance. To be an SRT member requires the individual to embody all of the Department's seven values, specifically commitment and support. The Deerfield Complex SRT continues to be at full strength, exhibiting a high level of morale and confidence knowing they have the full support of facility staff and administration. As Captain Harris, DFCC SRT Commander noted, "New staff come in the door eager and excited to join the team and demonstrate the camaraderie they see amongst team members."

Conference Session Extracts

From the consideration of the case study with conference participants

Speaker: I've got a question, based on your Working Dialogue. Which gate did you feel like it was the most difficult to get out of the current situation?

Dianne Motley: Although we are a new facility, our staff were not new to dialogue and some people were already introduced to the concept, so there was not a struggle with either. Normally in a Working Dialogue you get people to talk about what they would like to see. I would say the first phase was getting people prepared and talking about the goals that we were trying to reach. After those were identified the rest flowed pretty smoothly during the two times that we met, and it was really great to come together for the follow-up and acknowledge the goals of the process. I would say the initial phase, the initial gate, was the gate that we probably had more issues with. But overall because people were already familiar with the process we didn't really get stuck. It was really an awesome Working Dialogue, I don't want to boast and say we didn't have any issues at all, but it went pretty smooth.

Joseph Owen: I'll follow what Ms. Motley said. We waited till we have been operating for about three or four months, during which we had new intakes coming in and learning from those experiences. Identifying the current situation and getting new staff comfortable with each other was therefore the biggest obstacle, but, like Miss Motley said, with everybody coming from a shared background with a foundation in dialogue, we were able to navigate through that pretty easily. We also had a topic that everyone was interested in and that was key.

Speaker: One of the things you mentioned was including the wants of offenders. Did you actually have them in the Working Dialogue and, if you did, how did you include them?

Joseph: Great question. They were not in our first three dialogues, which were developed by staff, because at that point people were coming in and going out fairly quickly because of the pandemic. So we only had secondhand information from the people who dealt with the population such as the probation officers who worked in the case management aspect, the spectrum substance abuse counsels who were working

	individually with them and security staff who were dealing with them day to day. Now that our population is going through the training the next layer is to bring them into the circle.
Speaker:	I would also add that we are at an advantage at our facility because it is a smaller facility. Most of the security staff, all the probation officers, work very closely together, and I'm one of the probation officers at the facility. So I was able to directly observe how it was impacting the probationers in our program.
Speaker:	I was looking through the screens to see who here is not from the DOC [Department of Corrections] and wondering what incentives mean to them.
Speaker:	I was wondering what the top three incentives for this dialogue were.
Joseph:	Food and being able to reach out to their families were the top two, and then casual dress-down day was a third option that really appealed to people. Those are the incentives in our environment here in corrections. Then again, if you are developing an incentive plan you have to look at your target population and what is important to them. You can take the framework we used here and apply it to any situation with any group you're working with, though. We had a larger benefit from dialogue because it is a new facility with the new staff. We were able to bond together and build stronger relationships of trust as well as communicating and hearing all the voices present at the table and passing on what came out of the dialogue to our other staff who then also got excited about the process. The shared meaning of developing something that could be impactful to the population that we serve really energized our staff too. In a way that was a big benefit of the dialogue process, bringing people together to have their voices heard towards the common mission or goal of creating each incentive.
Speaker:	Are any of the other CCAPs [Community Corrections Alternative Programs] in the state modeling your program?
Joseph:	Yes. We have periodic steering committees where the CCAP groups meet together, and the information has been passed on to each one of those. CCAP are also developing their incentive plans to impact their population.

Speaker: I had an experience several years back where, as a unit manager, I did not have the right people in the process when developing incentives. The incentive plan was not going well because the incentives we came up with were not what the inmates were interested in obtaining. I now realize whether it is inmates or staff it seems that food is a big motivating factor, and in some female facilities we are actually paying money to wear jeans on Fridays. Some people outside of an institution might think that is insane, but if you're never allowed to wear them it is an incentive that definitely works and use the money to raise funds. So really looking at who your target is and knowing your target is important.

Postscript
The authors' reflections, written some months after the conference

Our theme, "Always Ready, Always There," emulates our approach. We are always ready for any task at hand, and always we are there to provide a special response when needed. Personal interaction with the Special Response Team (S.R.T.) keeps the team in front of staff—answering questions, providing examples and modeling the way. An optimistic and informative approach supports an avenue for those seeking personal development or S.R.T. Program graduation. Ongoing recruitment provides a fresh set of eyes throughout the journey, and this approach shows that it is always an asset to have the right people at the table.

What we realized during the process was that "learning is a journey." The impact of staff engagement has proven to be a pivotal approach to success. As leaders and Dialogue Practitioners in the industry, we realize the importance of involving others in problem resolution. Employee engagement allows the process to become easy, flowing, targeted and inclusive.

After presenting at the conference, our team exhibited the same excitement. They displayed the same passion to recruit and maintain a well-equipped, established and trained S.R.T. The practices continued and many benefited from the lessons we learned as a Deerfield family. Building from the ground up allowed us to lay a foundation that will provide potential growth for years to come. As a result of this experience, our S.R.T. membership has increased, and positive outcomes continue to be realized.

In summation, this experience was a great example of leadership. Many of us have moved on to new work locations; however, this approach can be used by any facility to strengthen their S.R.T. and enhance their operation.

Section Nine

Putting Dialogue to Work to Improve Operations

This section echoes the first section in this book, 'Putting Dialogue to Work in Organisations'. In the opening of the book, we considered putting Dialogue to work in commercial and social organisations, but the same challenge of fragmentation is present in every organisation of any size. In this section we consider how this plays out in local government, and specifically in the Virginia Department of Corrections. The traditional way decision-making is distributed in organisations – through hierarchy, specialisation and location – leads to dislocations and misunderstandings across organisational boundaries. As a process, Dialogue extends acr0oss organisational lines and can bring everyone affected by a decision into the consideration. The participation and contribution of different perspectives results in better solutions, and the consequent impact of any decision can be assessed before finalising the decision. In this section we consider five such examples.

TyKeshae Fowlkes Tucker, Andrea D Wilson and Karen Fleming held an interface Dialogue to restore clear communications between operations and the medical / dental staff. They successfully resolved conflicts that had interrupted appointments, outside work and inmate movements across the prison.

A Community office with seasoned staff and low turnover can become complacent – unless **Alfreda M Shinns, Jillian Mackling and Caitlin M Sweeney** are on hand! In their Working Dialogue they used SWOT analysis to determine the 'current situation', leading to enhanced participation and learning.

Shakita Bland, Tama Celi and Warren McGehee used a dialogic approach to improve the 'research peer reviews' that help the creation of information needed for a data-driven agency like VADOC. They found adequate time, clarity of purpose and thorough documentation make all the difference.

Putting Dialogue to Work to Improve Operations

The $100m question is why does VADOC struggle to hire and retain staff? **Matt Burgess, Michelle Hicks and Angela Hill** raised staff awareness, and found employees desire more communication, mutual respect between employees, and that new employees need trusted colleagues or mentors.

Shannon Fuller and Gregory Holloway addressed concerns of the experienced Chiefs of Housing and Programs (CHAPs) that operational, tracking and classification activities distracted them from their treatment accountabilities – resulting in better understanding and a balanced new work profile.

Mind the Gap: Bridging Communication between Medical and Operations

TyKeshae Fowlkes Tucker, Andrea D. Wilson and Karen Fleming

Situation

Central Virginia Correctional Unit 13 (CVCU) plays an integral part in assigning inmates to outside work employment, as well as maintaining consistent movement within the institution. The operation and management of these areas are critical in ensuring that a schedule is adhered to by all staff daily. The facility experienced conflicts with medical and dental appointments, which interrupted outside work activities and movement within the institution, inconsistency with the delivery of the master pass list and staffing issues. A breakdown in communication between the medical department and security staff led to a need for both areas to work together in bridging the gap between communication and operation.

Objectives

Both medical and security had its own perspectives and mindset on responsibilities, processes and procedures. Due to the breakdown in communication, a lack of understanding, a lack of knowledge and inconsistencies, there was a need to bridge the gap in order to improve functionality of operations and management. Our goal at Unit 13 was to bring cohesion and clarity to a painful division between uniformed staff, which are medical and security. When medical and security staff work together, the institution is more effective and efficient in delivering services for the facility.

Method

In the midst of the pandemic, participants assembled during December 2020 for this occasion. This marked the first time within the Covid-19 pandemic where all security supervisors were physically together from all shifts. All participants were safely seated exactly six feet from one another by color-coded chairs. At the onset of the meeting, both medical personnel and security were instructed to sit in specific colored chairs. This seating arrangement allowed each staff person to face a person from the opposite department. Partners had the opportunity to tell a story about themselves and then tell the entire group what they learned about their partner. This approach set the atmosphere for co-workers to learn something about each other, which offered insight rather than adversity.

The group quickly learned that they had many things in common as well as learning some surprising things about each other. Partners immersed into each other's experiences while engaging in conversation and gained new perspective about their partner, as well as other participants. One might ask how storytelling about oneself contributes to the communication and operation of the facility. Glad you asked—here's how.

Sharing experiences allows others to gain better knowledge with the storyteller and come to an understanding of their point of view. When a person retells someone else's story, that person takes the voice of a bystander and removes self from the story. Through this exercise, a tone was set that allowed both departments to identify how a lack of understanding and knowledge of roles and responsibilities causes mass confusion from the other department's perspectives.

Outcomes

Approximately one month later, participants had the opportunity to check in if they needed clarification or wanted to discuss the changes created from this dialogue. Although no participants responded, it is evident that both groups walked away with a better understanding of medical and security needs. They also established a better working relationship between the departments, which enhanced communication. Each department is now committed to making a daily effort in working together when problems arise. When a problem arises with transportation for outside workers or a duplicate master pass list is created, security supervision and medical have been working in partnership to ensure the process is followed properly.

Learnings

Our efforts in bringing the teams together gave participants ownership not only of understanding each other, but also of understanding the needs of the operation. A couple of the participants who doubted that change was possible emerged from the dialogue as leaders. A security supervisor and a medical supervisor paved the way for this new journey in bridging the gap between the two departments.

A change in attitude and appreciation was gained from the dialogue. The story of medical and security supervision continues. The commitment to work in unity prevails.

The term "mind the gap" originated in London, used to inform travelers throughout the day to watch out for the space between the platform and train when exiting and entering trains daily. Minding the gap at CVCU takes repetition, practice, and habituation to efficiently and effectively complete tasks, adjust to daily challenges and communicate our needs to each other.

Conference Session Extracts
From the consideration of the case study with conference participants

TyKeshae Fowlkes Tucker: The biggest eye-opener was a lot of people in areas that worked together every single day really didn't understand the complexities of what each person's responsibility was in getting things done. People communicated as far as saying, "I need this," or "I need that," but not really understanding what's behind each other's requests, or what goes into it.

Speaker: I agree. I'm a supervisor and I have to be very conscious to be respectful of what my people say and how they feel. It could be something about the way that I'm supervising them or there might be something that I should do differently. I welcome the feedback because after the dialogue is over, when the whispering starts, that is when the real dialogue starts.

Speaker: I found, on more than one occasion, that the big voices just started solving the problems. The majors are used to jumping in and just fixing things. So, to make sure everybody goes by the steps, follows the gates and the practices, and gets to voice their challenges, you have to be aware that we're a bunch of go-getters in this business. We want to fix it: "We are just going to tell you how, we're gonna fix it." But to get group thinking going, you have to pump the breaks and hold on: "Let's hear everybody's voice." In the last dialogue I was in I had to step out because I had a meeting to go to. I stepped out for 20 minutes and when I came back, they were all done. I was like, "Whoa, wait a minute. You're not done. I know you didn't follow these steps and you didn't do this and that." We had to go back, retrace it all and really go through the process. It's a challenge because it is not how people normally behave or solve problems. Most folks, especially those with authority, just want to give you the answer and you must go do it. It is a case of command and control.

Speaker: Like you said, we are all go-getters. We are where we are because we see that there needs to be an effective change—we want to be a change agent and we are able to make decisions the way they should be made. I think it's really important that we also realize that there's a process for a reason, and that we need to ensure we authentically stick to the process. The biggest voices might be the ones that get heard the most and solve the problems but it might be the really quiet ones that never talk who really have the best ideas, and we need to hear them.

Speaker: We love the focus of the dialogic practice, but there are some people who were already here before dialogue existed. They are used to command and control, and some of them fear using dialogue the way we hope the department will do now. I know because I have been there. It has not been my experience, but I know that there are people I worked with that have felt concerned and are not always willing to share openly and authentically about what they think is going on or could be done.

Speaker: I individually talked to everybody, by themselves, in a little interview to say, "Hey, how's things going? How's things been going since the Working Dialogue?" That's where I got input from people, through individually talking about their experiences. I found that folks who were not getting along are best buddies now, and they're doing the process like it is supposed to be done. I think my "aha" moment, which I did not expect to see, was how relationships were formed from this, professionally and personally, and how these relationships played a big part as well.

Speaker: I wanted to add that we can't think that we're in Utopia, that we will go and do a Working Dialogue and then things are perfect. Sometimes Working Dialogues take multiple sessions to get to the desired outcome, and something, which affects multiple departments, is that people have different levels of discipline. There's a level of understanding that needs to be obtained before you can even get to solutions, and desired outcomes can take a while. I've been involved in regional Working Dialogues that have taken several months.

Andrea Wilson: In this Working Dialogue people only met once. They experienced a pause, giving them time to think and talk together, to talk things through. It's a small facility and there were some glitches and some confusion but by them getting together, by talking it out and seeing things from a different perspective, they were able to say, "Okay, we can do this." Did some things happen afterwards? Yes. They figured out, if this happens, then this is what we need to do. And they started to do that.

Speaker: A lot of the time you'll have a Working Dialogue but once you get through all the gates there's no end result. But with this case study, it looks like everyone did a great job on creating that end result because the superintendent didn't have to do anything else—they carried it forward by themselves.

Postscript
The authors' reflections written some months after the conference

Not Shown: Karen Fleming

When a collective group of people comes together, without a doubt some form of communication will join the assembly. The impact of our check-in informed the trajectory of how this dialogue began, and it was a monumental start to change in the making. Good, bad or indifferent, stories shape the identify of a group. The participants had an opportunity to voice their challenges through storytelling. In this manner, stories transformed lives in a challenging, compelling and inviting manner.

In addition, communication between departments is the foundation of good teamwork. A team environment where people are able to respect each other and get along well is more productive. This process provided some additional insights on problem-solving through traditional communication and through the sharing of stories. There was a need to collaborate, and learning from others while listening and thinking together allowed perceptual differences to yield solutions that fully satisfied the concerns of all stakeholders.

Reviewing the extract, a speaker comment jumped out for me: "I think my aha moment, which I did not expect to see, was how relationships were formed from this, professionally and personally, and these relationships played a big part as well." I find myself agreeing as it is my belief that in the age that we currently live in, with its unique collection of values, beliefs, behaviors and attitudes in the workplace, these types of dialogue are needed to foster how we work together.

Using SWOT and Working Dialogue to Improve and Strengthen Our Work Unit

Alfreda M. Shinns, Jillian S. Mackling and Caitlin M. Sweeney

Situation

Alexandria Probation and Parole consists of 15 employees: eight Probation Officers, two Senior Probation Officers, one Chief, one Deputy Chief and three administrative staff. Through community partnerships and collaborative relationships, the District strives to build a healing environment for probationers and parolees, their families, and for the community at large. This office is fortunate to have a large team of seasoned officers with very little turnover. By completing the SWOT analysis (Strengths, Weaknesses, Opportunities and Threats) as a unit, staff were able to identify those areas that have become challenging as well as those areas where they excel. Their analysis identified complacency as a big challenge for the District.

Objectives

Alexandria Probation and Parole utilized a Working Dialogue along with the SWOT skills to solicit staff's voices towards identifying where we have become complacent and areas that could use more concentration to benefit the department, our District, and the population we serve. The Alexandria Management team met for a dialogue at which time it became evident that there was a concern about the possibility of staff reaching complacency. At that time, leadership decided that utilizing the SWOT would be appropriate for a Working Dialogue with staff. Promoting growth within the District has been the biggest challenge with a seasoned staff; therefore it was imperative to recognize and affirm our strengths in conjunction with pinpointing areas that staff associated with opportunities, weaknesses and threats. The end result would be that changes were required.

Method

We started our Working Dialogue with our entire office in May of 2019. To examine our current situation, we went through each section of the SWOT and identified items for each. Each staff member offered their authentic voice on what they thought fit in the SWOT for the District and came to an agreement at the end of that part of the process. Some items included in the current-situation phase of the Working Dialogue included the following: *Strengths*—Staff are able to express what they do in their own words; the staff offers great re-entry services and re-entry collaboration; and personnel feel appreciated and supported. *Weaknesses*—Staff are not fully knowledgeable about the Department's business practices; staff do not see where we can improve as a District; and new initiatives, practices or trainings being introduced takes a toll on our small office. *Opportunities*—Training to stretch staff growth; receiving notice when outside agencies will be in our office; and building better relationships with neighboring Districts. *Threats*—Relationship with community stakeholders as a whole needs strengthening; expectations need to be identified and a transparent environment needs to be created on all levels; also, more opportunity for promotions is needed within the District.

Once we were done exploring the current situation, we discussed what we wanted for our desired outcomes. These included: all staff feeling supported and heard; staff being open to being stretched and experiencing growth; being less complacent; creating an environment and District where everyone is connected to and supportive of our purpose, vision and mission; and strengthening our relationship with neighboring Districts.

We performed the first two sections of the Working Dialogue on one day and reconvened on another day to continue our work on the Working Dialogue. While looking at changes required we identified the following items to include in our action plan: learning teams will conduct dialogues based on ideas suggested by staff members; trainings regarding each business practice will be reviewed and conducted during staff meetings; staff will continue to volunteer to attend trainings and meetings outside of our office, including volunteering on committees, projects and initiatives or business practices; learning teams will incorporate the use of role plays to improve staff being comfortable with aspects of case supervision; and staff will participate in at least one collaborative event each year with a neighboring District.

Outcomes

We are proud to report we were successful in implementing our action plan. Despite the challenges presented by Covid-19, staff continued to participate on committees, special projects, and department initiatives and business practices. Examples include the Domestic Violence Intervention Program, Opioid Workgroup, and High Intensity Drug Trafficking Area. Staff meetings and learning teams provided the opportunity to enhance our knowledge and skills. We incorporated in-service training on a variety of topics, including Medication-Assisted Treatment and Preliminary Parole Violation Hearings. We conducted role plays related to case supervision, such as reviewing risk needs assessment results with probationers. We also held dialogues based on suggestions from staff. In the summer of 2021, we celebrated Probation and Parole Officer Week with a kickoff picnic with Arlington Probation and Parole. We hope to continue this as an annual tradition, including the possibility of expanding it to include additional neighboring Districts.

Learnings

Through their own voice, staff recognized their strong relationships with stakeholders and, even though we are a small office, we are able to assign specializations to individual staff members. We also learned in some instances that introducing new techniques or changes to the VADOC prompts our seasoned staff to pause. Staff also recognized the areas where we have incorporated the Department's business practices into daily operations.

We found that combining SWOT analysis and Dialogue enhanced our ability to identify and develop strategies to address areas of improvement while simultaneously celebrating Unit accomplishments.

Conference Session Extracts
From the consideration of the case study with conference participants

Jillian Mackling: Part of the outcome of our goals was to have at least one collaborative event each year with a neighboring district. We agreed on outcomes when we created our goals in the Working Dialogue. You should always leave a Working Dialogue knowing what each person's role is, how each person going to achieve that task and by when is it due. Then you have to make sure that you follow up to make sure those tasks were done, or if any other actions are needed. Every single staff member in that district participated in a SWOT. First we gathered their collective voices with the SWOT, which then prioritized what went into our Working Dialogue. So there was buy-in that this is something that will help our district grow and develop, to be even better than we already are. None of us are perfect and there's always room for growth but staff were very open to doing these things because they were things which everyone thought were needed for the district.

Speaker: In our group, we talked about the SWOT analysis in terms of how it creates an important structure, which is very important not just for the dialogue, but also to include other stakeholders. You cannot have only a certain level of leaders, or whoever, folks need to be included from the top down and from the bottom up.

There is also an accountability piece. Once you do the analysis, you must know how you are going follow up. I've done SWOT analysis for quite a few years and part of strategic planning is measuring if you follow through on what you say you are going to do. Follow up is key, and you should also allow enough time for completion. Sometimes there is pressure to do things quickly but I think it's important to also make sure you are patient and do things slowly so you can capture everyone's point of view rather than just a select few.

Speaker: Our conversation shifted and went to the question of succession planning, and one of the members in our group said that it is the biggest threat to our agency. When all this wisdom leaves the department, when you have people with 40-plus years leave, then all their knowledge is gone. That is why it's so important for us to have these discussions, and also write down the succession planning. People are retiring left and right, and the folks that are still here are left picking up the pieces. There is no manual on how to be chief or how to be deputy or how to be a warden, so we need these things in place for people that are coming after us.

Speaker: In another dialogue I was in, a question came up about community relationships and how to strengthen those who are in places that are being affected. What I then heard was there are ways in which what is happening outside is affecting people's experience on the inside. It made me wonder if there are SWOT analyses and Working Dialogues that can be done at the Community level with folks who are within the DOC [Department of Corrections] and without.

Alfreda Shinns: Succession planning was one of the things that came out of both the SWOT and the Working Dialogue. The follow-up to that was that the leadership team met and we did a Working Dialogue on succession planning. We then created action plans to help put this into fruition because our goal is to try to figure out how to put all this in writing. I want to go back to when someone asked how we could use SWOT or a Working Dialogue with some of our community stakeholders who are outside of DOC. Well, what I would tell you is that we have not done a SWOT or a Working Dialogue with any of our community stakeholders, but what we have done is conducted a Dialogue with our re-entry council to discuss bringing in someone that was on probation or parole into our re-entry council. I'm going to pitch this over to Jillian, because I believe she facilitated that Dialogue.

Jillian: I don't know how familiar you are with a Working Dialogue? First you ask what the current situation is, and then you ask, "What do you want it to be?"—not, "How are you going to get there?" A lot of people who go into the second phase of Working Dialogue immediately ask, "How do you fix it?" But no, first you should just verbalize what is needed. The next question is, "How do we get there?" How do we go from point A to point B? So, once you have the current situation and the desired outcome, only then do you go into how you are going to get there and create an action plan on what you are going to do. Our Working Dialogue with the re-entry council happened right before Covid hit and although we were able to start it, we still had a second day before it was finished go into the Working Dialogue to finish working on it. We created an initial action plan, and we are still working on those items. One of the main items was about getting re-entering citizens onto our re-entry council, and it is a work in progress.

Postscript

The authors' reflections written some months after the conference

When I first introduced the SWOT, as a Working Dialogue to my staff, I had no idea that it would lead us to this place and time. Moving forward, when I submitted it to be considered for the "World Needs Dialogue!-4" conference, I did not know what impact it would have on the participants and if it would be a success. I discovered that putting a case study together takes time and needs specific details in order for it to successfully reach others. In addition, I realized how important it is to have all voices at the table who will be impacted by a decision. During the entire process I realized the importance of not only having dialogues but also the positive effects it has when shared with others. At the conference, the participants shifted the conversation to succession planning and shared how they could use our case study to create a succession plan for their unit.

Jillian Mackling described the process as meaningful. She found the process of working together as an intricate unit produced an amazing product due to the use of communication between us. She added that the one thing that was reinforced throughout the process was relying on and trusting your team. Jillian implored everyone to use the Dialogic Skills (especially the practices) in order to continue to grow to become the best version of themselves.

I found the creation of this paper to be the epitome of what working together as a team looks like, and why it's important to empower others to act so that they can also see the worth. There is no doubt that Dialogic skills are needed if you want to be inclusive, grow and have positive life-changing impacts.

Caitlin Sweeney found one impactful takeaway from our case study work: the reminder that Dialogue can and should be used as a proactive tool, not just as a reaction or response to events that may occur.

We would like to thank Jillian Mackling and Caitlin Sweeney of the Virginia Department of Corrections for collaborating with me on this case study and Director Harold Clarke for supporting this process.

Research Peer Review as Part of the VADOC Healing Environment

Shakita Bland, Tama Celi and Warren McGehee

Situation

The Virginia Department of Corrections (VADOC) is responsible for the care, security, and well-being of over 30,000 inmates, 60,000 supervisees, and 13,000 staff. Our mission is to help people do better. To accomplish this, each person within the VADOC is accountable to ensure that the organization works efficiently, effectively, and continuously, with minimal disruptions. Agency culture and environment are critical to achieving the agency's mission. VADOC has adopted a Healing Environment that is "purposefully created by the way we work together and treat each other, encouraging all to use their initiative to make positive, progressive changes to improve lives. It is safe, respectful, and ethical—where people are both supported and challenged to be accountable for their actions."*

Objectives

VADOC is a data-driven agency and makes evidence-based decisions. The Research Unit plays an important role in establishing, measuring and supporting the agency's evidence-based decisions. Quality assurance and accuracy are integral to making solid, informed decisions and, accordingly, the Research Unit has established a rigorous internal peer review mechanism. Dialogue is an important part of this process.

Method

The peer review process is a method that offers support, and challenges, staff to create information that is user friendly and easily understood by the targeted audience. There are multiple layers of the peer review process, starting with peer feedback to the staff member, followed by manager review, and finally Assistant Director and/or Research Director review prior to moving on to the other agency leadership.

---

* VADOC Healing Environment statement

282 | Putting Dialogue to Work to Improve Operations

In order for the process to work, participants need to be willing to provide and accept candid feedback from their peers. Prior to the introduction of Dialogue, Unit leadership was finding that even after peer review, reports were rising through the review process without appropriate corrections occurring. A Dialogue was held in July of 2021 to discuss the Healing Environment and staff accountability in the peer review process.

To set the tone, the Dialogue started with a check-in: "Looking at the VADOC Healing Environment statement, name one part that is important to us—and why. Avoid following [merely agreeing with another] if you can." For this Virtual Dialogue we split into two smaller groups to explore the following: "Part of the Healing Environment is accountability. In the Peer Review process, who is accountable for the content of reports? The staff? The reviewer? Or both? What can we do to ensure the integrity of the peer review process and hold each other accountable?"

Outcomes

The Dialogue groups determined that, while the main responsibility for accuracy is on staff members, the reviewer also shares responsibility for ensuring that the final product is accurate and on point. The Dialogue groups made several recommendations critical to an effective peer review process. First, we need to ensure that reviewers have enough time to review thoroughly. Second, it is important that the reviewer understands the purpose of the report and the analysis behind the results in the report. Third, it is important for the staff to keep thorough documentation and make it available to the reviewer.

Learnings

Through this process, we learned important lessons. An effective check-in helped set the tone and mindset for the Dialogue. Staff involvement in developing the peer review process improved the process and outcomes. The resulting process is clear and understandable to all, and staff understand the expectations. Additionally, effective Dialogues can be held in a virtual environment successfully. Simply put, Dialogue worked.

Conference Session Extracts
From the consideration of the case study with conference participants

Tama Celi: What was behind our Working Dialogue was that in order for research to be meaningful, it needs to be accurate. In order to help with that we had a peer review system. And then, after that was done, then the work would then go to the manager and then, finally, it would come up to me, before we send it out to other parts of the Agency.

I was receiving reports filled with errors, ranging from typos to formatting issues to numbers not being consistent or making sense. One, people weren't reviewing the reports like they were supposed to or, two, they weren't being candid about what they were seeing or, three, they didn't know better. I really didn't believe that they didn't know better. It had to be either they weren't reviewing them or they were just not being candid. So, I finally decided that I was going to take the problem to the group and do a Working Dialogue with them and let them figure out the solution to the problem.

Warren McGehee: We noticed that the person doing the review had no context. There was very little, if any, supporting information. We also noticed that people were not answering the question that was being asked for in the report. Without seeing the original request, the person who wrote the report might write it perfect and correct, but it wasn't what the requester asked for.

Shakita Bland: As an analyst looking at this, I believe we have to be fair. Dialogue teaches us about safe container building and trust, and about utilizing our voice. So, through this process we recognized that there are a lot of individuals that need to be held accountable. Speaking as a peer reviewer, I have to hold myself accountable for giving my fellow co-workers and analysts 100% candid information and candid feedback. It's only fair to them.

Tama: And the best way I can have your back is to give you that candid feedback and not just give a polite response.

We are going into the breakout rooms next. The questions that we'd like you to talk about are: Have you ever had staff be polite instead of holding each other to account? Why is this occurring, and what do you do about it?

(After return from the breakout rooms)

Shakita: Does someone want to give us some feedback? What did you all discuss?

Speaker: We talked about a couple different things about being polite instead of accountable. And one of the things we talked about was perspective. You know our politeness or our kindness can be perceived as weakness, sometimes. It can be easily misconstrued when we're trying to relay important information. We need this information...

Speaker: We also talked about how the Healing Environment starts with you, and with you being accountable, so when you're doing a peer-to-peer review you have to understand that just because a person is not your supervisor does not mean that they can't hold you accountable.

Shakita: I recognized within myself that I had responsibilities, but I wasn't holding myself accountable, because I was being polite. That was doing more harm than it was doing good.

Speaker: We looked at the fact that authentic voice is very important. There are lots of occasions that an answer is generated because it's what you think people *want* to hear instead of what really *needs* to be said. So authentic voice is huge, but with authentic voice comes respect and suspension. You must respect what people are saying, and you must use suspension to really see where a viewpoint is coming from. The authentic voice with respect and suspension are probably the most important things we talked about.

Speaker: But we do still have a strong chain of command, and I think this might also reinforce people being polite instead of being authentic.

Tama: I really like the idea of coaching up and coaching down: "You have a typo there, you spelled this wrong," or, "Hey, I don't understand this!" To me, that's an accomplishment because it means we've established enough relational trust that people are comfortable giving me feedback. And I need that feedback. None of us are perfect. I don't care how good you are, you are not perfect. We always need to be looking at each other's work and trying to get the best product that we can. We are a data-driven agency, we use research and we use information. It is imperative that we work this out right, because, otherwise, people are going to make some bad decisions. So, I really like the idea of coaching up and coaching down. I think it is critically important.

Postscript
An author's reflections written some months after the conference

The Peer Review process was designed as a method of accountability when reviewing work before it is presented to a manager. The level of accountability from the peer reviews, however, was sometimes inaccurate as some reviewers did not want to conduct an accurate review or hurt the feelings of those reviewed. This led to managers finding errors within the work, causing a delay in the response time and potentially delaying the deadline of the assignment.

During this process I learned that accountability is not something to be taken lightly. It is the responsibility of all to make sure that anything that is conducted and sent from our department is an accurate depiction of our unit. We all have a duty to make sure that the work we present is presented flawlessly.

This process has stimulated me to make sure that I provide my co-workers with honest, straight-forward, detailed and thorough feedback when conducting a peer review. I was fortunate to have the opportunity to work with both the Director of Research, Dr. Tama Celi, and the Assistant Director of Research, Warren McGehee. Professionally, it deepened my respect for both as they are truly great leaders. They make sure that we all have the tools to go as far as we want and to do the best job we can within the VADOC.

Employee Retention: How Do We Recover?

Matt Burgess, Michelle Hicks and Angela Hill

Situation

The Virginia Department of Corrections (VADOC) strives to hire trustworthy, dedicated staff and retain their employment for 20 to 30 years of professional service. While this employment strategy contrasts with the five-years-of-service trends in private industry, in corrections the employer and the employee greatly benefit from a long career history. Recently, the VADOC has struggled to hire and retain professional corrections employees. This challenge is widespread across the Department and has been exacerbated by the Covid-19 pandemic.

There are many advantages to being a VADOC corrections employee. Applicants, regardless of higher education levels, previous professional experience, or prior law enforcement training, are trained to become excellent security and nonsecurity employees, opening additional opportunities for career advancement and promotion. VADOC offers its employees competitive benefits packages, including health benefits, financial savings plans and retirement packages. Employment in the corrections field is truly a *professional career.*

With all of its perks, why does the Virginia Department of Corrections struggle to hire and retain staff to fill its rosters? Staff shortages have created a myriad of issues that are adding unprecedented stress throughout the entire Department. Staff shortages mean necessary security posts are inadequately filled, overall security is potentially lessened, and effective scheduling for inmate needs is becoming increasingly difficult. Existing staff is being overworked, resulting in staff burnout; seasoned, professional employees are leaving VADOC for their own mental and physical well-being. The result is even more vacant positions, even less staff to fill them, and even more employee burnout.

Newly hired and trained employees are leaving the Department soon after completing their extensive (DOC-funded), $40,000 training. They receive superior training from the VADOC, and then they use that training to receive superior pay from other law enforcement agencies. Furthermore, VADOC has excellent staff who have dedicated their entire career history to serving in corrections, but these staff are leaving because of stress from being overworked and underappreciated.

This employment breakup is the most detrimental to the Department because VADOC loses excellent staff and all of the wisdom and experience within them, meaning years of wisdom and experience can then no longer be shared with new employees.

The Virginia Department of Corrections needs to turn its employment epidemic around. How can VADOC competitively offer employment to surrounding communities? How can VADOC retain existing employees, both newly hired and seasoned professionals? The Department is seeking innovative solutions for attracting new employees and retaining its seasoned professionals.

Objectives

In 2020 the Greensville Correctional Center, Virginia's largest correctional facility, facilitated in-depth Dialogues regarding employee retention. The Dialogues aimed to gather data from current staff (both new and seasoned) and staff who have left their VADOC employment. During the sessions, Dialogue practitioners focused on employment components that can promote change rather than explore issues such as pay, over which participants have no control.

Method

The process for these Dialogues included in-person, Working Dialogue sessions, virtual interviews and phone interviews. We began with an in-person Working Dialogue with about 10 participants, then moved to Virtual meetings due to pandemic-related restrictions. These meetings consisted of two Practitioners and five or six staff members. Seeking to gather data from many employees, the participant pool was made of all ranks of security staff, from both breaks and shifts, and all departments of nonsecurity. Participation included a broad range of years of VADOC service. Adequately trained Dialogue Practitioners utilized several different practices to build safe containers, encourage authentic voice, and continually maintain fidelity.

For the Dialogues and the interviews, a series of questions were asked to all participants and the responses were recorded as given. Each Dialogue opened with the same check-in question:

On a scale of one to 10 (with one being the least and 10 being the greatest), where would you rate your overall job satisfaction?

The interviews were conducted in the form of Skillful Conversations and Generative Dialogues. Interview questions addressed specific areas of concern. The content of the questions related to staff retention, staff morale, overall employee focus, pros and cons of working at Greensville Correctional Center, and the expectations and needs of employees from their employer—in this case, Greensville Correctional Center and the VADOC.

The check-out was designed to bring a measure of personal accountability into the Dialogue. The check-out question was:

What can you do to raise your level of job satisfaction?

The duration for this particular dialogic case study was approximately 45 days. The Dialogue for employee retention, however, is ongoing. Another Dialogue session will be scheduled for the fall of 2021.

Outcomes

Outcomes of the check-in averaged a satisfaction ranging from four to seven. Check-in answers were based on the relationship that employees have with their direct supervisors. An employee's specific department, the length of VADOC service, and his or her personal views also played a role in employees' feelings of value and appreciation.

Outcomes of the Dialogue's questions included 1) employees' desire for increased communication and 2) mutual respect (giving and receiving) among all correctional employees. Staff shortages were recognized as a concern by many individuals. Professionalism and being a part of a team were seen as positive motivators.

Outcomes of the check-out question mostly focused on the employee's responsibility to maintaining a positive attitude and assisting others in their job duties.

Learnings

In conclusion, many staff members had the same concerns regardless of their role, position or time in the Department. Specifically related to employee retention, the Dialogue illustrated reasons why employees do not seek promotion, recruit others to work for VADOC, or fully dedicate themselves to their corrections career.

Our intention was to open lines of communication and to raise staff awareness on this multifaceted, department-wide concern. We have accomplished this on an institutional level, and we continue to encourage staff to share ideas and feedback.

This Dialogue also showed a need for new employees to have trusted colleagues to address concerns as they integrate into VADOC employment. The relationship between new employees and Dialogue Practitioners could be a starting point to retention of new employees.

Conference Session Extracts

From the consideration of the case study with conference participants

Speaker: Rather than just training new supervisors we need to help create leaders, as opposed to having policy lead us. Obviously, we have policies that we have to follow, but sometimes being too policy-driven and rigid can make staff feel like they can't come to their supervisor and be open and speak freely. I'm a firm believer in being there and being present for your staff, asking those questions and saying, "Hey, I can only get better if you give me the feedback." I think when they know their supervisors are available it helps staff to feel supported and safe. Sometimes, unfortunately, supervisors don't have that mentality, though. They are promoted to fill the spot, as opposed to looking at how they can be the leader that the district and or the institution needs.

Matt Burgess: That resonates with me. We need leaders, not just supervisors, because people will follow leaders. If they set the model, if they live it, if they're working it, if they're using dialogue and if they're showing people that they know how to communicate, people will follow them.

Speaker: We talked about checking on everyone, not just on brand new people. I think it's important to realize that even though someone's passed their probation period it doesn't mean they will stay forever. Whether it's two years or 10 years, be proactive. Let's not wait till somebody's fussing or they're walking off the plank on the side of the ship. Let's check in, let's dialogue. Let's be sure that we're monitoring everyone's pulse and trying to accommodate them as best we can, and hopefully that'll help everyone want to stay.

Speaker: If you've been to Louisa [Virginia] lately you may have seen the McDonalds there is paying $21 an hour, but a correctional officer gets paid $18.27. That is a pretty stark contrast. It's not necessarily what somebody will say in an exit interview, because they know there's not more money, but we are not blind to that. Often the Feds offer money after we trained people and then they go for triple the salary we can't pay.

I do like the idea of checking in, which the previous speaker just mentioned. We don't want it to be an exit interview. We want an interim progress review, and to then for them to have a meeting with their supervisor and address some of their concerns. It might be a problem though if they assume their concerns are going to be run up the chain. But we have to come up with some ideas because there's only so many fingers and toes to fill the holes in the dam.

Matt: I agree, we need to address not just the salary needs of new correctional officers but also salary needs across the whole department, and salary increases for the people who have been in the department for a long time. I agree that we don't want to have exit interviews, we want interviews with people.

Speaker: I'm following a lot of what has already been said. In our smaller group, we actually had three people from the institutions who said that they were overworked and underappreciated. It was also mentioned that it would be nice if officers were told exactly what they were getting into before they said, "Okay, I'm gonna be a corrections officer." Then there wouldn't be the uncertainty of having to do something you never thought you would have to do before the day it happened. We also talked about the dynamic not necessarily being great when we first started. Some of us wanted to leave, but luckily things turned around because there was also a family dynamic. Someone mentioned that when your brothers and sisters are in the room you get on each other's nerves, which is to be expected, but at the end of the day you are a family, you work things out. You dialogue and you move forward.

The officers also mentioned that they want to hold people accountable when they don't come to work, but right now, they need them. How do you address the issue of holding people accountable when some people are constantly coming to work, day in and day out, doing what they're supposed to do, and then you have others who don't, but you need them anyway?

Speaker: A member of our group put forward the idea of "stay" interviews. You know, we're focused on why people are leaving, but we're not necessarily focused on why people are staying. And even in a dialogue, regardless of whether those people felt disrespected or whether they were happy or not, they are currently still employed with the department. So why are they staying and putting up with all that when they have a choice to leave? We could possibly follow up on exit interviews with people who are still not comfortable to come forward with why they're leaving. Is there a follow up process, shortly down the road, where we could say, "Hey, can we have another conversation about why you left?" We can provide training all day long, but if somebody doesn't come to you and say, "Hey, this person thought what you said was disrespectful to them," you are not going to know how to adjust your behavior, and then it continues on indefinitely.

Postscript

The authors' reflections written some months after the conference

Last year we conducted and presented a case study on a prevalent problem in the VADOC, which is the hiring and retention of employees. We held Working Dialogues and examined the issue from several viewpoints to gain a comprehensive understanding of some of the issues we faced as a department. We felt that we have examined the question in some depth; however, we were posing the question for the upcoming forum and not providing answers or solutions.

This was a serious challenge, and I was a little apprehensive about presenting it as a case study. The response indicated that this was a subject that many individuals were examining, not just within VADOC. Some of the ideas presented were exactly what we needed, a different and fresh perspective. These included proposals for interviews with employees, chosen randomly, to find out what is working and where we are falling short of meeting employee expectations. They could be small-group or individual Dialogues—if done in a timely manner, we could address recurring issues before they lead to an employee seeking a new career. We also are observing new initiatives in the field; for example, we have seen that the legislature has provided substantial pay adjustments for security officers and supervisors, and across-the-board increases for all staff.

We are still short-staffed, yet this is a step in the right direction. We are seeing new employees entering the department. Our ongoing challenge is to retain them and provide positive avenues of growth and development. As Dialogue practitioners, in accord with Department Healing Environment Ambassadors, we are seeking ways to connect with and encourage not only new but all current staff members in institutions and Probation and Parole offices throughout Virginia. Employment and careers with VADOC will require an ongoing effort to reveal areas where we can continue to expend energy and effort to improve and make employment attractive to staff.

The conference afforded an opportunity to obtain information we did not have, and that was our intent. Since the case study I have observed that this is a nationwide challenge. Segments of the population are seeking a different style of employment, including work from home, freelance etc. We have limited availability of these types of positions and need staff to be present at our facilities. Many other employers are facing similar challenges and we will do well to observe and learn methods used by others to navigate through the changing face of employee/employer interactions.

Learning from my experience at the last conference I have chosen to try and address other concerns in our Criminal Justice System. I look forward to engaging with members and guests to gain perspective regarding this subject.

Remaining Focused on What Has Proven to Work Best

Shannon Fuller and Gregory Holloway

Situation

In 2018, the Chief of Housing and Program Managers (CHAPS) participated in a survey initiated by the Virginia Department of Corrections (VADOC) to look at a number of challenges the managers were facing. The survey revealed that operational and housing unit issues and inmate classification, along with managing and tracking learning teams for all staff members at their assigned facilities, required a majority of their time. The large amount of time required for operational issues, in turn, hindered the time available for implementing evidence-based (scientifically based) practices. At the time of the survey there were 24 CHAPS across the state. The 24 CHAPs had been employed by VADOC for an average of 19 years and ranged from six to 28 years of total service.

Objectives

Multiple desired outcomes were identified during the Working Dialogue which included: 1) Re-structure CHAP's role in classification, 2) Hold true to CHAP's Employee Work Profile as it related to evidence-based practices, programs, and re-entry, 3) For all leadership and staff to have a better understanding of the CHAP's role, and 4) To have statewide consistency for CHAP's role and duties at each facility.

Method

Following the survey, Regional Operations Chief Gregory Holloway identified and pulled together Wardens, Assistant Wardens, Chief of Housing and Program Managers and Statewide Evidence-Based Practices Managers from all three regions to participate in a Working Dialogue to think together to improve the CHAP's focus on implementation of evidence-based practices.

The successful Working Dialogue was completed in May of 2018 at the Academy of Staff Development. Crystal Butler and Shannon Fuller facilitated the Working Dialogue.

Following the Working Dialogue, a work group was coordinated to restructure the CHAP's role in inmate classification and to revise the CHAP's employee work profile. The work group was led by Shen-fen-Lee, Nikita Bradshaw and Monica Robinson. The work group met and sent revisions to the Employee Work Profile and recommendations, to reduce the CHAP's role in Inmate Classification, to Department of Corrections Leadership. The revised Employee Work Profile and Inmate Classification revisions were reviewed and approved by DOC Leadership.

Outcomes

The Chief of Housing and Programs Manager positions have developed into a staple position for the Department of Corrections at all major facilities within the department. Staff and Leadership have an increased understanding of the positions, role and duties of CHAPs. The CHAP's employee work profile was revised and included the following revisions: Operations Management decreased from 30% to 20%, application of evidence-based practices increased from 40% to 45%, quality control services increased from 15% to 20% and additional sections were revised to include more specific duties related to evidence-based practices.

Learnings

We learned from the Working Dialogue that Chief of Housing and Program Managers were heavily involved with operations and also held the responsibility to implement evidence-based practices at their assigned facilities. Many of the CHAPs indicated that they did not have a back-up person to assist with implementing evidence-based practices, and they felt alone in this process. We also learned that the Chief of Security positions were not equally trained in evidence-based practices and in operations, as CHAPs were in their positions. We learned that not all staff had a full understanding of the CHAP position, and that it is important for the Chief of Security and Chief of Housing and Programs to have a dual role in implementing evidence-based practices at their assigned facilities. We learned that it is important for Assistant Wardens and Wardens to support the whole process equally.

Shen-fen-Lee stated, "I knew that CHAPs were heavily involved in operational and tasks other than implementing evidence-based practices, and the Working Dialogue really shed light on all of the different things that CHAPs were doing. I don't know what others learned from this. As for me, this was one of the first few Working Dialogues I participated in, so I learned more about the Working Dialogue process." Monica Robinson stated, "I learned that having staff involved that are actually doing the job made this work group very successful."

Conference Session Extracts
From the consideration of the case study with conference participants

Speaker: I'll just go ahead and add to what life was like before this Working Dialogue. As a Lieutenant I really didn't know who to report to and just as we didn't know what we were supposed to take to the CHAPS [Chiefs of Housing and Programming]. I felt like we were taking double issues to both the major and the CHAP for the same exact thing. I'm sure the CHAPS didn't know what they were supposed to do either, but the Working Dialogue streamlined their position and gave them more focus goals. We definitely operate a lot smoother as a facility now.

Speaker: I agree with you. The Chief of Security we play a dual role and it's nice to know that if I'm not here the Chief of Security or somebody else can take care of what I usually taken care off. However, a lot of times the CHAPS didn't know who to come to. It is much better now most people know who to go to, and when to go to who.

As far as Working Dialogues go, we do a lot of them here. One that comes to mind was addressing that our staff dining area was not what we wanted it to be. It wasn't a great place to go and enjoy a lunch. We had a Working Dialogue to talk about how we could improve it. Everybody had a voice and spoke what was on their mind. We talked about what needed to be done and how we were going to do it. You can go out there today and it is a completely different area. People enjoy going there and spending their lunch break, and it has improved morale as far as I'm concerned.

Shannon Fuller: Excellent feedback, thank you.

Speaker: That is a really good example of why a Working Dialogue needs to be specific, which is something we can easily lose sight of. Instead of talking about how we improve staff morale, which can seem like a huge obstacle or challenge, we could make it smaller and more manageable. We coul say, "Okay, what can we do to improve staff dining?" In turn this could then improve staff morale. When the focus of a Working Dialogue is not kept manageable and specific, we might just keep going and going and going, and then we are not able to see some measurable items come out of it.

Speaker: A project addressed by the Healing Environment ambassadors was to increase the participation of learning teams. Because a CHAP is responsible for scheduling it would be great if all the CHAPs had a Working Dialogue with staff to discover some of the roadblocks they encounter in their participation. Rather than something coming down from the warden, a proposal to increase participation comes from the participants.

Speaker: We talked about the relationship between a CHAP and a major, especially where a lot of things overlap in housing units with security and non-security. I also wanted to speak about follow-up. We have a lot of great DPS (dialogue practitioners) here and our staff expects follow-up from them. When staff expect follow-ups, they get more involved as they don't think one or two Working Dialogues a quarter is a waste of their time.

Speaker: I was asked, "How do you address it when someone doesn't want to go along with the program and the decisions made in a Working Dialogue?" I replied that early on when the director first arrived, we went through the importance of effective communication and motivational strategies. Part of effective communication is to meet people where they are, find out why they are resistant to the process of change and to try get their buy-in as much as possible. However, although I think Working Dialogues must have a cross-section of people bring ideas to the table, once decisions are made and people agreed to these we must move forward with the follow-up. We can't just wait for everybody to get on board because administration has to make the best decisions for the staff and inmates.

Shannon: That is a good point. I know that many of us have seen this through the years and I think Mr. Clark answered that well today when he talked about needing a plan and being strategic. He also explained how sometimes when he worked in another state he had to focused on some staff at a lower level and the outcomes from that level were then used as a way to motivate the supervisors to get involved.

Postscript
An author's reflections written some months after the conference

When tasked by Regional Operations Chief Holloway to facilitate the Working Dialogue to improve the focus of Chief of Housing and Program managers (CHAPs) on the implementation of evidence-based practices, I was excited and willing to assist. I had previous experience facilitating Working Dialogues assigned by Mr. Holloway and was inspired by his energy to make positive improvements for the agency. I felt that my role was purposeful and that I had an opportunity to assist with making positive changes. In previous Working Dialogues with Mr. Holloway I had observed his follow-through with action items and was confident that the work that we were doing would impact change for the agency.

The Working Dialogue flowed and was very easy to facilitate. The staff selected to participate were able to articulate challenges that CHAPs faced with focusing on the implementation of evidence-based practices and we were able to identify action plans to address these challenges.

Writing the paper was easier than I initially anticipated. This was mainly due to the structure of the Working Dialogue process that was already in place and the initial report that we had prepared at the conclusion of the Working Dialogue. When writing the paper it was refreshing to reflect back on this experience and to the positive changes that had occurred since the initial Working Dialogue.

During this process I learned that Working Dialogues have more impact on staff and agencies than can be observed by the facilitators and / or the staff participating in the Working Dialogue only. When presenting the case study, staff who were not involved in the Working Dialogue provided feedback about the changes that had been implemented from the Working Dialogue. This information was new information that had not been heard prior and validated the positive impacts of the Working Dialogue on the different levels of the agency. I also learned that Working Dialogues are more effective when specific, manageable and not too complex.

www.ingramcontent.com/pod-product-compliance
Lightning Source LLC
Chambersburg PA
CBHW061128170426
43209CB00014B/1700